Macmillan English

Tina Thoburn

Rita Schlatterbeck

Ann Terry

SERIES **E** ™

Macmillan English

California State Series
Published by
California State Department of Education
Sacramento 1981

Macmillan Publishing Co., Inc.
866 Third Avenue
New York, N.Y. 10022
Collier Macmillan Canada, Ltd.

Printed in the United States of America

ISBN 0-02-245670-8

ACKNOWLEDGMENTS

The publisher gratefully acknowledges permission to reprint the following copyrighted material:

"Rumors" form *Jataka Tales* by Nancy DeRoin. Copyright © 1975 by Nancy DeRoin. Reprinted by permission of Houghton Mifflin Company.

"A Giant Firefly" from *An Introduction to Haiku* by Harold G. Henderson. Copyright © 1958 by Harold G. Henderson. Reprinted by permission of Doubleday & Company, Inc.

"Stillness," "Grasshopper," "The moon is in the water," and "The bat" from Translation of haiku from *Haiku* Vols. 1-4 by R.H. Blyth, copyright © 1949-52 R.H. Blyth, reprinted by permission of The Hokuseido Press, Tokyo.

"The National Pastime" reprinted by permission of Scholastic Magazines, Inc. from *The Cartoon Book of Sports* by Clare and Frank Gault. Text copyright © 1977 by Clare S. Gault and Frank M. Gault.

"What Happens in the Spring" from the Book for Young Explorers, *What Happens in the Spring*, © National Geographic Society.

Excerpt of "Mr. Maybe" by Sally Jarvis from *Little Plays For Little People*. Text copyright © 1965 by Parents' Magazine Press. By permission of Parents' Magazine Press.

"Marian Anderson" adapted from *Marian Anderson* by Tobi Tobias. Copyright © 1972 by Tobi Tobias. By permission of Thomas Y. Crowell.

"Prairie Blizzard" by Louise Budde DeLaurentis. Copyright © 1975 by Louise Budde DeLaurentis. Permission courtesy of the author.

"Ribsy and the Lube Job" adaptation reprinted by permission of William Morrow & Company, Inc. from *Henry and Ribsy* by Beverly Cleary. Copyright 1954 by Beverly Cleary.

Illustration credits:

Kevin Chadwick	Jan Naimo
Phyllis Demchick	Anthony Rao
Paulette Giguere	Charles Shaw
William Harmuth	Joel Snyder
Phyllis Nathans	

Photography credits:
Michael Collier, Stock Boston, Inc. 70/71
© Jerry Cooke, Photo Researchers, Inc. 288/289
Ingbert Grüttner, viii/1, 36/37, 110/111, 150/151, 190/191, 224/225
NASA 258/259

TABLE OF CONTENTS

UNIT 3

UNIT 4

UNIT 5

UNIT 6

UNIT 7

UNIT 8

UNIT 9

Grammar and
Related Language Skills

Practical Communication

Creative Expression

Learning About Sentences

Some groups of words state a complete idea. Other groups of words may suggest part of an idea. Such groups of words are not sentences.

> A **sentence** is a group of words that states a complete idea.

● Look at the groups of words in the box.

The telephone.	The telephone rings under the bed.
The detective.	The detective opens the drawer.
The detective.	The detective searches for his glasses.

The groups of words on the left name a person or a thing. They do not say what action the person or thing does. The groups of words on the left are *not* sentences.

● Now look at the groups of words on the right. They name a person or a thing. They say what action the person or thing does. These groups of words are sentences.

Every sentence has two parts. Each part states only half an idea. You need both parts to state a complete idea.

● Read this sentence. Look carefully at its two parts.

The detective   searches for his glasses.

Notice that the first part of the sentence names whom the sentence is about. The sentence is about the detective. The second part of the sentence tells what action the first part is doing. What action is the detective doing?

Suppose you want to know if a group of words is a sentence. You have to answer the following questions:

Whom or what does the group of words name?
What action does that person or thing do?

Talk About It

Tell whether or not each group of words is a sentence. Give reasons for your answers.

1. A clown visits the detective.
2. A circus mystery.
3. The clown saws a box in half.
4. Loses half the box.
5. A missing part.
6. The bottom of the box.

Skills Practice

Some of the groups of words below are sentences. Other groups are not. Write each group of words that is a sentence. If a group of words is not a sentence, write **not a sentence.**

1. Needs the missing part.
2. The detective searches.
3. Looks for clues.
4. Peeks into animal cages.
5. Hears strange noises.
6. The detective sees footprints.
7. The detective finds a clue.
8. Opens the trunk.
9. The detective opens the trunk.
10. The clown lifts the lid.
11. Looks inside.
12. Finds the bottom of the box.

Sample Answers 1. not a sentence 2. The detective searches.

Four Kinds of Sentences

You know that a sentence states a complete idea. Did you know that there are different kinds of sentences? Some sentences tell something. Other sentences ask something.

A **declarative sentence** is a sentence that makes a statement or tells something.

● Look at the picture. Find two sentences in the picture that are declarative sentences.

A **question sentence** is a sentence that asks something.

● Look at the picture again. Find two sentences that are question sentences.

Some sentences tell someone to do something. Other sentences show excitement or strong feeling.

A **command sentence** is a sentence that tells or asks someone to do something.

● Look in the box. Find three sentences that are commands.

Do not touch the furniture.	I will open the window.
Are there more footprints?	Watch your step.
Look for other clues.	How scared I am!
What a lot of dust there is!	I want to leave.

An **exclamation sentence** is a sentence that shows excitement or strong feeling.

● Look in the box again. Find two sentences that are exclamation sentences.

Talk About It

Tell what kind of sentence each one is. Give reasons for your answers.

1. The football disappeared.
2. Who took it?
3. A person ran away.
4. Did he climb out the window?

5. What a strange sight that was!
6. Call the detective.
7. She will solve the mystery.
8. What a detective she is!

Skills Practice

Read each sentence. Decide what kind it is. Write whether each sentence is **declarative, question, command,** or **exclamation.**

1. Do you know Mr. Holmes?
2. I see him on Baker Street.
3. He is a great detective.
4. How smart he is!
5. Tell me about him.
6. He works with Dr. Watson.

7. He finds clues everywhere.
8. How does he solve his cases?
9. He plays the violin and thinks.
10. What a person he is!
11. Has he solved the mystery?
12. Ask the police.

Sample Answer 1. question

Sentence Signals

Traffic lights tell a driver or a walker when to start and when to stop. A green light means *go*. A red light means *stop*. When you write sentences, you use special signals. They tell the reader where your sentences begin and where they end.

● Look at each sentence in the box. What kind of letter is at the beginning of each sentence?

The island was quite small.	What a strange building it is!
We stand on the beach.	Does someone still live here?
Who made the hut?	Look around.

Use a **capital letter** to begin the first word of every sentence.

● Look again at each sentence in the box. What signal, or punctuation mark, is used at the end of each sentence?

Use a **period (.)** at the end of a declarative or a command sentence.

Use a **question mark (?)** at the end of a question sentence.

Use an **exclamation mark (!)** at the end of an exclamation sentence.

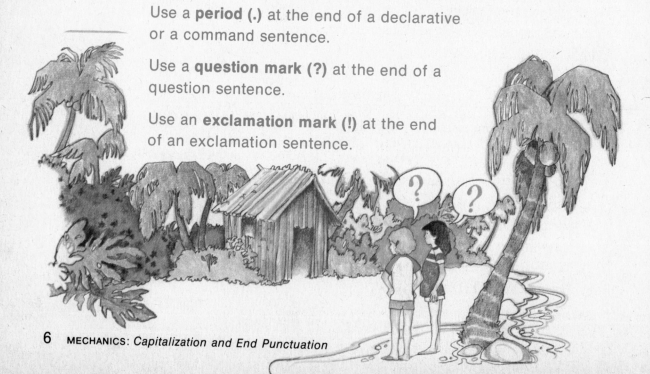

Talk About It

Read each sentence. What punctuation mark should you use at the end of each one? Give reasons for your answers.

1. A fire burned in the fireplace
2. We saw a potato baking
3. Who could have cooked it
4. What a strange place this is
5. Look in the other room
6. Is there butter for the potato

Skills Practice

Write each of the following sentences. Begin each sentence with a capital letter. End each sentence with the correct punctuation mark.

1. have you heard about Bigfoot
2. what is that
3. it is a big furry creature
4. what a strange creature that is
5. how does it walk
6. it walks like a person
7. no one has caught it
8. people are looking for it
9. what a catch that would be
10. i would like to see it

Writing Sentences

Imagine you are a detective. All the lights in your house just went out.

1. Write two declarative sentences. Tell how you would feel.
2. Write one command sentence. Tell someone to do something.
3. Write two question sentences. Ask someone two questions.
4. Write one exclamation sentence. Tell what you would say in your excitement.

Sample Answer 1. Have you heard about Bigfoot?

Skills Review

Some of the groups of words below are sentences. Other groups are not. Write **sentence** if the group of words is a sentence. If a group of words is not a sentence, write **not a sentence.**

1. A mystery story on TV.
2. Two girls went hiking together.
3. The beach.
4. The girls heard scary noises.
5. A dark cave.
6. Returned with a flashlight.
7. The girls entered the cave.
8. Pat led Sandy through the dark.
9. A strange sound.
10. Pat slipped on a rock.
11. The flashlight.
12. Fell on the ground.
13. The girls saw mysterious lights.
14. Pat stood very still.
15. Sandy peeked through a hole.
16. Friends sat around a campfire.

Read each sentence. Decide what kind it is. Write whether each sentence is **declarative, question, command,** or **exclamation.**

17. Did you see that mystery story about the cave on TV?
18. What an exciting show it was!
19. Would you be afraid to go into the cave?
20. Pat and Sandy climbed on the big round rocks.
21. Look at the large waves pounding the shore.
22. The water from each wave went into the cave.
23. Did Pat and Sandy get their feet wet in the cave?
24. They dried their shoes by the campfire.
25. We went to the town dump yesterday.

26. What a lot of old furniture we saw there!
27. Please take me there today.
28. Why do you want to go there?
29. I want to find a table and a chair.
30. Why do you need a table and a chair?
31. I want to put them in my hideout.
32. Take a shortcut through the woods.
33. What a long way it is!

Write each of the following sentences. Begin each sentence with a capital letter. End each sentence with the correct punctuation mark.

34. what a great place this is
35. help me look for the chair and table
36. i see some tables and chairs over there
37. what a lot of broken furniture there is
38. will you help carry the chair
39. we can carry the furniture in my wagon
40. where is your hideout in the woods
41. will you keep it a secret
42. i will not tell anyone.

When you finish
    Writing a sentence . . . . use . ? or !
    Talking on a CB radio . . . . say 10–4.
    Writing a newspaper story . . . . put ③⓪
       after final sentence.
    Writing a book . . . draw # on the last page.
    Can you think of other words or signs
       that mean "I am finished"?

Exploring
Language

Subject Parts and Predicate Parts

Every sentence has two parts. Each part has a special job. One part names whom or what the sentence is about. This part is the *subject part*. The other part names what action the subject part does. This part is the *predicate part*. You need both parts to state a complete idea.

> The **subject part** of a sentence names whom or what the sentence is about. The subject part may have one word or more than one word.

● Look at the following sentence. What is the sentence about?

A bright light │ flashes in the sky.

The sentence is about a bright light. *A bright light* is the subject part of the sentence.

> The **predicate part** of a sentence tells what action the subject part does. The predicate part may have one word or more than one word.

● Look at this sentence again. What action does the subject part do?

A bright light │ flashes in the sky.

The subject part is *A bright light*. The bright light *flashes in the sky*. The predicate part of the sentence is *flashes in the sky*.

Most of the time the subject part of a sentence is stated in words, but in a command sentence the subject *you* often is not stated.

Stop that.   Look at the sky.

Talk About It

Read each of the following sentences. Look at the group of words in each box. Tell whether each group is the subject part or the predicate part. Give reasons for your answers.

1. Many people | see the flash of light.

2. Television sets | break.

3. Cars | stop.

Skills Practice

Write each sentence. Draw a line between the subject part and the predicate part. Draw one line under the subject part. Draw two lines under the predicate part.

1. Juanita Lopez | reads a book.   4. An object | floats overhead.
2. Juanita | hears a noise.   5. Green lights | blink on and off.
3. Juanita | goes to the door.   6. The object | stands still.

Writing Sentences

You see something in the sky. It has flashing lights and makes noise. You are not sure what it is.

1. Write one sentence that tells about the objects. Use one of these subject parts in your sentence.
   a. The flashing lights   **b.** The loud noise
2. Write another sentence that tells more about what you see or hear. Use one of these predicate parts in your sentence.
   a. hear something   **b.** see flashing lights

Sample Answer 1. Juanita Lopez | reads a book.

Understanding New Words
in Sentences

The meaning of words is important when you read and write. To find the meaning of a word, you may do three things. You may ask someone. You may look up the word in a dictionary. You may figure out the meaning by thinking about the other words in the sentence.

● Read the following sentences.

> Workers put up a new traffic light. The
> light is at the underline intersection of Ash Street
> and Madison Avenue.

Suppose you do not know the meaning of *intersection*. Notice the words *traffic light* in the sentence. Where do you usually find a traffic light? You usually find it where two roads cross. Therefore, *intersection* means a place where two roads cross.

Sometimes the meaning of a new word is not clear. The other words in the sentence do not help you. Then you have to read the sentence that comes before or after. Sometimes you have to read several sentences. These sentences may help you understand the new word.

● Read the following sentences.

> Last year we painted our whole house.
> During the winter we painted the inside of
> the house. When the warm weather came, we
> painted the exterior.

Suppose the new word is *exterior*. The first sentence tells you that the whole house was painted. The second sentence tells you that the inside was painted. What part of the house was left to paint? You can figure out that *exterior* means *outside*.

Talk About It

Read each of the following sentences carefully. Try to figure out the meaning of each underlined word.

1. The snow and sleet made driving very <u>hazardous</u>.
2. The helicopter pilot took an <u>aerial</u> picture of the city.
3. Our team is in <u>competition</u> with two others for the prize.
4. The noise was a <u>disturbance</u> to the readers in the library.
5. We looked for seats, but all of them seemed to be taken. Finally we found two seats that were <u>vacant</u>.
6. The <u>majority</u> of students went to school by bus. Only a few students walked.

Skills Practice ✓

Write the underlined word in each sentence. Then write what you think each underlined word means.

1. I could see the <u>luminous</u> numbers on my watch in the dark.
2. We saw the moon <u>emerge</u> from behind the clouds.
3. The <u>fragile</u> glass broke even though she moved it carefully.
4. You need light, water, and soil to <u>nourish</u> plants and trees.
5. I grow all my own food. I do not <u>depend</u> on buying it at the market.
6. Dishes and furniture shook from the <u>vibrations</u> of the earthquake.
7. A garbage truck turned over and spread <u>debris</u> everywhere.
8. The library had too many books. It gave the <u>surplus</u> books away.
9. Dana wanted to leave the room. First she had to <u>obtain</u> permission from her teacher.
10. We all had to bring flowers to class today. Some of us brought real flowers. Some of us brought <u>artificial</u> ones.

Sample Answer 1. luminous—glowing with light

The Beginnings of Language

Linguists are people who study languages. Linguists are really language detectives. They gather clues that tell about the beginnings of languages. Their detective work makes a good story.

Long ago a group of people all spoke one language. It was called *Indo-European,* because the people lived between India and Europe. As time passed, small groups of people moved to new places. Slowly the language of each group changed a little as the people had new experiences. People added new words to describe new things. The sounds and spellings of words changed. In time Indo-European was no longer spoken. Each small group spoke its own language. Some languages that grew from Indo-European are French, Spanish, Italian, German, and Hindi.

Talk About It

English has *borrowed,* or taken, many words from other languages. Use each word in a sentence. Can you think of other words?

1. patio (Spanish)
2. veranda (Hindi)
3. sausage (French)
4. violin (Italian)
5. ranch (Spanish)
6. mosquito (Spanish)
7. spaghetti (Italian)
8. kindergarten (German)
9. sauerkraut (German)

The English language also grew from Indo-European. However, early English does not sound like the English we speak today. It almost sounds like a foreign language. Early English is also called *Old English*. It was made up of the languages used by groups of people called the Jutes, Angles, and Saxons who moved to England starting in 449 A.D. England was called Angle-land for a long time. In 1066 A.D. Old English started to change into *Middle English*. At that time a French duke named William conquered England. Many French people then moved to England. French words replaced some Old English words. The English language changed a great deal.

Talk About It

Say each Middle English word just the way it looks. Spell each word in modern English.

1. poyson   **3.** botel   **5.** citee   **7.** melodye

2. nyght   **4.** dayes   **6.** ende   **8.** thyng

Soon Middle English began to sound more like modern English. But English has not stopped changing. We still add many words to our language. Sometimes we still borrow words from other languages.

Talk About It

Here are some words borrowed from other languages. Use each word in a sentence. Tell your sentence.

1. skunk   (Native American)

2. chipmunk   (Native American)

3. raccoon   (Native American)

4. boomerang   (Native Australian)

5. almanac   (Arabic)

6. shawl   (Persian)

7. kimono   (Japanese)

8. judo   (Japanese)

Skills Review

Write the subject part of each sentence.

1. An alarm sounds in the police station.
2. People jump up from their desks.
3. Police officers rush out the door.
4. The officers race to their cars.
5. The cars leave the parking lot.
6. The sirens make noise.
7. The police drive to the building.
8. Police cars turn the corner.
9. A detective drives into the driveway.

Write the predicate part of each sentence.

10. Officers surround the building.
11. Some officers enter the dark building.
12. The officers climb the stairs.
13. The officers stomp on the wooden floors.
14. A box falls in a room.
15. The police officers turn on their flashlights.
16. Officer Conway opens the door to the room.
17. A ragged cat comes out of the room.
18. The cat looks up at the officers.

Read each sentence. Write the underlined word in each sentence. Then write what you think each underlined word means.

19. The flood did a lot of <u>damage</u> in our town. Many houses were ruined.
20. No one could make any sound. Retta put her hand to her mouth to <u>stifle</u> a laugh.
21. People who read a lot are <u>enlightened</u> on many subjects.
22. You always <u>lag</u> behind and are always the last one at school.
23. We watched the kite <u>ascend</u> high into the sky.
24. Kim was lost. She stopped to <u>inquire</u> how far the next town was.

25. Carlo could not find his missing gloves. He had to <u>rummage</u> through the closet until he found them.

26. How can you write with that pencil? The point is too <u>blunt</u>. You need to sharpen it.

27. Chris did not know what he would do the next day. He <u>pondered</u> the problem all night.

28. It is <u>customary</u> for us to spend the Fourth of July with our grandparents. It is unusual for us to spend this holiday alone.

29. We rent our house from the <u>landlord</u>.

30. Mr. Rivera stepped hard on the brakes. His car came to an <u>abrupt</u> stop.

31. Timmy does not go to school alone. His sister and brother <u>accompany</u> him.

You have learned that language is always changing. One way you can change the meaning of a word is to add another word to it.

For example, how does the word that is added change the meaning of <u>ship</u>?

steamship   airship   spaceship   starship

How does the addition of the word <u>sea</u> change the meaning of each of these words?

seaweed   seafood   seaplane   seashell

Exploring Language

Parts of a Book

There are many kinds of books. Most books that you use in school contain information. Other books that you read often contain stories, plays, or poems. Books are organized so that you can find the information you need.

Almost every book has a title page at the front of the book. The *title page* usually shows the name of the book, the author, the publisher, and the place of publication.

A copyright date is on the back of the title page. The *copyright date* tells when a book was published. It is particularly useful to know how long ago a book was published. Perhaps some of its information has become outdated.

The table of contents comes next in most books. The *table of contents* lists the names of the chapters or units. It tells on which page each chapter or unit begins. By looking at the table of contents, you can often tell if a book has the kind of information you need.

The main part of a book is called the *body* of the book. In school books this part is made up of chapters or units of information. In other books it is the story, play, or poems.

How To Be a Detective
R. F. Lancer

Limon Publishing Co.
Chicago

TITLE PAGE

Copyright © 1975
Limon Publishing Co.
All rights reserved.

COPYRIGHT PAGE

Contents

1. Training of a Detective 3
2. What a Detective Does 17
3. Working with the Law 32
4. True Adventures 58

TABLE OF CONTENTS

School books often have special information sections at the back, such as a handbook and an index.

A *handbook* lists the important rules or facts from the body of the book. These rules or facts are organized so that you can refer to them quickly and easily.

An *index* is an alphabetical list. It tells on what page you can find a certain subject or name.

> A **sentence** is a group of words that state a complete idea.
> The Alberts prepared to go on a picnic.
> James searched everywhere for his sneakers.

HANDBOOK

> Pronouns, 50–58
>   defined, 50
>   list of, 52
>   correct usage of, 56

INDEX

Talk About It

Use this English book to discuss the following:

1. Name the publisher and the copyright date.
2. Tell on what page Unit 7 begins.
3. Tell where in the handbook you can find the definition of a noun.
4. Use the index to tell the pages that tell about adverbs.
5. How many units are in the body of this book?

Skills Practice

Look at the sample pages on the opposite page. Write the answers to these questions about the parts of a book. Identify the part of the book in which you found the answer.

1. What is the title of the book and name of the author?
2. Who is the publisher?
3. In what city was the book published?
4. What is the copyright date?

Putting Ideas in Order

You have lots of ideas. Everyone does. You can express your ideas in sentences and paragraphs. But you would confuse people if you wrote like this:

The telephone rang. I ate bananas for breakfast. My favorite TV show is *News 47*. I visited friends in Texas last summer. I love to go swimming.

This paragraph is confusing because the ideas are not related. When you write, related sentences are grouped together in a paragraph.

Your paragraph should have a main idea. The sentence that states this main idea is called a *topic sentence*. The topic sentence is often the first sentence in the paragraph. The other sentences in the paragraph are called *detail sentences* because they give details to tell more about the main idea. Here is an example of a topic sentence and two detail sentences.

Topic Sentence:	Sherlock Holmes solved cases that stumped Scotland Yard.
Detail 1:	He sometimes used a bloodhound to help him find clues.
Detail 2:	Sherlock Holmes was a brilliant thinker.

Sentences in a paragraph sometimes tell about things in the order in which they happen. Some time-order words that help you follow the action are *first, next, then, finally,* and *at last.*

Here is an example of how a group of sentences in a paragraph work together. Notice that the topic sentence comes first and that the detail sentences begin with the time-order words.

Topic Sentence:	Rob discovered his shoes were missing.
Detail 1:	*First* he looked upstairs for them.
Detail 2:	*Next* he searched the downstairs.
Detail 3:	*Then* he looked in one last place.
Detail 4:	*Finally* he found them in the puppy's bed.

Talk About It

Read these sentences. Find the topic sentence first. Then tell how to put the other sentences in the correct order. Use the time-order words to help you.

1. Next she questioned her neighbor who was a detective.
2. Finally she decided to study to be a police officer.
3. Marin wanted to be a detective.
4. First she read many books about detectives.
5. Then she thought about the problems of the job.

Skills Practice

Read the group of sentences below. Write the topic sentence first. Write the detail sentences in the correct order after the topic sentence. Use the time-order words to help you.

1. First Larry and Marin checked the valve.
2. Larry's bike had a flat tire everyday.
3. Finally the mystery was solved.
4. Next they questioned the neighborhood children.
5. Then they discovered a box of tacks on the floor.

Now write this group of sentences in the correct order.

6. Next she called the paper girl.
7. Mrs. Flynn's newspaper disappeared Sunday morning.
8. First she called the newspaper dealer.
9. Finally a newspaper was recovered.
10. Then she looked in the doghouse.

Time Order in Paragraphs

Thinking About Paragraphs

When you have an idea for a story, you can always talk about it. Sometimes you might want to write about your idea so others can read it. You can write a paragraph. A good way to begin writing is to organize your paragraph. Remember that a paragraph can be made up of a topic sentence and detail sentences. The *topic sentence* states the main idea of the paragraph. The *detail sentences* in the paragraph tell more about the main idea.

There are different ways to arrange sentences in a paragraph. One good way is to use *time order*. First you write the topic sentence. Then you order, or arrange, the detail sentences according to *time*. You tell what happened first and what happened next until you get to the last detail of what happened.

Words that show time can help you know how to order your sentences. Look for these time-order words at the beginning of detail sentences:

First	Second	Next	Finally

Can you think of more words that might signal time order?

You should also notice that the first line of a paragraph looks different from the other sentences. It is important to remember to *indent* the first word. Indenting means leaving a little space. It signals your reader that you are starting a new topic or paragraph.

●Read the paragraph below.

Michael followed clues to find his friends in the woods. First he saw the broken ends of the bushes. Next he found some marshmallow sticks left over from their campfire. Finally he found his friends asleep behind a group of trees.

Talking About Paragraphs

1. Find the topic sentence in the paragraph about Michael. It is the first sentence of the paragraph: *Michael followed clues to find his friends in the woods.*
2. Read the detail sentences. What are the time-order words in the detail sentences?

Writing a Paragraph

Read the sentences below.
1. Then it searched the tabletop.
2. First it looked in its food dish.
3. Finally it opened the refrigerator.
4. The cat was trying to find food.

Find the topic sentence. Write it on your paper. Now write the three detail sentences in the order that they happened. You have just written a time-order paragraph!

A Class Paragraph

Thinking About Your Class Paragraph

Your class is going to write a time-order paragraph together. The pictures will help you. You will use time order to arrange the sentences in your paragraph.

Writing Your Class Paragraph

1. Start your paragraph with this topic sentence: *The girl went swimming on a cold morning.* You or your teacher should write all the sentences on the board.

2. Think of a detail sentence that tells about the first picture. Choose a time-order word to begin your detail sentence.

3. Think of detail sentences that tell about the next three pictures. The topic sentence and the four detail sentences will make up your class paragraph.

4. Copy the paragraph on your paper. Remember to indent the first word.

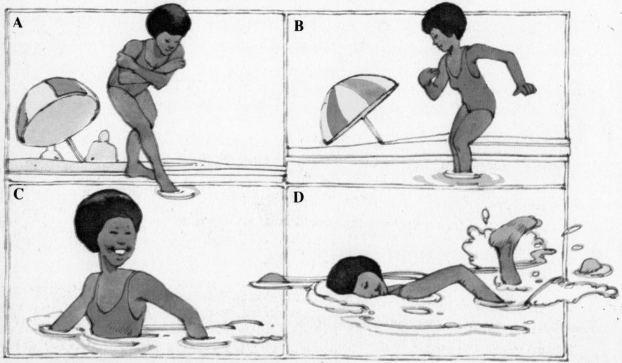

Your Own Paragraph

Thinking About Your Paragraph

Now you are ready to write your own paragraph. The pictures will help you. The Word Bank shows how to spell some of the words you may want to use.

Writing Your Own Paragraph

1. Begin your paragraph with this topic sentence: *John had a very busy day*. Write the topic sentence on your paper. Remember to indent the first word.
2. Look at the four pictures. They are arranged in time order.
3. Write a detail sentence that tells about each picture. Remember to use the time-order words to show the order of the pictures.
4. Use the Word Bank to help you spell your words.
5. Save your paragraph.

Word Bank

next
baseball
friend
later
finally
school
reading
then
breakfast

How to Edit Your Work

Have you ever wanted to change a paragraph you have written? You decide that you want to improve it. This important step in writing is called *editing*. It means you must read your paragraph carefully and correct any mistakes. The final step in editing is copying your paragraph neatly so that it can be read by others.

Look at the time-order paragraph you wrote about John's day. Check your paragraph with these editing questions:

1. Look at your topic sentence. Does it tell what all the pictures are about?
2. Are your detail sentences in a time order that makes sense?
3. Did you use time-order words?
4. Does each sentence state a complete idea?
5. Did you indent the first word?
6. Did you start each sentence with a capital letter?
7. Did you end each sentence with the correct punctuation mark?
8. Did you spell all the words correctly? Remember to use your Word Bank.

Read the time-order paragraph below. The writer made some mistakes. The mistakes have been corrected.

> Margaret was looking for her bracelet. First she looked under the bed. Next she looked on her dresser. Third she looked in her closet. Finally she found it in her pocket.

Look at the way the paragraph is corrected. Some marks are used to show mistakes. These marks are called *editing symbols*. Two editing symbols are used in this paragraph.

∧ —A caret means something has been left out. You add the missing words above it.

sp —These two letters are short for the word spelling. They mean the word is misspelled. You should cross out the word and spell it correctly.

Look for the carets in the edited paragraph. What words were left out? Find the two misspelled words.

Use the eight editing questions to help you correct your time-order paragraph. Use the two editing symbols if you need them. When you have made all the changes and corrections, copy your paragraph neatly.

Careers

Some writers have become famous as authors of mystery stories. Dame Agatha Christie is a well-known author of mystery stories. Two famous detectives, Hercule Poirot and Miss Jane Marple, appear in many of her stories. But the best-known author of mystery stories may be Sir Arthur Conan Doyle. His most famous character is Sherlock Holmes. *The Hound of the Baskervilles* is one of the most famous novels about this detective and his friend, Dr. Watson. Both writers were British and wrote many short stories, novels, and plays.

Culver Pictures. Inc.

Checking Skills

Some of the groups of words below are sentences. Other groups are not. Write **sentence** if the group of words is a sentence. If a group of words is not a sentence, write **not a sentence.** *pages 2–3*

1. Arnold hears a noise.
2. Calls his sister.
3. Doris looks under the bed.
4. Arnold walks to the closet.
5. Opens the closet door.
6. Doris walks to the window.
7. A branch.
8. Brushes against the window.
9. Sees the tree branch.
10. Doris smiles.

Read each sentence. Decide what kind it is. Write whether each sentence is **declarative,** a **question,** a **command,** or an **exclamation.** *pages 4–5*

11. The flower grows in a crack in the sidewalk.
12. What a mystery it is!
13. Did someone plant a seed?
14. Smell the flower.
15. How pretty it is!

Write each of the following sentences. Begin each sentence with a capital letter. End each sentence with the correct punctuation mark. *pages 6–7*

16. dinosaurs disappeared millions of years ago
17. how do people know what they looked like
18. people found dinosaur bones
19. how large they are
20. why did dinosaurs disappear
21. did it get too cold for them
22. some people think dinosaurs got sick

Write the subject part of each sentence. *pages 10–11*

23. Stephanie goes to the store.
24. The money falls out of her hand.
25. The sad girl looks on the sidewalk.

Write the predicate part of each sentence. *pages 10–11*

26. Stephanie looks under the cars.
27. The girl finds the money.
28. Stephanie buys some food.

Read each sentence. Write the underlined word in each sentence. Then write what you think each underlined word means. *pages 12–13*

29. Jan won a <u>scholarship</u>. Now she has enough money to go to school.
30. My brother is <u>thrifty</u>. He doesn't waste his money.
31. Eleanor Anders was a <u>hermit</u>. She lived all alone in the woods.

Read the following sentences. Find the topic sentence. Then put the detail sentences in the right time order. Write the paragraph. *pages 22–27*

32. a. Next he put all his books and games on the shelf.
    b. First he made his bed.
    c. Paul straightened his room today.
    d. Finally he hung his clothes neatly in the closet.

Read the following sentences. Find the topic sentence and then put the detail sentences in time order. Write the paragraph. *pages 22–27*

33. a. Last she stands up straight again.
    b. Then she tucks her head between her legs.
    c. Jessica can do a perfect somersault.
    d. First she puts her hands flat on the ground.
    e. Next she pushes with her feet and rolls over.

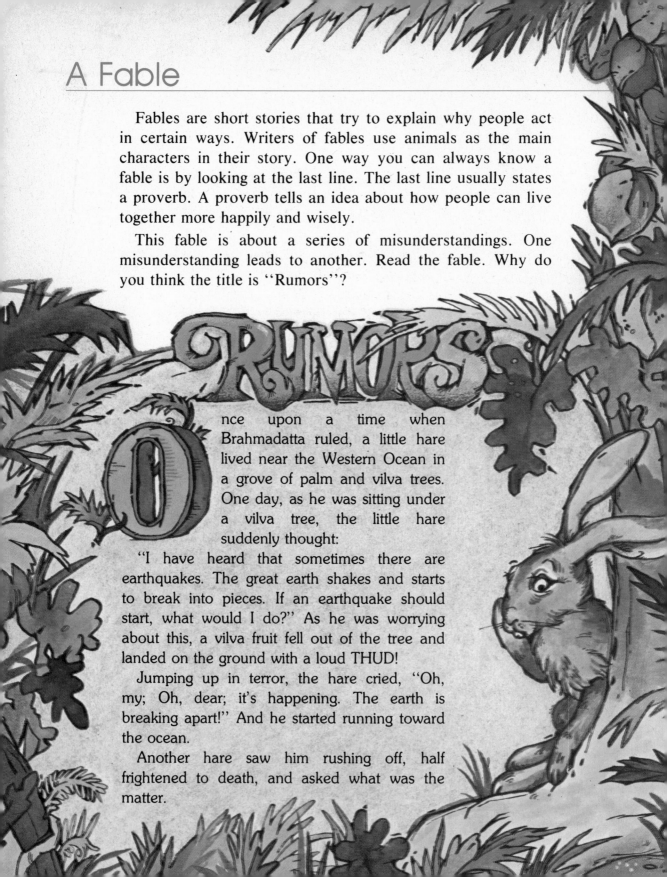

A Fable

Fables are short stories that try to explain why people act in certain ways. Writers of fables use animals as the main characters in their story. One way you can always know a fable is by looking at the last line. The last line usually states a proverb. A proverb tells an idea about how people can live together more happily and wisely.

This fable is about a series of misunderstandings. One misunderstanding leads to another. Read the fable. Why do you think the title is "Rumors"?

RUMORS

Once upon a time when Brahmadatta ruled, a little hare lived near the Western Ocean in a grove of palm and vilva trees. One day, as he was sitting under a vilva tree, the little hare suddenly thought:

"I have heard that sometimes there are earthquakes. The great earth shakes and starts to break into pieces. If an earthquake should start, what would I do?" As he was worrying about this, a vilva fruit fell out of the tree and landed on the ground with a loud THUD!

Jumping up in terror, the hare cried, "Oh, my; Oh, dear; it's happening. The earth is breaking apart!" And he started running toward the ocean.

Another hare saw him rushing off, half frightened to death, and asked what was the matter.

The first hare cried, without stopping, "The earth is breaking apart!" Hearing this, the second hare began to run, too. And so, first one, then another hare joined in until 100,000 hares were all racing toward the ocean.

They were seen by a deer, a boar, an elk, a buffalo, a wild ox, a rhinoceros, a tiger, and an elephant. When these animals, in turn, heard that the earth was breaking apart, they too started to run.

And so, one by one, the number grew and grew until the earth seemed covered with running, terrified animals.

A young lion who was asleep in his cave high on the hillside was awakened by the thundering of so many feet. He looked out of his cave and was amazed to see the headlong flight of so many thousands of animals.

"Why," he said, "they are all running toward the ocean. If I don't do something, they will all drown themselves."

So, bounding down from the mountain, the lion ran in front of the stampeding animals and gave the mightiest roar ever heard before or since. The animals, paralyzed with fright, stopped dead in their tracks.

"What is the matter here?" the lion demanded.

"The earth is breaking apart," They cried, all together.

The lion thought, "The earth does not seem to me to be breaking apart," and he began asking questions starting with the largest animals. "Why are you running?" he asked the elephants.

"The earth is breaking apart," trumpeted the elephants.

"Who saw it breaking apart?" the lion asked.

"The tigers know all about it," the elephants replied.

"The tigers said, "The rhinoceroses know."

The rhinoceroses said, "The oxen know."

The oxen said, "The buffaloes know."

The buffaloes said, "The elks know."

The elks said, "The boars."

The boars said, "The deer."

The deer said, "The hares."

When the hares were questioned, they pointed to the little hare and said, "He told us."

The young lion said to the hare, "Is it true, sir, that the earth is breaking apart?"

"Oh, yes, sir," the little hare replied, "I heard it with my own ears!"

"Where?" the lion asked.

Where I live, sir, a grove of palm and vilva trees. I was lying beneath a vilva tree when I heard the earth start to break apart."

The lion turned to the animals and said, "All of you, wait here. I myself will go to the very spot and see if this is true. Then I will come back and tell you."

Placing the hare on his back, the lion sprang forward with great speed and soon arrived at the palm and vilva grove. "Come," said the lion, "show me the place where the earth is breaking apart."

The hare jumped off his back, not daring to go too near the vilva tree and pointed. "Over there, sir, is where I heard the awful sound."

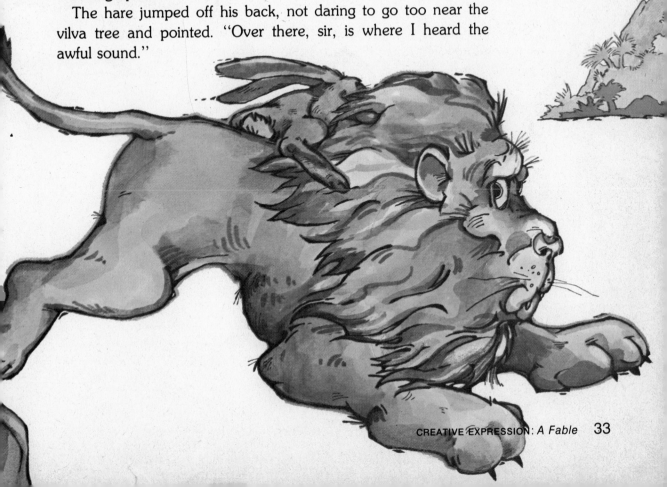

The lion went to the place and found the ripe vilva fruit that had fallen to the ground. Picking it up, he said, "Here, sir, is your world breaking apart—no more than a ripe fruit that fell upon the ground." Then, putting the hare on his back once more, the lion raced back to the frightened herd of animals and said:

"Do not be afraid any longer. You are perfectly safe. The world is not breaking apart. This hare only heard a ripe vilva fruit fall upon the ground." Then he said:

One foolish creature starts a rumor;
Ask yourself who is the worst:
He who takes it for the truth,
Or he who started it at first?

Activities

1. Think about how the animals acted in the story. How did the rumors get started? What does the proverb at the end of the story tell you about rumors? Try playing this game. Six or more people can play. The first person should write a sentence and then whisper it to a second person very quickly. The second person whispers quickly what is heard to the third person. Keep whispering the sentence to each person until you reach the last player. The last player says the sentence aloud. See if the sentence is the same one the first player said.

2. A famous story teller named Aesop told a great many fables. Go to the library and try to find a book of his fables. After you read more fables, try writing your own. Remember that the proverb is the last line.

3. This fable, "Rumors," is fun to read aloud. Pick a person to read the story. That person will be called the narrator. Choose a person to read what each animal said. The narrator could read the proverb. Remember that the animals become more and more excited. Your voices should show you are becoming more and more excited, too. You might practice your fable, tape-record it, and share it with another class. Maybe you could even add background music to your tape.

4. An old English folk tale tells the story of Chicken Little. Ask a librarian to help you find this story. See how it is like the fable "Rumors."

Grammar and Related Language Skills

Learning About Nouns
Singular and Plural Nouns
Common and Proper Nouns
Possessive Nouns

Practical Communication

Using the Dictionary
Writing a Friendly Letter

Creative Expression

Haiku

Nouns

Imagine living in a world where there were no people, places, or things. There would be no lawyers, no kings, no kitchens, no zoos, no ballparks, no money, no kites. The world would be a pretty dull place. But the real world does have lots of people, places, and things. We call words that name people, places, and things *nouns*.

●Look at the picture.

Notice the people, places, and things in the picture. The words that name them are nouns. Do you see Sarah riding down the trail on the mule? *Sarah* is a noun that names a person. *Trail* is a noun that names a place. *Mule* is a noun that names a thing.

●Think of some nouns that name other people, places, or things you see in the picture.

You can see and touch people, places, and things. But some nouns name things you cannot see or touch. They name ideas. *Anger, pain, peace,* and *love* are examples of nouns that name ideas that you cannot see or touch.

●Look at the underlined word in each sentence in the box.

> A trip to the Grand Canyon brings <u>joy</u> to people.
>
> Do the mules share the <u>pleasure</u>?

The underlined words are nouns that name ideas.

> A **noun** is a word that names a person, place, thing, or idea.

Talk About It

Find each noun. Tell whether it names a person, place, thing, or idea.

1. Elliot pointed to a river.
2. Sarah walked to the water.
3. Angelo rented canoes.
4. Ed liked the beauty of the river.

Skills Practice

Read each sentence. Write each noun. After each noun, write whether it names a **person, place, thing,** or **idea.**

1. Nina paddled the canoe.
2. The canoe hit a rock.
3. Elliot waded into the water.
4. Elliot fixed the canoe.
5. Nina paddled quickly.
6. Mike stayed behind with Elliot.
7. The children chose mules.
8. The riders rode horses.
9. Sarah looked for a cave.
10. Sarah wanted peace and quiet.

Add a noun to fill each blank. Write each sentence. Make sure that the sentence makes sense.

11. The group walked into a dark ___.
12. ___ saw a mole on a ledge.
13. A beaver gnawed the ___ of a birch tree.
14. The children walked past an old ___.

Sample Answer 1. Nina, person; canoe, thing

Forming Plural Nouns

The child eats an apple on the beach.
The children eat apples on the beaches.

The nouns in the first sentence name only one person, place, and thing. Only one child eats one apple on one beach. These nouns are called *singular nouns*.

> A **singular noun** is a noun that names one person, place, thing, or idea.

The nouns in the second sentence name more than one person, place, and thing. More than one child eats more than one apple on more than one beach. These nouns are called *plural nouns*.

> A **plural noun** is a noun that names more than one person, place, thing, or idea.

● Look at each noun below.

thought → thoughts   forest → forests
beach → beaches   fox → foxes

What has been added to the singular nouns *thought* and *forest* to make them plural?

> To make most singular nouns plural, add **s**.

What has been added to the singular nouns *beach* and *fox* to make them plural?

> If a singular noun ends with **s, ss, x, ch, sh,** or **z,** add **es** to form the plural.

Some singular nouns form the plural in a different way.

child → children   man → men
mouse → mice   woman → women
goose → geese   foot → feet
tooth → teeth   ox → oxen

Talk About It

Read each sentence. Look at each underlined word. Tell how each plural was formed?

1. The <u>children</u> visited a forest.
2. The <u>women</u> talked to Sally.
3. Some <u>geese</u> flew overhead.
4. The man looked at three <u>mice</u>.

Skills Practice

Write each noun in each sentence. Then write **singular** if the noun is singular. Write **plural** if the noun is plural.

1. The children went to a park.
2. Squirrels roamed freely.
3. Two squirrels climbed a pine.
4. Virgil climbed a tree.
5. Virgil perched on a branch.
6. Jo looked at the feet of Virgil.
7. Randy spotted the lake.
8. Waves pounded the shore.
9. Sally tied knots in a rope.
10. Tony made hamburgers.

Write the plural form of each noun.

11. box
12. person
13. tree
14. bus
15. blanket
16. church
17. foot
18. ash
19. kiss
20. boy
21. child
22. peach

Writing Sentences

Imagine you are visiting a place that has many animals. The place might be a farm, a forest, or a zoo.

1. Write two sentences telling about things you see. Use only singular nouns in your sentences.
2. Write two sentences telling about things you do. Use only plural nouns in your sentences.

Sample Answers 1. children, plural; park, singular. 11. boxes

More About Plural Nouns

Not all singular nouns can be made plural in the same way. Here are some other ways you can form plural nouns.

Singular nouns that end in *y* form the plural in two different ways. Some nouns that end in *y* are like *sky*. *Sky* ends in a consonant and *y*.

> If a singular noun ends with a consonant and **y,** change the **y** to **i** and add **es** to form the plural.

sky⟶skies   fly⟶flies

Some nouns that end in *y* are like *toy*. *Toy* ends in a vowel and *y*.

> If a singular noun ends in a vowel and **y,** add **s** to form the plural.

toy⟶toys   boy⟶boys

• Look at each noun.

valley	dairies
baby	holidays
tray	territories
colony	ways

How would you change each noun in the left column to the plural form? *Valleys, babies, trays,* and *colonies* are the plurals. How were the nouns in the right column changed from the singular to the plural form? *Dairies* and *territories* were made plural by changing the *y* to *i* and adding *es. Holidays* and *ways* were made plural by adding *s.*

Many singular nouns ending in *f* or *fe* add *s* to form the plural in the usual way.

roof → roofs   safe → safes   cliff → cliffs

For some singular nouns that end in *f* or *fe,* change the *f* to *v* and add *s* or *es* to form the plural.

knife	knives	shelf	shelves	half	halves
life	lives	leaf	leaves	loaf	loaves
		thief	thieves		

Talk About It

Spell the plural form of each noun.

1. alley   3. body   5. navy   7. cliff
2. army   4. reply   6. half   8. shelf

Skills Practice

Write the plural form of each noun.

1. penny   4. spray   7. city   10. thief
2. birthday   5. life   8. belly   11. leaf
3. factory   6. reef   9. boy   12. safe

Write each sentence with the plural form of the noun.

13. On ___ the children go to the zoo.   (Sunday)
14. The goats eat ___ from the plants.   (leaf)
15. The monkeys climbed on the ___ of the buildings.   (roof)
16. Sophie laughed at two ___ on the rope.   (monkey)
17. Evan stared at the fat ___.   (turkey)
18. Phyllis and Adam saw a mother lamb with ___.   (baby)
19. Ira and Debby rode two ___.   (donkey)
20. Laura was as tall as the knees of the ___.   (giraffe)

Sample Answers 1. pennies 13. On Sundays the children go to the zoo.

Compound Nouns

Sometimes new nouns are made by joining two or more words together. A *compound noun* is a noun made up of two or more other words. You can usually figure out the meaning of a compound noun if you know the meanings of the smaller words that form it.

● Look at these compound nouns.

spaceship liftoff splashdown

The words *space* and *ship* make up the compound noun *spaceship*. *Spaceship* means a *ship* that moves in *space*. *Liftoff* means the *lift* up *off* the ground. *Splashdown* means coming *down* in the water with a *splash*.

Sometimes compound nouns can help you say things in a short way.

● Look at each sentence.

Don saw a <u>ground for making</u> a camp.   Don saw a <u>campground</u>.
Kim gathered <u>wood for a fire</u>.   Kim gathered <u>firewood</u>.
Lu ate by <u>the light of the moon</u>.   Lu ate by <u>moonlight</u>.

The underlined words in each sentence show both a long and a short way to say the same thing.

Talk About It

Think of a compound noun to replace the underlined words in each sentence.

1. The trip started in the <u>time after 12 o'clock noon</u>.
2. The children saw <u>falls of water</u> at Yellowstone Park.
3. Suddenly a <u>storm of rain</u> started.
4. The children ran back to the <u>ground where people</u> camp.

Skills Practice

Write the compound noun in each sentence. Draw a line between the two words that make up each compound. Then write what each compound noun means.

1. Wendy walked up the hillside on Tuesday.
2. Andy collected wood for a campfire.
3. Andy got a terrible backache.
4. Matt ate blueberries.
5. Roy made a fruitcake.
6. The children saw a lot of wildflowers.
7. Winona spotted a hummingbird.
8. Wendy looked for earthworms for bait.
9. Matt hung a worm on a fishhook.
10. Chin and Cal played with horseshoes.

Write a compound noun to replace each group of underlined words.

11. Andy fed a deer by the <u>side of the river</u>.
12. Roy walked to the <u>side of the lake</u>.
13. Roy heard a <u>snake that rattles</u>.
14. Debbie climbed to the <u>top of a tree</u>.
15. The climb gave Debbie an awful <u>ache in the head</u>.
16. Wendy wrote about the event in a <u>book for making notes</u>.

Sample Answers 1. hill/side, the side of a hill 11. riverside

Skills Review

Write each noun in each sentence. After each noun, write whether it names a **person, place, thing,** or **idea.**

1. The friends went to camp together.
2. The campers lived in cabins.
3. The children had fun.
4. The children explored the mountains.
5. Miko found a golden rock near a cave.
6. The surprised girl ran down the hill.
7. Angela approached the place.
8. Nina saw golden rocks on the ground.
9. Elliot found many strange stones.
10. Then Angela discovered a can of golden paint.

Write each noun. Then write **singular** if the noun is singular. Write **plural** if the noun is plural.

11. The campers swim in a large lake.
12. The children play near the shore.
13. The campers paddle the canoes.
14. Virgil stays near the beach.
15. Tony jumps in the waves.
16. A friend swims near an island.
17. Trees cover the island.
18. Randy swims across the lake.
19. Sally climbs into the boat.
20. A boy rows the boat.
21. A lifeguard watches the children.
22. A girl dives off the raft.

Write the plural form of each noun.

23. ability	27. tooth	31. monkey	35. bush
24. man	28. lady	32. girl	36. chief
25. bench	29. fox	33. knife	37. beach
26. delivery	30. cliff	34. shelf	38. horse

Skills Review

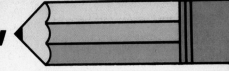

Write the compound noun in each sentence. Draw a line between the two words that make up each compound. Then write what each compound means.

39. Joe and Tina play basketball.
40. They like to play outside.
41. They play in the backyard.
42. The babysitter watches them play.
43. They hear a watchdog bark.

Write a compound noun to replace the underlined words in each sentence.

44. Animals in the <u>house on the farm</u> ran away.
45. Hens scampered through the <u>fields of corn</u>.
46. The hens scared the <u>insects that hop in the grass</u>.
47. A <u>figure used to scare the crows away</u> fell down.
48. The <u>soil at the top</u> of the land washed away.

You know that nouns name people, places, things, or ideas. You know that other words show action. Did you know that sometimes the same word that is a noun can show action? Look at the word *walk* in these sentences.
1. *Walk* a mile for your health.
2. I found an alligator on the front *walk*!
In which sentence is *walk* a noun? In which sentence does *walk* show action? Read these words: *fly, hurry, iron, fight*. Can you use each word in a sentence as a noun? Can you use each word to show action? Make a list of other words that are nouns and that show action.

Exploring Language

Common and Proper Nouns

- Look at the sentence below.

A young woman liked a building in her town.

Find the nouns. The nouns in this sentence are *woman, building,* and *town.* These nouns are called *common nouns* because they name any person, place, and thing.

> A **common noun** is a noun that names any person, place, thing or idea.

- Now look at this sentence.

Samantha Carlsen liked the Sears Tower in Chicago, Illinois.

The nouns in this sentence are *Samantha Carlsen, Sears Tower, Chicago,* and *Illinois.* These nouns are called *proper nouns* because they name a special person, place, and thing.

> A **proper noun** is a noun that names a special person, place, thing, or idea. A proper noun can be one word or more than one word.

- Look at the nouns below. How does each proper noun begin?

George Washington Bridge	the bridge
Ritz Theater	the theater
Museum of the American Indian	the museum

Each proper noun begins with a capital letter. If a proper noun has more than one word, each important word begins with a capital letter.

Talk About It

Find the nouns in each sentence. Tell whether each noun is a common noun or a proper noun. Give reasons for your answers.

1. Henry Thoreau lived in the woods.
2. Thoreau lived near Walden Pond.
3. Walden Pond is in Massachusetts.
4. Thoreau studied plants.
5. Thoreau wrote a book.
6. The book is called *Walden*.

Skills Practice

Read each sentence. Write each noun. After each noun write whether it is **common** or **proper.**

1. The class went to Bear Mountain Park.
2. Frank Perez rented the bus.
3. The bus driver drove over the George Washington Bridge.
4. The group traveled along the Hudson River.
5. Amy pointed out a farm.
6. The class saw chickens, horses, and cows.
7. A big dog barked.
8. The children saw many towns.
9. The children liked Montrose.

Writing Sentences

Imagine that your friends lost their dog when they went to the store.

1. Write two sentences to describe how they lost their dog. Underline the common nouns in the sentences.
2. Write two sentences to describe how your friends found their dog.

Underline the proper nouns in the sentences.

Sample Answer 1. class, common; Bear Mountain Park, proper

Abbreviations

Sometimes people use shortened words to write the names of people, places, or things. For example, you might write *Rd.* for *Road* or *Wm.* for *William*. These shortened words are called *abbreviations*.

An **abbreviation** is a short form of a word.

Abbreviations are often used in writing. We write *Mr.* and *Mrs.*, for example. Some abbreviations are used only in addresses and lists. We write *Ave.* on an envelope, but we write *Avenue* in a sentence.

Here are some common abbreviations. Notice that you must put a period after an abbreviation.

Abbreviations Used in Writing	Title Stands for	Abbreviations Used in Addresses, Lists	Stands for
Mr.	a man	Ave.	Avenue
Dr.	Doctor	Blvd.	Boulevard
Rev.	Reverend	Dr.	Drive
Sr.	Senior	Rd.	Road
Jr.	Junior	Rte.	Route
Ms.	a woman	St.	Street
Mrs.	a married woman	Co.	Company
		Inc.	Incorporated

●Look at the address that appears on the envelope.

In the address, *Mr.* stands for *Mister*. *Jr.* is short for *Junior*. *St.* is an abbreviation for *Street*. A comma (,) is placed between the name of a city and the name of a state.

Calendars often use abbreviations for the days and months.

DAYS: Sun. Mon. Tues. Wed. Thurs. Fri. Sat.
MONTHS: Jan. Feb. Mar. Apr. Aug. Sept. Oct. Nov. Dec.

The words *May, June,* and *July* are not usually abbreviated.

The abbreviation A.M. stands for the Latin words *ante meridiem*. Ante meridiem means "before noon." The abbreviation P.M. stands for *post meridiem*. It means "after noon." Are you in school at 11 A.M. or 11 P.M.? Are you sleeping at 4 A.M. or 4 P.M.?

Talk About It

Find the abbreviations in these phrases. Tell what each abbreviation stands for.

1. Dr. Anna Lopez
2. 487 Jackson Blvd.
3. Mrs. Hannah Bell
4. 6470 Jones Ave.
5. Mon., Aug. 12
6. 12:30 P.M.

Skills Practice

Change each underlined word to an abbreviation. Write the new phrase.

1. <u>Route</u> 66
2. Lakeville <u>Boulevard</u>
3. <u>Friday</u>, <u>October</u> 31
4. 98765 Twist <u>Road</u>
5. Fifth <u>Avenue</u>
6. 1:45 <u>ante meridiem</u>
7. <u>Reverend</u> Stan Nichols
8. 420 Bradley <u>Drive</u>
9. Pet Food <u>Company</u>, <u>Incorporated</u>
10. <u>Doctor</u> Jason Benton, <u>Junior</u>
11. <u>Thursday</u>, <u>January</u> 11
12. 2:30 <u>post meridiem</u>

Sample Answer 1. Rte. 66

Possessive Nouns

If you own a bicycle, you possess it. *Possess* means the same thing as *have* or *own*. Nouns can be used to show *possession*. Nouns that show possession are called *possessive nouns*.

● Look at each sentence.

> Jay found the bicycle <u>of the boy</u>. Jay found the <u>boy's</u> bicycle.

The underlined words in the first sentence show that the bicycle belongs to the boy. The underlined word in the second sentence is a *possessive noun*. It shows that the bicycle belongs to the boy.

> A **possessive noun** is a noun that names who or what has something.

● Look again at the second sentence in the box above. The noun *boy* is singular. An apostrophe and an *s* have been added to the singular noun *boy* to form the possessive.

> Add an **apostrophe** and **s** ('s) to form the possessive of most singular nouns.

Form the possessive of singular proper nouns in the same way.

John—John's   Ross—Ross's   Sally—Sally's

● Look at each sentence.

The pet <u>of the villagers</u> escaped.   The <u>villagers'</u> pet escaped.

> Add an **apostrophe** (') to form the possessive of plural nouns that end with **s.**

Form the possessive of plural proper nouns in the same way.

the Bernsteins   the Bernsteins' pet
the Rileys   the Rileys' pet

The plural forms of certain nouns do not end in *s*. For example, the plural form of the noun *child* is *children*.

● Look at each sentence.

The wagons <u>of the children</u> move quickly.
The <u>children's</u> wagons move quickly.

> Add an **apostrophe** and **s** ('s) to form the possessive of plural nouns that do not end with **s**.

Talk About It_____

Read each sentence. Use the possessive form of the noun. Spell the possessive noun.

1. Several ___ children played together.   (neighbors)
2. The ___ fathers played too.   (children)
3. The children played in the ___ yard.   (Leibers)
4. Mom found the ___ bicycle.   (girl)
5. ___ parents served lunch.   (Gerry)

Skills Practice _____

Change each word at the end of the sentence to make a possessive noun. Write each sentence.

1. The ___ children walked to the zoo.   (neighbor)
2. A ___ eyes winked hello.   (monkey)
3. The ___ meat fell to the floor.   (lion)
4. The ___ mother paced back and forth.   (cubs)
5. The ___ roars frightened the cubs.   (elephants)
6. The ___ feet clattered on the rocks.   (buffalo)
7. The zoo keeper pointed to the ___ cage.   (snake)
8. The children fed lettuce to the ___ baby.   (camel)
9. The ___ paws splashed water.   (bear)

Sample Answer 1. The neighbor's children walked to the zoo.

Suffixes

A new word can sometimes be made by adding one or more letters to the end of a word. The added letters give a new meaning to the old word.

A **suffix** is one or more letters added to the end of a word.

●Look at each sentence.

A news <u>reporter</u> wrote about the floods in Arizona.
The famous <u>inventor</u> created a machine.

The underlined word in each sentence has a suffix added to it. What is the suffix in each word? The first suffix is *er*. The second is *or*. The suffix *er* or *or* means *a person who*. A *reporter* is a person who reports. An *inventor* is a person who invents. Most words use the suffix *er* instead of *or*. Some common words with the *or* suffix are *actor, governor, director,* and *sailor*.

●Look at the sentence below.

The girls found their way in the <u>darkness</u>.

Can you find the suffix in the underlined word? The suffix *ness* means *the state of being*. *Darkness* means the state of being dark. *Coldness* means the state of being cold.

●Look at each sentence.

Many people were <u>helpless</u> for days.
Sal spent a <u>cheerless</u> winter in the mountains.

What suffix is in each underlined word? The suffix *less* means *without*. *Helpless* means without help. *Cheerless* means without cheer.

Suffix	Meaning	Example
er	one who	printer (one who prints)
or	one who	sailor (one who sails)
ness	the state of being	happiness (state of being happy)
less	without	senseless (without sense)

Talk About It

In each sentence find the word that has the suffix **or, er, ness,** or **less.** Tell what the word means.

1. The rain pleased the farmer.
2. The rain brought gladness to our town.
3. Green grass grew from the colorless ground.
4. The governor came to the town.

Skills Practice

In each sentence find the word that has the suffix **er, or, ness,** or **less.** Write the word and then write what it means.

1. The wetness of the rain cleaned the streets.
2. The street sweeper swept the rubbish.
3. A shoeless boy planted a garden.
4. The traffic director watched.

Add the suffix **er, or, ness,** or **less** to the incomplete word in each sentence. Write the word.

5. The people lost their fond ___ for rain.
6. A store own ___ pumped water from his basement.
7. A sail ___ fixed boats.
8. The cheer ___ people stared at the rain.

Sample Answers **1.** wetness, state of being wet. **5.** fondness

Skills Review

Write the nouns in each sentence. After each noun write whether it is **common** or **proper**.

1. The family visited Carlsbad Caverns.
2. Karla explored the cavern in New Mexico.
3. A cowboy named Jim White discovered the cave.
4. Jim saw bats in the cave.
5. Betsy explored the large rooms.
6. The family saw some statues.
7. One room contained carvings.
8. Jim saw walls of limestone.
9. Guides took people through the caverns.
10. Mike took pictures with a new camera.
11. Jim tripped on a rock.
12. Many people from the United States visited the caverns.

Change each underlined word to an abbreviation. Write the new phrase.

13. <u>Wednesday</u>, <u>January</u> 11
14. State <u>Street</u>
15. 463 Rocky <u>Road</u>
16. <u>Mister</u> Arthur Green
17. 2:30 <u>post meridiem</u>
18. 79 Norton <u>Drive</u>
19. <u>Doctor</u> Lynn Stanton
20. John Fox, <u>Senior</u>
21. <u>Route</u> 21
22. 4:29 <u>ante meridiem</u>
23. Colfax <u>Avenue</u>
24. White Paper <u>Company</u>
25. <u>Thursday</u>, <u>November</u> 2
26. 21104 Bay <u>Avenue</u>
27. Car Wreckers, <u>Incorporated</u>
28. Northern <u>Boulevard</u>
29. <u>February</u> 18, 1950
30. <u>Mister</u> Mel Practice, <u>Junior</u>
31. <u>Reverend</u> Summers
32. Baker <u>Street</u>
33. <u>Doctor</u> Anna Washington
34. Zip <u>Company</u>, <u>Incorporated</u>

Change the word at the end of the sentence to make a possessive noun. Write the possessive noun.

35. The ___ smiles showed happiness. (children)
36. Tara saw the ___ cages. (bears)
37. The ___ mother protected her children. (goats)
38. One bear ate a ___ hat. (stranger)
39. Tara counted the ___ stripes. (raccoon)
40. The children laughed at the ___ tricks. (monkeys)

In each sentence find the word that has the suffix **er, or, ness** or **less.** Write the word and then write what it means.

41. A climber went up Mount Rainier.
42. The breathless woman sat down.
43. The coldness of the wind caused the woman pain.
44. A visitor waved from the ground.
45. The fearless woman smiled.
46. The lifeless mountain glowed in the sunset.
47. At the top the woman met a hiker.
48. The woman laughed with happiness.
49. The stranger took the dullness out of the climb.

Have you ever wondered how the months and days got their names? Here are some names that some months and days come from.

1. January—Janus, Roman god of gates and beginnings and endings.
2. August—Augustus Caesar, a Roman emperor
3. Thursday—Thor, the Norse god of Thunder
4. June—Juno, Roman queen of the gods
5. March—Mars, Roman god of war

Exploring Language

Using the Dictionary

A dictionary is an important tool. It is helpful to you in reading, writing, spelling, and speaking. A dictionary is really a long list of words. Each word in the list is called an *entry word*. Entry words are arranged alphabetically.

● Look at the dictionary sample page below.

dobbin/doctor

dob·bin (dob′in) *n.* a horse, especially a gentle, plodding one.

Do·ber·man pin·scher (dō′bər mən pin′shər) a dog belonging to a breed developed in Germany, having a long head, slender legs, and usually a sleek, black or brown coat. [From Ludwig *Dober-man*, a nineteenth-century German dog breeder.]

dock¹ (dok) *n.* a structure built along the shore; wharf.

dock² (dok) *n.* the solid, fleshy part of an animal's tail. -*v.t.* to cut the end off or shorten: *to dock a horse's tail.*

dock³ (dok) *n.* the place in a criminal court where the defendant stands or sits during a trial. [Flemish *dok* cage.]

dock⁴ (dok) *n.* any group of plants related to buckwheat. [Old English *docce.*]

doctor (dok′tər) *n.* **1.** a person who is licensed to practice medicine, such as pediatrics. **2.** a person who is licensed to practice any of various related sciences, such as dentistry. **3.** a person who holds the highest graduate degree given by a university.

Notice that the word **dobbin** is the first entry word on the sample page. At the top of the sample page there are two words printed in dark type: **dobbin/doctor.** These words are called *guide words.* The guide words are the first and last word on a particular dictionary page. Notice that **dobbin** is the first word and that **doctor** is the last word on the sample page. All the entry words on this page began with **dob** or **doc.**

You can use a dictionary to help you find the meaning of words that you do not know. Entry words usually have more than one meaning.

1. Often the meanings of a word are related. They are usually numbered after the entry word. Look at the word **doctor** on the sample page. Three related meanings are listed.
2. Sometimes a word has two or more unrelated meanings. Then there is more than one entry for the same word. Look at the word *dock*. The word *dock* is spelled and pronounced the same way four times, but the meanings are different. The numbers above the last letter of *dock* show the four unrelated meanings.
3. A part of a sentence or a sample sentence will sometimes show how the entry word is used. Look at the second meaning of *dock* to see how you could use it in a sentence.

Talk About It

Use the sample dictionary page to answer these questions.

1. What are the guide words?
2. Which word has the most related meanings? How do you know?
3. Which words have only one meaning in the dictionary?

Skills Practice

Below are guide words on two pages of a dictionary.

acceptable/accomplishment	7	eyeball/Ezra	341

On which page would you find each of these entry words?

1. accompany   2. eyetooth   3. accident   4. eyebrow

Look at the sample dictionary page.

5. What is the third meaning of *dock*?
6. What is a synonym of the first meaning of *dock*?
7. What is a *dobbin*?
8. What is the third meaning of *doctor*?

Sample Answer 1. Page 7

Descriptive Paragraphs

Thinking About Paragraphs

Writing is one way to help you say clearly what you think or how you feel about an idea. A painter uses colors to make a picture. A writer paints pictures with words. As a writer, you must choose words that help you tell about or describe your idea. You could say, "It was windy today." It is more interesting to say, "A breezy wind laughed in my ear all day." A good description helps your reader to picture exactly what you have in mind.

● Read this paragraph. Can you picture what the writer is describing?

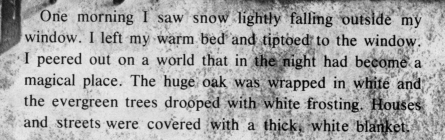

One morning I saw snow lightly falling outside my window. I left my warm bed and tiptoed to the window. I peered out on a world that in the night had become a magical place. The huge oak was wrapped in white and the evergreen trees drooped with white frosting. Houses and streets were covered with a thick, white blanket.

These are ways you can describe an idea.

1. Use words that describe how things look, smell, taste, sound, or feel. (The *huge* oak was wrapped in *white* and the evergreen trees drooped with *white frosting*.)
2. Use action words that describe what someone is doing or how something acts. (I left my warm bed and *tiptoed* to the window.)
3. Use a dictionary to find new words. Avoid using words over and over again, such as nice, terrible, awful, and wonderful.

Talking About Paragraphs

Read the paragraph about the snow again.

1. Find the topic sentence.
2. Read the detail sentences. What detail words are used to describe the snow?
3. What action words are used? You should have noticed the words *tiptoed, wrapped,* and *drooped.*
4. What word in the paragraph means the same thing as the word *looked?*

Writing a Paragraph

1. Look at the pictures above. Think of detail words and action words to describe each picture. Write this topic sentence: *The grassy meadow is a home for many animals.*
2. Write each of the following detail sentences after the topic sentence. Fill in the blank spaces with words that describe the pictures.

   The ___, ___ pony ___ across the ___ meadow.

   The ___, ___ rabbit felt ___ and ___.

   The ___ hawk ___ through the ___ sky looking for food.

A Friendly Letter

Thinking About a Letter

Sometimes you might want to write a letter to a friend. You could share an experience by describing what happened to you. When you write to a friend, you would use a special form of writing called a friendly letter. Study the letter below. The five parts in a friendly letter are listed on the left. Notice where each part is placed on the page.

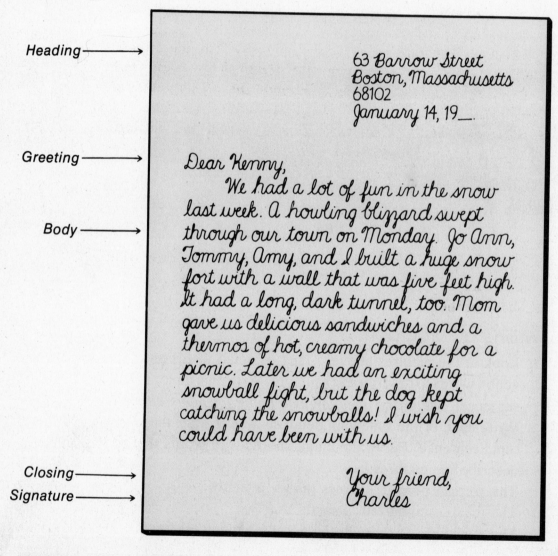

Heading →

63 Barrow Street
Boston, Massachusetts
68102
January 14, 19___.

Greeting →

Dear Kenny,

Body →

We had a lot of fun in the snow last week. A howling blizzard swept through our town on Monday. Jo Ann, Tommy, Amy, and I built a huge snow fort with a wall that was five feet high. It had a long, dark tunnel, too. Mom gave us delicious sandwiches and a thermos of hot, creamy chocolate for a picnic. Later we had an exciting snowball fight, but the dog kept catching the snowballs! I wish you could have been with us.

Closing →
Signature →

Your friend,
Charles

Think about the different parts of a friendly letter.

1. **Heading.** The heading is your address. It is placed in the upper right corner. The date should be the day you write the letter. Leave a space between the heading and the greeting.

2. **Greeting.** The greeting is your "hello" to the person to whom you are writing. The person's name is followed by a comma.

3. **Body.** The body is your message to the person to whom you are writing. Remember to indent all paragraphs and to use complete sentences.

4. **Closing.** The closing is your "good-by" to the friend. Place it under the body of the letter to the right and directly under the heading. Follow the closing with a comma.

5. **Signature.** Write your name directly under the closing. Use your first name in a friendly letter.

Talking About a Letter

Study the friendly letter that Charles wrote.

1. What information is found in the heading?
2. Why do you think the first name of a person is used with a friendly letter?
3. Look at the body of the letter.
   a. What is the topic sentence of the paragraph?
   b. How many detail sentences are there?
   c. What detail word describes the blizzard? What action word describes what the blizzard did?
4. What other words could you use in the closing?

Your Own Friendly Letter

Thinking About Your Letter

Have you ever written a friendly letter? One way to make a new friend is to write a friendly letter to a pen pal. A pen pal is a person (pal) to whom you write (pen) letters. Probably you won't actually meet your pen pal, but your letters may help you to become friends. It is a good way to learn about new and interesting people. Choose one of these imaginary people to be your pen pal:

Ann-Marie Chapman; London, England; age 10
Jim Tucker; Honolulu, Hawaii; age 11
Carlos Martinez; San Rafael, California; age 9
Barbara Homes; Washington, D.C.; age 10

Writing Your Letter

1. Write the heading in the correct place. Remember that your address always needs a ZIP code. Use today's date.
2. Write the greeting. Remember that you use the first name of the pen pal in a friendly letter.
3. Write the message to your pen pal in the body of the letter. Use this topic sentence: My name is ___ and I am ___ years old. Fill in the blanks with your name and age.

   Remember to indent the first word in your paragraph. You might include the following information in the detail sentences:

   a. Describe what you look like. Remember to use details.
   b. Describe what you like to do. Use action words if possible.
   c. Describe a pet or a favorite animal.
4. Write the closing.
5. Write your signature. Use your first name only.

Edit Your Letter

Look at your friendly letter. Read it carefully to check the following editing questions. Remember the two editing symbols. Use the *caret* (⌄) if you leave out words, and the *spelling sign* (sp) if you misspell a word.

1. Did your topic sentence tell the main idea?
2. Did each detail sentence state a complete idea?
3. Did you use good describing words in your sentences?
4. Did you use action words and details?
5. Did you follow the letter form correctly?
6. Did you indent the first word of the first paragraph?
7. Did you capitalize all proper nouns and the first word in each sentence?
8. Did you use the correct end punctuation?
9. Did you check your spelling?

Careers

Public health is concerned with protecting the cleanliness and safety of food, liquids, and air. People who work in public health test food that is eaten in public places such as hospitals, schools, or restaurants. Others test air and water samples for pollution. Another word for the protection of public health is *sanitation.* People who work to remove garbage are often called *sanitation workers. Sanitation engineers* design plants to treat sewage, which is water containing waste matter.

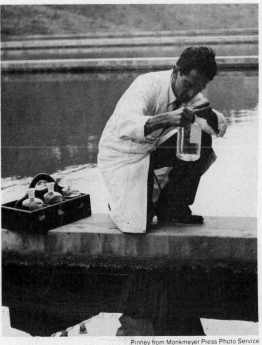

Pinney from Monkmeyer Press Photo Service

Checking Skills

Write each noun in each sentence. After each noun, write whether it names a **person, place, thing,** or **idea.** Then write **singular** if the noun is singular and **plural** if the noun is plural. *pages 38–41*

1. The people stayed on an island.
2. The families lived in huts.
3. Kim liked adventure.
4. The children explored the land.
5. Nick saw flowers near a cave.

Write the plural form of each noun. *pages 40–43*

6. daisy
7. ribbon
8. dress
9. dish
10. tie
11. journey
12. foot
13. woman
14. leaf

Write the compound noun in each sentence. Draw a line between the two words that make up each compound. Then write what each compound word means. *pages 44–45*

15. The children traveled to a playground.
16. The sunshine beamed brightly.
17. Marsha saw a mountaintop.

Write each noun in each sentence. After each noun write whether it is **common** or **proper.** *pages 48–49*

18. Ben Rogers visited the museum.
19. Lisa Rogers liked the Whitney Museum.
20. A guide pointed to a statue.

Change each underlined word to an abbreviation. *pages 50–51*

21. Friday, March 25
22. Doctor Rudolph Poe
23. 77 Oak Drive
24. Route 66
25. Quick Dry Company
26. December 25

Change the word at the end of the sentence to make a possessive noun. Write the possessive noun. *pages 52–53*

27. The children rode ___ trolleys.   (San Francisco)
28. Charlie watched the ___ faces.   (people)
29. Yoko painted ___ faces.   (strangers)
30. The children loved ___ art.   (Yoko)

In each sentence find each word that has the suffix **er, or, ness,** or **less.** Write each word and then write what it means.   *pages 54–55*

31. A traveler goes many places.
32. A sailor travels on the sea.
33. A fearless sailor faces danger on the sea.
34. The darkness brings gloom.

Below are the parts of a friendly letter. They are not in the right order. Put the parts in their proper order. Then write the letter. Be sure to use the correct punctuation in each part of the letter. *pages 62–65*

1. Phyllis
2.   I am busy making plans for summer camp. First I am deciding what clothes to take with me. I am sure I am going to need a new bathing suit. Then I have to sew labels with my name and address onto all my clothes. Last year I lost a swimming cap and my favorite hat.
3. 1601 15th Street
   Auburn Montana
   June 8 19___
4. Dear Sue
5. Your friend

Haiku

Haiku is a form of poetry which describes things in nature such as birds, butterflies, the sun, the moon, or even the seasons of the year. Haiku comes from Japan. Each haiku has three lines. The number of words may differ in each haiku. In Japanese the haiku always has seventeen syllables. However the haiku may not have that number when it is written in English.

Read the following haiku slowly and thoughtfully. Try to picture in your mind what the poet is describing.

Stillness:
The sound of petals
Sifting down together
　　　　—Chora

A giant firefly:
that way, this way, that way, this—
and it passes by.

　　　　　　　—Issa

Grasshopper,
Do not trample to pieces
The pearls of bright dew.
　　　　—Issa

P.G.

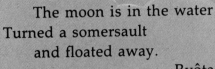

The moon is in the water
Turned a somersault
   and floated away.

            —Ryôta

The bat
Lives hidden
   Under the broken umbrella.

           —Bushon

Activities

1. Choose something in nature that you would like to
   describe. Here are some suggestions:

       a lake   a snowflake   a rainbow   a bee

   Think about the colors, sounds, and movements of your
   chosen object. Write the important words that describe
   these things. Then write your own haiku about the object.
   Try to use five syllables in your first line, seven syllables
   in your second line, and five syllables in your third line.

2. The tanka is another form of poetry like the haiku. A
   tanka has five lines. The first line has five syllables. The
   second line has seven syllables. The third line has five
   syllables, the fourth line, seven syllables, and the fifth
   line, seven syllables. Try writing a tanka. This first
   line may help you begin:

       Snowflakes falling down . . .

Grammar and Related Language Skills

Learning About Verbs
Objects of Verbs
Present and Past Tense of Verbs
Synonyms

Practical Communication

Using the Library
Writing a Business Letter

Creative Expression

A Sports Article

Action Verbs

A sentence has two parts, the *subject part* and the *predicate part*. The *subject part* names whom or what the sentence is about. The *predicate part* tells what action the subject part does. The word in the predicate that names an action is called the *action verb*. Words like *run, jump, fly, eat, talk,* and *sing* show action. Can you think of some others?

● Look at this picture. What action do you see in it? What words could you use to tell about the action?

> An **action verb** is a word that names an action. It may contain more than one word. It may have a main verb and a helping verb.

● Read each sentence below. The underlined word names an action. The underlined word is a verb.

A player <u>carries</u> the ball.　　The player <u>falls</u> down.
Runners <u>grab</u> his leg.　　Another player <u>stumbles</u>.

● Which word names the action in each of the following sentences?

One runner carries the ball.　　The player throws the ball.
His shoe flies in the air.　　His teammate catches the ball.

Talk About It

What is the action verb in each of the following sentences?

1. The children play flag football.
2. Cindy takes a cloth.
3. Suki ties the knot.
4. Cindy carries the cloth.
5. The knot hangs down.
6. Cindy runs with the ball.
7. Althea grabs for the cloth.
8. Cindy drops the ball.
9. The ball bounces.
10. Jack catches the ball.
11. Jack throws the ball quickly.
12. The ball flies high.
13. The ball hits a tree.
14. Jack climbs the tree.

Skills Practice

Read each sentence. Write the action verb.

1. Al saw a football game.
2. The Bears played the Colts.
3. Al drove to the stadium.
4. Al sat in the last row.
5. The teams came on the field.
6. The captains met.
7. The official tossed a coin.
8. The Colts kicked the ball.
9. The Bears caught the football.
10. The carrier ran down the field.
11. The Bears reached the goal.
12. The Colts defended their goal.
13. The Colts got the ball.
14. The teams played well.
15. The Colts scored a touchdown.
16. The teams rested.
17. A band came out.
18. The band played rock music.
19. Al listened to the music.
20. The teams returned.
21. The game continued.
22. The Bears scored a touchdown.
23. Both teams played hard.
24. The Colts won the game.

Write an action verb to complete each of the following sentences. Write the complete sentence.

25. The player ___ the ball.
26. The fans ___ loudly.
27. One runner ___ on the field.
28. Both teams ___ well.
29. The ball ___ in the air.
30. The game ___ in a tie.

Sample Answer 1. saw

Objects of Verbs

The verb in a sentence names an action. Sometimes there is a person or thing that receives the action. The person or thing that receives the action of the verb is called the *object* of the verb.

● Look at these sentences.

Nina bumps Nancy.   Magda guards Nina.

The verb in the first sentence is *bumps*. Whom does Nina bump? She bumps Nancy. Therefore Nancy is the object of the verb. Who is the object of the verb in the second sentence?

● Now read these sentences.

Nina shoots the ball.   The ball hits the hoop.

The verb in the first sentence is *shoots*. What does Nina shoot? Nina shoots the ball. Therefore *ball* is the object of the verb. The object is often a noun. What is the object of the verb in the second sentence?

The **object** of a verb receives the action of the verb. It answers the question *whom*? or *what*? after an action verb.

Sometimes there is no object of a verb in a sentence.

• Look at these sentences.

Verbs with No Objects
The ball <u>bounces</u>.
The team <u>scores</u>.

Verbs with Objects
Lois <u>bounces</u> the ball.
Nina <u>scores</u> two points.

The sentences on the left are complete as they are. The sentences on the right use objects to tell more about the action.

Talk About It

Read each sentence. Name the verb. Name the object of the verb.

1. Nina throws the ball.
2. The ball hits the wall.
3. Joanne pushes Magda.
4. Magda loses her shoe.
5. Her shoe hits the basket.
6. Lois catches the shoe.

Skills Practice

Read each sentence. Write the verb. Then write the object of the verb.

1. The fans filled the gym.
2. Ali and Bob found seats.
3. Children sold peanuts.
4. The coaches shook hands.
5. The referee blew a whistle.
6. The team missed a basket.
7. Magda raced Nina.
8. Nina grabbed the ball.
9. Nina passed the ball.
10. Joanne scored two points.
11. The fans cheered Joanne.
12. The team won the game.

Write an object of the verb for each sentence below. Make sure that the word you use is a noun. Try to vary your answers.

13. Nancy passed ___.
14. Magda threw ___.
15. Magda missed ___.
16. Lois lost ___.
17. Nancy scored ___.
18. The fans cheered ___.

Sample Answers 1. filled, gym 13. the ball.

Present Tense

A verb names an action. A verb also tells when an action happens. The *tense* of a verb shows when the action takes place.

- Look at the verbs in these sentences.

The runners <u>race</u> around a track. A boy <u>throws</u> a heavy ball.
The winner <u>breaks</u> the tape. Some girls <u>jump</u> high over a bar.

In these sentences each verb shows action that happens now. These actions all take place at the present time.

The **present tense** of a verb names an action that happens now.

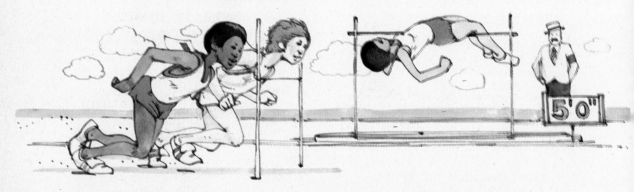

- Read the sentences in the box. Notice the differences in the way the verbs end.

Jon win<u>s</u> the race. The jumpers rest.
He break<u>s</u> the tape. I give you a heavy ball.
The coach cheer<u>s</u>. You throw the ball.
Anne leap<u>s</u> in the air. The girls race next.
She land<u>s</u> in the sand. They run fast.
Wing Lee jump<u>s</u> with a pole. We cheer the winners.

Verbs in the present tense have certain forms. In the sentences in the box, notice that an *s* is added to the end of each verb in the first column. When the subject is a singular noun or *he, she,* or *it,* an *s* is added to form the present tense verb. Notice the verbs in the second column. When the subject is a plural noun or *I, you, we,* or *they,* the verb doesn't change in the present tense.

You already know how to add *es* to words that end in *s, ss, x, ch, sh,* or *z.*

● Notice the endings of the verbs in these sentences.

Jon cross<u>es</u> the finish line.
The racers cross the finish line.

Cal finish<u>es</u> the race.
The runners finish the race.

Talk About It

Complete each sentence with a verb in the present tense.

1. Shana ___ the race. (watch)
2. Juanita ___ fast. (run)
3. Mel ___ the winner. (guess)

4. Terry ___ a number. (wear)
5. Terry ___ up the shoes. (mix)
6. The coach ___ the shoes. (fix)

Skills Practice

Write each sentence. Use the correct form of the verb in the present tense.

1. Molly ___. (jump)
2. Molly ___ the bar. (miss)
3. The teams ___ again. (race)
4. A runner ___ a stick. (pass)
5. Eva ___ for a win. (wish)
6. The jumper ___. (leap)
7. Wing Lee ___ the pole. (drop)

8. The coach ___ the pole. (catch)
9. Davy ___ his arm. (stretch)
10. Davy ___ the ball. (toss)
11. The last runner ___. (finish)
12. A runner ___ the line. (cross)
13. A fan ___. (clap)
14. A new race ___. (begin)

Sample Answer **1.** Molly jumps.

Past Tense

A verb in the present tense names an action that happens now. Another tense tells about actions that happened before now. These actions ended in the past.

●Look at the verbs in these sentences.

The teams <u>played</u> baseball yesterday. Tracy <u>pitched</u> for the Tigers. The rain <u>ended</u> the game. Our team <u>remained</u> the champion. The coach <u>smiled</u> at Tracy.

Each verb shows an action that already happened. These verbs are in the past tense.

The **past tense** of a verb names an action that already happened.

Verbs in the past tense have a special form. Most verbs that show action in the past end in *ed*. The verbs end in *ed* when the subject is either singular or plural.

The pitcher start*ed* the game.   The players want*ed* a run.

●Notice how the past tense of these verbs is formed.

compare   compared
share   shared
race   raced

Remember that verbs that already end in *e* drop the *e* and add *ed* to form the past tense.

Talk About It

Find the verb in each sentence. Then change the verb to the past tense.

1. The fans like baseball.
2. The Lions want a home run.
3. The Tigers start the game.
4. The coach smiles.
5. Tracy pitches a ball.
6. The batter misses the ball.
7. The runner races to second.
8. The catcher shows a signal.

Skills Practice

Read each sentence. Then write the verb in the past tense.

1. Baseball amuses the fans.
2. The fans compare the players.
3. The players share the lockers.
4. The game starts on time.
5. The umpire needs a nap.
6. Tracy asks a question.
7. The coach moves his head.
8. Tracy looks at the runner.
9. Jenny chases the ball.
10. The fans cheer.
11. The players join the coach.
12. Tracy finishes the inning.
13. The rain ends the game.
14. The game lasts an hour.

Writing Sentences

Imagine that you played baseball with two famous ball players. They can be real or make-believe baseball players.

1. Write a sentence telling what one famous pitcher did. Use a verb in the present tense.
2. Write a sentence telling what two batters did. Use a verb in the past tense.
3. Write a sentence telling what one player did. Use a verb in the past tense.
4. Write a sentence telling what the fans did. Use a verb in the past tense.

Sample Answer 1. amused.

Skills Review

Read each sentence. Write the action verb.

1. Sam played ping-pong with Susie.
2. Sam beat Susie in each game.
3. Sam slammed the ball hard across the table.
4. The ball flew by Susie too quickly.
5. Now Susie tries harder.
6. Susie holds her paddle tightly.
7. Sam hits the ball very hard to Susie.
8. This time Susie returns the ball.
9. Sam yells in surprise.
10. Susie laughs at the look on his face.

Read each sentence. Write the verb. Then write the object of the verb.

11. Hugo coaches the racers.
12. The teams sail boats.
13. Hugo blows the whistle.
14. One boat races the other.
15. The sails catch the wind.
16. The wind fills the sails.
17. Hugo watches the winner.
18. The boat crosses the line.

Write each sentence. Use the correct form of the verb in the present tense.

19. The students ___ funny games in gym.   (play)
20. Mrs. Williams ___ the games to the class.   (teach)
21. Mrs. Williams ___ two large sacks.   (take)
22. Mrs. Williams ___ one sack to a student.   (give)
23. The student ___ her legs into the sack.   (put)
24. Mrs. Williams ___ the sack tightly.   (tie)
25. Another student ___ the second sack.   (use)
26. The two students ___.   (race)

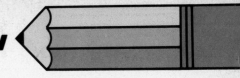

Read each sentence. Then write the verb in the past tense.

27. Emily races Mara.
28. The girls jump madly across the floor.
29. Their friends cheer.
30. Emily looks down.
31. Her toes show through the sack.
32. These games amuse Mrs. Williams.
33. Emily uses a different sack next time.

Have you ever wondered . . .
If the past of grow is *grew*,
why isn't the past of snow *snew*?
If the past of give is *gave*,
why isn't the past of live *lave*?
If the past of sit is *sat*,
why isn't the past of hit *hat*?
Can you think of other questions like these?

Exploring Language

Present and Past of <u>Have</u>

The verb *have* is a special verb. *Have* forms the present and past tense in a different way from most verbs.

- Look at these sentences. The verb *have* is in the present tense in each sentence.

Manuel <u>has</u> a game.

It <u>has</u> rules.

He <u>has</u> a friend, Marina.

She <u>has</u> good cards.

The game <u>has</u> two players.

The children <u>have</u> a game.

You <u>have</u> the rules.

I <u>have</u> the scorecard.

We <u>have</u> a good time.

They <u>have</u> fun, too.

When the subject is a singular noun or *he, she,* or *it,* the present tense form of this verb is *has.* When the subject is a plural noun or *I, you, we,* or *they,* the form is *have.*

- Look at these sentences. The verb *have* is in the past tense in each sentence.

He <u>had</u> a good day yesterday.

The children <u>had</u> fun.

They <u>had</u> good cards.

Marina <u>had</u> four cards.

The past tense of the verb *have* is always *had.*

Talk About It

Complete each sentence. Use the correct form of the verb *have*.

1. Today Marina ___ good cards. (present)
2. The table ___ a flat top. (past)
3. Manuel ___ trouble with the cards. (past)
4. The players ___ two decks of cards (present)
5. You ___ the queen of hearts (present)
6. Marina ___ the ace of clubs. (present)
7. Yesterday they ___ a good time. (past)

Skills Practice

Write each sentence. Use the correct form of the verb *have*.

1. The friends ___ a new hobby now. (present)
2. They ___ a small puppy. (present)
3. It ___ the name "Dinky." (present)
4. The puppy ___ brown eyes and soft fur. (present)
5. The friends ___ a lot of fun with Dinky. (present)
6. Marina ___ some unusual pets. (past)
7. She ___ a pair of hamsters last summer. (past)
8. The hamsters ___ a family. (past)
9. They ___ six baby hamsters. (past)
10. The hamsters ___ a great time inside their cage. (past)

Sample Answer 1. The friends have a new hobby now.

Past Tense with <u>Have</u>

There is a special way of talking about the past. Sometimes you want to tell about an action that began in the past and is still going on. Sometimes you want to talk about an action that did not happen at a definite time in the past.

The rain <u>has</u> <u>started</u>. } still going on
The teams <u>have</u> <u>played</u> many games. } not at a definite time

The underlined verbs are examples of the *past tense with have*. They have a main verb and they use the helping verb *have* or *has*. The main verb is in the past tense. Notice how the past tense with *have* is formed.

Verb	Past tense with *have*
race	has or have raced
play	has or have played
ask	has or have asked
move	has or have moved

● Find the verbs that are examples of the past tense with *have*.

Irene has played first base this season.
Tom has pitched well.
The outfielders have received much praise.

Talk About It

Complete each sentence. Use the correct form of the verb in the past tense with *have* or *has*.

1. The game ___. (has started, have started)
2. The coach ___ the weather. (has checked, have checked)
3. The players ___ well this year. (has played, have played)
4. Practice ___. (has helped, have helped)

Complete each sentence. Use the correct form of the verb in the past tense.

5. The coach has ___ hard. (work)
6. The team has ___ all season. (practice)
7. The players have ___. (improve)

Skills Practice

Write each sentence. Complete each sentence by using the correct form of the verb in the past tense with *have* or *has*.

1. The stadium ___. (has filled, have filled)
2. The fans ___. (has arrived, have arrived)
3. The cheers ___. (has started, have started)
4. The umpire ___. (has appeared, have appeared)
5. The teams ___ for the game. (has dressed, have dressed)

Write each sentence. Complete each sentence by using the correct form of the verb in the past tense.

6. Sam has ___ many Green Sox games. (watch)
7. The players have ___ Sam. (notice)
8. Sam has ___ the dugout. (share)
9. The players have ___ a ball for Sam. (sign)
10. Sam has ___ the ball on his bookshelf. (place)

Sample Answers 1. The stadium has filled.
6. Sam has watched many Green Sox games.

More About the Past Tense

The past tense of some verbs is not formed in the regular way. These verbs do not change to past tense by adding *ed*. They have special forms that do not follow any rules. You must learn these special forms. Ten of these verbs are in the left-hand column of the chart below. The middle column shows their form in past tense. The right-hand column shows the past tense with *have*.

Verb	Past Tense	Past Tense with Have
begin	began	has, have begun
break	broke	has, have broken
do	did	has, have done
drink	drank	has, have drunk
fly	flew	has, have flown
give	gave	has, have given
grow	grew	has, have grown
lose	lost	has, have lost
run	ran	has, have run
sit	sat	has, have sat

- Look at each pair of sentences below. Notice the special way each verb changes from present to past tense.

The players <u>lose</u> every game.   The team <u>lost</u> again last night.
Their fans <u>do</u> a lot of crying.   They <u>did</u> a lot of crying last night.

The past tense with *have* of these verbs is not formed in the regular way.

- Look at each sentence below. Notice the special way each verb changes from the present tense.

<u>begin</u>   The team <u>has</u> <u>begun</u> to leave.
<u>break</u>   Some players <u>have</u> <u>broken</u> a lot of records.

Remember that this special past tense with *have* tells about action that started in the past and is still continuing. It also tells about action that did not happen at a particular time.

Talk About It

Complete each sentence. Use the correct form of the verb in the past tense.

1. Yesterday the team ___. (lose)
2. The team has ___ again. (lose)
3. Fans have ___ to cry. (begin)
4. Last week Bob ___. (run)
5. The players have ___ home. (fly)
6. Bob has ___ up hockey. (give)

Skills Practice

Write each sentence. Use the correct form of the verb in the past tense.

1. Ali ___ taller last year. (grow)
2. Ali has ___ taller. (grow)
3. The fans have ___ down. (sit)
4. The puck ___ over the ice. (fly)
5. Bob ___ away his stick. (give)
6. Amy has ___ her stick. (break)
7. Guy has ___ some water. (drink)
8. Bob has ___ away. (run)
9. The coach ___ down. (sit)
10. Maya ___ a song. (begin)
11. Maya has ___ well. (do)
12. Goalies ___ badly. (do)
13. Fans ___ soda. (drink)
14. Jill ___ her toe. (break)

Sample Answer 1. grew

Forms of Verbs: Present

An *s* or *es* is often added to a verb to agree with a singular subject or *he, she,* or *it.* Sometimes you change the spelling before you add *es.*

● Look at each pair of verbs. How is the spelling changed?

tidy	bury	carry
tidies	buries	carries

If a verb ends with a consonant and *y,* change the *y* to *i* and add *es* to make the correct form of the present tense.

● Now look at each pair of verbs below. How is the spelling changed?

stay	obey	destroy
stays	obeys	destroys

If a verb ends in a vowel and *y,* add *s* to make the correct form of the present tense.

Talk About It

Complete each sentence with the correct form of the verb in the present tense.

1. He ___ to school.   (hurry)
2. It ___ the clothes.   (dry)
3. He ___ the bone.   (bury)
4. It ___ in the wind.   (sway)

Skills Practice

Use the correct form of the verb in the present tense. Write each sentence.

1. The van ___ the fans.   (carry)
2. Joe ___ along.   (hurry)
3. Mary ___ at home.   (stay)
4. Joe ___ his coach.   (obey)
5. Mitsu ___ very hard.   (study)
6. Rain ___ the field.   (destroy)

Sample Answer 1. The van carries the fans.

Forms of Verbs: Past

The past tense of most action verbs is formed by adding *ed*. With some verbs you change the spelling before you add *ed*.

● Look at each pair of verbs. How is the spelling changed?

reply   study
replied   studied

If a verb ends in a consonant and *y*, change the *y* to *i* and add *ed* to form the past tense.

If a verb ends in a vowel and *y*, add *ed* to form the past tense.

The sick player stay<u>ed</u> in bed.

● Now look at each pair of verbs below. How is the spelling changed to form the past tense?

clap   beg   bat   fan
clapped   begged   batted   fanned

If a verb ends in consonant, vowel, consonant, double the last consonant and add *ed* to form the past tense.

Talk About It

Spell each verb in the past tense.

1. spy   **2.** fry   **3.** flip   **4.** play   **5.** pin

Skills Practice

Write each of these verbs in the correct form of the past tense.

1. tidy   **3.** obey   **5.** spray   **7.** replay   **9.** grab
2. chop   **4.** flop   **6.** cry   **8.** destroy   **10.** sway

Sample Answer 1. tidied

Prefixes

A *prefix* is a letter or a group of letters added to the beginning of a word. Adding a prefix changes the meaning of the word.

● Look at the underlined words in these sentences. What prefix can you find in each word?

Jack <u>misuses</u> the equipment.
Jack <u>misbehaves</u> on the golf course.

The prefix added to these verbs is *mis*. *Mis* means *badly* or in the wrong way.

Our language has many other prefixes. Here are three of the most common prefixes used with action verbs:

Prefix	Meaning	Example
mis	badly, in the wrong way	Did you know you <u>misspelled</u> my name?
re	again	Please <u>rewrite</u> my name.
un	opposite of	Jack <u>untied</u> his shoelaces.

● Look at these sentences. Let the prefixes help you understand the meaning of the verbs.

Jack <u>misplaces</u> his golf ball.
Jack <u>reopens</u> his locker.
Jack <u>unzips</u> the pocket of his jacket.

● Look at these sentences. Notice how helpful the prefix is.

Jack does the opposite of pack his lunch.
Jack unpacks his lunch.

The first sentence sounds clumsy. Prefixes help you speak and write clearly.

Talk About It

Tell what the underlined word means in each sentence.

1. Jack <u>misjudges</u> the ball.
2. The workers <u>replace</u> the grass.
3. Jack <u>unfolds</u> a handkerchief.
4. Jack <u>unbuttons</u> his shirt.

Skills Practice

Find the verb that has a prefix in each sentence. Write the verb. Then write what the verb means.

1. Jack misplaced his golf clubs one morning.
2. Jack unlocked his locker to look there.
3. He rechecked his locker in the afternoon.
4. He unwrapped some boxes and found his clubs.

Write each sentence. Change each group of underlined words to one word that has a prefix.

5. Jack <u>understands in the wrong way</u> the game of golf.
6. Jack does <u>the opposite of cover</u> his equipment in the rain.
7. Jack <u>plays in the wrong way</u> and hits three people.
8. Jack <u>reads again</u> his book on playing golf.

Writing Sentences

Imagine that you are playing a game.

1. Write a sentence using an action verb with the prefix *mis*.
2. Write a sentence using an action verb with the prefix *re*.
3. Write a sentence using an action verb with the prefix *un*.
4. Write a sentence using an action verb with any prefix you like.

Sample Answers 1. misplaced, placed wrongly
5. Jack misunderstands the game of golf.

Synonyms

Life would be dull if we used the same words over and over again. Words wear out. For this reason our language has different words that have similar meanings. A *synonym* is a word that has nearly the same meaning as another word.

● Look at the words below. All of them are synonyms. Each verb names almost the same action.

say   talk   speak   mention   tell

● Now look at each word below. Do all of these synonyms mean exactly the same thing?

laugh   snicker   giggle   smile   titter   chuckle

Words may be synonyms even when they do not name exactly the same action.

Sometimes in your writing you may be able to think of more than one verb to tell about an action. When you have a choice, always use the verb that best names the action.

● Look at these sentences below. Each one tells about the picture.

Cho <u>hits</u> the ball.   Cho <u>knocks</u> the ball.
Cho <u>taps</u> the ball.   Cho <u>strikes</u> the ball.
Cho <u>sends</u> the ball.   Cho <u>slams</u> the ball.

The verbs in the six sentences are synonyms. The verbs mean nearly the same thing. But the verb *slams* most closely names the action. *Slams* is the only verb that tells how hard the ball is hit.

Talk About It

Each sentence is followed by two verbs that are synonyms. Either verb completes the sentence. Which verb most closely names the action? Give reasons for your answer.

1. Shawn ___ across the court in record time. (walked, sped)
2. The hard-hit ball ___ by. (whizzed, went)
3. Shawn ___ the ball as hard as he could. (slammed, tapped)
4. The other player ___ at the ball in surprise. (looked, stared)

Skills Practice

Choose the verb in parentheses that most closely names the action. Write each sentence with the verb you have chosen.

1. The big tennis match ___ the eager watchers. (pleased, thrilled)
2. Hundreds of fans ___ the small stadium. (jammed, filled)
3. Trina just barely ___ between two other people. (squeezed, sat)
4. The players ___ quickly to and fro. (ran, darted)
5. Jake ___ the ball as hard as he could. (hit, smacked)
6. Shawn's leg hurt. He ___ off the court. (limped, walked)

Writing Sentences

Imagine you are playing some kind of ball game. Use an action verb in each sentence.

1. Write a sentence using the action verb hit.
2. Write a sentence using a synonym for hit.
3. Write a sentence using the action verb run.
4. Write a sentence using a synonym for run.

Sample Answer 1. The big tennis match thrilled the eager watchers.

Skills Review

Complete each sentence. Use the correct form of the verb *have*.

1. Two teams ___ a tug-of-war.   (present)
2. Our team ___ strong pullers.   (present)
3. The other team ___ luck.   (present)
4. Last year we ___ a tie.   (past)
5. We ___ a line between us.   (present)
6. Last time I ___ the rope end.   (past)

Write the correct past tense form of each verb in parentheses.

7. The team has ___ a goal.   (score)
8. The score has ___ quickly.   (grow)
9. The fans have ___.   (cheer)
10. The fans have ___ down.   (sit)
11. Ali ___ orange juice.   (drink)
12. One player has ___ the puck.   (chase)

Use the correct form of the verb in the present tense. Write the verb.

13. The sun ___ out all day.   (stay)
14. The field ___ after the rain.   (dry)
15. The truck ___ the equipment to the game.   (carry)
16. The player ___ the rules.   (obey)
17. The team ___ the equipment.   (share)
18. Joe ___ to the coach's question.   (reply)

Write each of these verbs in the past tense.

19. flip   21. scar   23. sway   25. beg   27. supply
20. drop   22. study   24. bury   26. grab   28. hurry

Find the verb that has a prefix in each sentence. Write the verb first. Then write what the verb means.

29. Jean unwrapped her team jacket.
30. Her name was misspelled on the jacket.
31. Jean sent the jacket back to the company to be redone.
32. The company worker unfolded the jacket.
33. The worker reprinted her name the right way.

Write the following sentences. Change each group of under-lined words to one word that has a prefix.

34. The Pirates <u>did the opposite of pack</u> their uniforms.
35. The Pirates <u>judged in the wrong way</u> the Rockets.
36. The Pirates will <u>play again</u> the Rockets next year.

Choose the verb in parentheses that most closely names the action. Write the verb you have chosen.

37. Our team ___ hard for the frisbee championship.
    (played, battled)
38. The frisbee ___ high in the air all day.   (went, sailed)
39. Our team ___ down the field quickly.   (rushed, moved)
40. The fans ___ loudly to the players.   (spoke, shouted)
41. Aladdin ___ the frisbee to June.   (tossed, gave)
42. June ___ over a rock.   (ran, stumbled)
43. Her arms ___ for the frisbee.   (reached, stretched)
44. Our team ___ the frisbee championship.   (won, captured)

The ABC Action Verb Ball Game
Make up a sentence using an action verb that begins with the letter "a." You might say: "I <u>aimed</u> the ball." Then you or another player might say: "I <u>batted</u> the ball," "I <u>caught</u> the ball," "I <u>dribbled</u> the ball," and so on, through the alphabet as far as you can go.

Exploring Language

Using the Library

The library is a good place to gather information and to find interesting books and magazines to read. Sometimes you will want to use the information to write a report. The books and magazines you might use are called *reference works*. You use them to find a *reference* about a subject.

An encyclopedia is one of the most useful reference works to use when gathering facts for a report. An *encyclopedia* is a book or set of books that gives information about many subjects. All the subjects in an encyclopedia are arranged in alphabetical order. Remember that there are pictures or photographs in encyclopedias that can help you, too. An encyclopedia often has an index in a separate book to help you find your subject. The index tells in which book and on what page of the book you can find the facts you need.

Mark

ENCYCLOPEDIA

Another good reference work is the almanac. An *almanac* is a single book that gives you the latest facts and figures about many subjects. Most almanacs are printed every year. They give you lists of facts about important records, events, and people. You can use an almanac to find interesting facts about your state or about a state you may be visiting.

Mark F

WORLD ALMANAC

To find a book in a library, use the card catalog. There are three cards for every book. The number in the upper left corner shows where you can find the book. Ask your librarian for help.

Look at these sample cards:

1. The **author card** lists the name of the author and the title of the book. The author's last name comes first.
2. The **title card** gives the name of the book and the author.
3. The **subject card** states the topic of the book and lists the author and title.

TITLE CARD

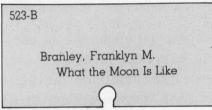

AUTHOR CARD

SUBJECT CARD

Talk About It

Look at the cards above and answer these questions.

1. What is the subject on the subject card?
2. What information is on every card?
3. What number would you give to a librarian to find the book?

Skills Practice

Decide whether you would use an encyclopedia or an almanac.

1. Where would you find a list of volcanoes in the world?
2. Where would you find facts about how peanuts grow?
3. Where would you look for facts on Native Americans?
4. Where would you find facts about your state's rainfall?
5. Where would you find a list of space flights?

Sample Answer 1. Almanac

Facts in Paragraphs

Thinking About Paragraphs

Writing is a good way to share information with others. One place to find information is in a library. You can use reference works to gather facts about your ideas. For example, you might use an encyclopedia to help you to write about a person in history. Or an almanac could give you information about the number of people who live in your state. Ask questions such as who, what, where, when, and how to find facts. You can then share your information by writing a paragraph using your facts. The topic sentence will state the main idea. Each detail sentence should give specific facts which support the main idea.

• Read the paragraph below. Look for facts about the main idea:

> Tennis is an old sport that is played all over the world. Tennis began in France in the twelfth century. It was called the "game of the palm." The players batted the ball over the net with the palms of their hands. In 1873, the English introduced "lawn tennis." It was played on grass courts. Now the sport is known by the name "tennis."

Talking About Paragraphs

1. The topic sentence tells you that tennis is an old sport. What did you expect the paragraph to be about?
2. Read the detail sentences. The facts in the paragraph should help you answer the following questions: Where and when did tennis begin? Why was it called the "game of the palm"? When was tennis introduced in England?

Writing a Paragraph

Facts tell you something specific about a main idea. Look at the picture below. A list of facts beside the picture tells about a great moment in sports.

Date: April 8, 1974
Time: 9:06 P.M.
Place: Atlanta Stadium
Teams: game between
      the Atlanta Braves
      and the Los Angeles
      Dodgers
Record: Hank Aaron's
      715th home run
      Hit on Al Downing's
      second pitch

United Press International

1. Think about how to arrange the facts in the paragraph. You can arrange the facts by using the answers to the questions: who, what, where, when, and how.

   a. Write this topic sentence on your paper: *Hank Aaron broke Babe Ruth's home-run record.*

   b. Write a detail sentence from the list of facts that gives information about *when* the event happened. Use the date and time.

   c. Write a detail sentence about *where* it happened. Use the place.

   d. Write a detail sentence about *who* was there. Use the names of the teams.

   e. Write a detail sentence about *what* and *how* it happened. Tell about the record.

A Business Letter

Thinking About a Letter

A business letter is different from a friendly letter. It is a serious *letter* often written to a business to ask for information or to order something you want. A paragraph in a business letter should use facts to explain the purpose of your letter.

Read the advertisement below.

SALE! Warm-Up Suits $20
red with blue stripes
green with yellow stripes
Sizes: small, medium, large
Order from: Brown's Sporting Goods.
472 Ocean Avenue; Johnson, New York 11005

The following business letter was written to Brown's Sporting Goods. How is this letter different from the friendly letter?

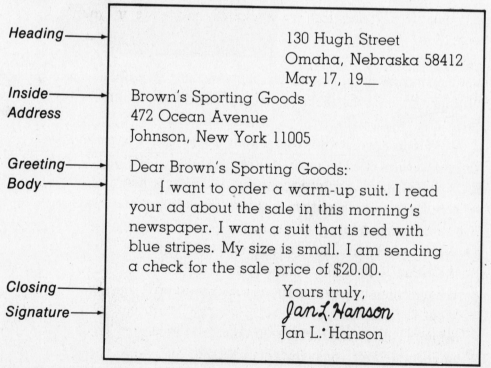

Heading ——→

130 Hugh Street
Omaha, Nebraska 58412
May 17, 19__

Inside ——→
Address

Brown's Sporting Goods
472 Ocean Avenue
Johnson, New York 11005

Greeting ——→
Body ——→

Dear Brown's Sporting Goods:
    I want to order a warm-up suit. I read your ad about the sale in this morning's newspaper. I want a suit that is red with blue stripes. My size is small. I am sending a check for the sale price of $20.00.

Closing ——→
Signature ——→

Yours truly,
Jan L. Hanson
Jan L. Hanson

Look at the business letter written to Brown's Sporting Goods. Notice that it has six parts.

1. **Heading.** The heading is in the upper right corner of the letter. It gives your address and the date. Notice that there is a comma between the city and state and the date and the year.

2. **Inside address.** The inside address starts at the left margin. This part is not found in a friendly letter. It is the address of the person or business receiving your letter.

3. **Greeting.** The greeting begins in the left margin and ends with a punctuation mark called a colon.

4. **Body.** The body of the letter states why you are writing the letter. It should be polite and short with all needed facts.

5. **Closing.** The closing comes after the body, directly under the heading. Write: "Yours truly," or "Sincerely."

6. **Signature.** Use your full name directly under the closing. Many business letters are typed. If so, you leave a space between the closing and the signature and write in your name.

Talking About a Letter

Study the business letter that Jan wrote. Use it to answer these questions.

1. How would Brown's Sporting Goods know where to send the warm-up suit? The correct address with a ZIP code in the heading is very important in a business letter.

2. What information is written in the inside address?

3. Notice that the greeting gives the full name of the business. What other kind of greeting could you use?

4. Look at the body of the letter.
   a. What is the topic sentence of the paragraph?
   b. What facts are in your detail sentences? Notice that the facts answer the questions where, when, and what.

5. What last two parts are needed in a business letter?

Your Own Business Letter

Thinking About Your Letter

Read the business letter to Brown's Sporting Goods in the last lesson. Imagine that you ordered a warm-up suit from the store. When you received it, you found that something was wrong with it. Now you want to return it and get your money back. Think of some reasons for returning the suit. For example, give facts such as the colors faded when you washed it, or the zipper was broken when you received it.

Writing Your Letter

Read again the business letter that Jan wrote. Write a letter to Brown's Sporting Goods saying that you want to return the warm-up suit. Follow these directions:

1. Write your heading with today's date.
2. Write to this inside address: Brown's Sporting Goods; 472 Ocean Avenue; Johnson, New York 11005.
3. Write the greeting. Remember to use a colon in a business letter.

Word Bank

advertised
ordered
problem
unhappy
wrong
style
money

4. Use facts in the body of the business letter.
   a. Write this topic sentence: *I am returning a warm-up suit.*
   b. Use detail sentences to give the facts clearly and briefly. Tell the store why you are returning the suit and ask for your money back. Try to arrange your sentences according to:
      When you ordered it.
      Where you read about it.
      What is wrong.
      What you want them to do.
      Remember that even though you may feel angry about returning the suit, it is important to be polite in a business letter.
   c. Be sure to indent the first sentence.

Edit Your Letter

Look at your business letter. Use the following editing questions to edit your letter. Remember to use the two editing symbols when needed. The *caret* (˄) is used if you leave words out, and the *spelling sign* (sp) shows a misspelled word.

1. Did you have a good topic sentence?
2. Did your detail sentences state facts clearly?
3. Did all your sentences express a complete idea?
4. Did you indent the first word of the paragraph?
5. Did you use any action words in your paragraph?
6. Did you follow the business letter form correctly?
7. Did you check the spelling of your words?
8. Did you use capitals to start every sentence?
9. Did you use commas in your heading correctly and use a colon in your greeting?

Careers

There are many different kinds of jobs in a small business. A business must have an *owner* who makes decisions about the way the business is run. Also two or more people could be responsible for the business and form a *partnership.* The owner needs other people to help run the store. A *clerk* helps people find what they want in the store. A *stock clerk* orders and takes care of the products that the store sells. A *bookkeeper* or *accountant* keeps records of sales and expenses.

Leinwand from Monkmeyer Press Photo Service

Checking Skills

Read each sentence. Write the action verb. *pages 72–73*

1. The player catches the ball.
2. Diane shoots the basketball through the hoop.
3. Diane scores two points for her team.

Read each sentence. Write the verb and the object of the verb. *pages 74–75*

4. Ché hit the ball.
5. Andrea grabbed the flag.
6. The judge blew her whistle.
7. Fans filled the stadium.

Write the correct form of the verb in the present tense. *pages 76–77*

8. She ___ an egg.   (toss)
9. He ___ the egg.   (catch)
10. He ___ the egg.   (throw)
11. She ___ the egg.   (drop)
12. A judge ___ the contest.   (watch)
13. The judge ___ him the winner.   (call)

Read each sentence. Write the verb in the past tense. *pages 78–79*

14. They begin the game over.
15. This time she tries harder.
16. The egg almost flies.
17. The judge declares her the winner.
18. She skips down the street.
19. The dog wags its tail.

Read each sentence. Write the correct form of the verb *have*. *pages 82–83*

20. Once I ___ a bird.   (past)
21. It ___ three eggs.   (past)
22. Now the bird ___ a nest.   (present)
23. The birds ___ a family.   (present)

Read each sentence. Write the correct past tense form of each verb in parentheses. *pages 84–87*

24. The team has ___ the game.   (finish)
25. The team ___ the game.   (lose)
26. The fans have ___ sad.   (grow)
27. A player has ___ his stick.   (toss)

28. Jan ___ her skates away.   (give)
29. The coach has ___ down.   (sit)
30. The players have ___ bags.   (pack)
31. Two players ___ home.   (run)

Write the following sentences. Change each group of underlined words to one word that has a prefix.   *pages 90–91*

32. The Tigers <u>did the opposite of fasten</u> their sails.
33. The Bears <u>handled wrongly</u> their boat.
34. The captain <u>arranged again</u> the sails.

Choose the verb in parentheses that most closely names the action.   *pages 92–93*

35. Mickey quickly ___ each number from one to ten.   (says, counts)
36. The other players ___ in all directions.   (scatter, leave)
37. Mickey ___ the ball hard at Linda.   (tosses, twirls)

Below are the parts of a business letter. They are not in the right order. Put the parts in their proper order. Then write the letter. Be sure to use the correct punctuation in each part.   *pages 100–203*

1. Yours truly
2. Camp Rodeo
   70 Oak Lane
   Pine Bluffs Utah 33601
3. Helen Swartz
4.   I would like to spend two weeks at your rodeo camp this summer. I need to know how much it costs, and what kinds of activities you offer. Also could I have my own pinto pony to ride? Please send all your information to the address above.
5. Dear Camp Rodeo
6. 601 West Orange Avenue
   Phoenix Arizona 68315
   May 5 19___

A Sports Article

People write for many reasons. An author who wants to explain something to the reader may write an *article*. In an article the author uses facts to tell about a subject. Articles appear in encyclopedias and other library books. You also find articles in newspapers and magazines.

This selection is a sports article about baseball. You already know some facts about baseball. Even so you will probably learn a few new things from reading this article.

THE NATIONAL PASTIME

Give people a ball and stick or just an old tin can, and they will make up a game to play.

When a game is played a lot and there is a set of rules people agree to play by, the game often becomes a sport. Some sports are played by teams. Others are played one against one, or two against two. There are sports for summer, sports for winter, sports for every time of the year.

What sport is so popular in the United States that it is called "the national pastime"? *Baseball!*

Millions of people watch baseball games on television, listen to baseball games on the radio, and go to see baseball games in the stadiums in big cities and in small towns.

Professional baseball players can make a lot of money. A star player may earn up to $200,000 a year!

Some baseball players become famous. Henry Aaron hit more home runs in his career than anyone else (755).

United Press International

Wide World Photos

Babe Ruth was the most powerful slugger ever. He still holds the record for the most total bases per time at bat for a slugging percentage of .690.

Ty Cobb was the greatest hitter of all. He still holds the record for the highest lifetime batting average (.367), the most base hits (4,191), and the most runs scored (2,244).

Culver Pictures, Inc.

Culver Pictures, Inc.

The Cy Young Award is named after one of the greatest pitchers of all time. Cy Young played in the major leagues for 21 years and won more games than any other pitcher (511).

A lot of people play baseball just for fun.

Softball is much like baseball. But the ball is larger
and softer than a baseball, and it is pitched underhand.
(A baseball is usually pitched overhand.) And in softball,
the playing diamond is smaller and the bases are closer
together.

For many people, softball is just as exciting as baseball.

Clare and Frank Gault

Activities

1. Imagine that you are a baseball. You want to describe
   what happened to you during a half-inning of a baseball
   game. Here is how your description might start:

   > The pitcher picked me up and rubbed dirt on me.
   > He threw me to the batter. I flew into center
   > field and landed in the player's glove.

   Think of five or six sentences to complete the inning.
   Tell what happened to you by the time the third out
   was made.
2. Imagine that you are a sports announcer. Give a
   play-by-play description of your favorite team's inning
   at bat or in the field.
3. Can you make up your own sport? Here is how you can
   invent your own game for people to play.

   a. Think of three things that you would need to
      play the game such as a ball, a stick, a pole,
      a hoop, or a net.
   b. Decide what the object of the game is.
   c. Make up five rules about the game.

   Explain your new game to the class. You might want to
   work with someone else when you develop your ideas.

Grammar and Related Language Skills

Learning About Pronouns
Subject and Object Pronouns
Possessive Pronouns
Using Pronouns

Practical Communication

Parts of a Newspaper
Writing an Editorial

Creative Expression

A Photo Essay

Pronouns

Think of how odd it would sound to repeat the same nouns again and again. A *noun* is a word that names a person, place, thing, or idea. There are special words that can be used to replace nouns. They are called *pronouns*.

> A **pronoun** is a word that takes the place of one or more nouns.

Suppose your name were Lisa. Without pronouns, you would have to speak about yourself like this:

> Lisa watches television often.
> Television teaches Lisa about many new things.

- Try saying the above sentences using your own name. Don't they sound strange?

- Now read the same sentences below. This time there is one difference.

> I watch television often.
> Television teaches <u>me</u> about many new things.

In the sentences above the pronouns *I* and *me* are used to take the place of the noun *Lisa*.

- Look at the word list in the box below. These are some pronouns that are often used.

I	me
you	
she, he, it	her, him
we	us
they	them

Talk About It

Read each pair of sentences. The second sentence in each pair has one or more pronouns. Name each pronoun. Then tell the noun or nouns each pronoun replaces.

1. The United States has three main television networks. They show the programs Americans watch.
2. Many viewers like news programs. They watch them daily.
3. Miguel watches funny programs. They make him laugh.

Skills Practice

Read each pair of sentences. The second sentence in each pair has one or more pronouns. Write each pronoun. Then write the noun or nouns each pronoun replaces.

1. Paul watches nature programs. They give him facts about plant and animal life.
2. One nature program described how bees live. It told how they build hives.
3. Maria came from Mexico to visit Paul. During the visit she watched American television with him.
4. Maria liked American television. She found it very different from Mexican television.
5. Maria watched a lot of television with Paul. He helped her with some of the language.
6. Maria saw a program about snakes. It described how they get new skin.
7. Maria and Paul watched a very funny show. It made them laugh for hours.
8. In America Maria learned a lot of English. She remembered it for many years.

Sample Answer 1. They, programs; him, Paul

Pronouns as Subjects

The *subject part* of a sentence names whom or what the sentence is about. What is the subject part in each of these sentences?

Pablo reads nature magazines. He enjoys stories about animals.

In the first sentence the subject part is the noun *Pablo*. In the second sentence the subject part is the pronoun *He*. *He* replaces the noun *Pablo*.

Only certain pronouns can replace nouns in the subject part of a sentence. These pronouns are *I*, *you*, *he*, *she*, *it*, *we*, and *they*. They are called *subject pronouns*.

> A **subject pronoun** is a pronoun that is used as the subject of a sentence.

It is important to choose the correct subject pronoun.

● Read each pair of sentences below. Which subject pronouns are used to replace nouns?

Lisa and Roberto read the newspaper together.
They learn many interesting facts.
Roberto reads the sports pages every day.
He discovers which teams win the games.

The pronouns and the nouns they replace are underlined.

A subject pronoun can also replace a noun and a pronoun that work together.

● Read the following pair of sentences.

Roberto and I buy a newspaper. We read the weather report.

In the second sentence above, the pronoun *we* replaces the noun *Roberto* and the pronoun *I*.

● Now look at the sentences on the next page. They tell you how to choose a subject pronoun.

Use *I* to talk about yourself.

Use *you* to talk directly to one or more persons.

Use *he* to talk about one male.

Use *she* to talk about one female.

Use *it* to talk about one thing.

Use *we* to talk about yourself and at least one other person.

Use *they* to talk about two or more persons or things.

Talk About It

In the second sentence of each pair, some words are underlined. Tell which subject pronouns can be used in place of the underlined words.

1. Mr. and Mrs. Mason work for a newspaper.
   <u>Mr. and Mrs. Mason</u> work for *The Sun*.
2. *The Sun* prints a great many facts.
   The Sun gives information about the world.
3. Chris and I read about foreign places.
   <u>Chris and I</u> read about nearby places, too.

Skills Practice

Read each pair of sentences. Write the second sentence. Use the correct subject pronoun in place of the underlined words.

1. Lisa and I read articles about dogs. <u>Lisa and I</u> raise dogs.
2. One article describes correct puppy care.
   <u>Puppies</u> need very special attention.
3. Lisa knows the puppies like soft food.
   <u>Lisa</u> feeds the puppies puppy meal.
4. One puppy eats no meal.
   <u>The puppy</u> only drinks milk.
5. Chuck loves the puppies.
   <u>Chuck</u> plays with the puppies every day.

Sample Answer 1. We raise dogs.

Pronouns as Objects

The *object of a verb* receives the action of the verb. It answers the question *whom?* or *what?* It comes after an action verb. What is the object of the verb in each of these sentences?

> Brian showed an ad to Diana.
> Then Diana showed it to Adam.

In the first sentence the object of the verb is the noun *ad*. In the second sentence the object of the verb is the pronoun *it*. *It* replaces the noun *ad*.

Special pronouns can be used as the object of a verb. These pronouns are *me, you, him, her, it, us,* and *them.* They are called *object pronouns.*

> An **object pronoun** is a pronoun that is used as the object of a verb.

It is important to choose the correct object pronoun.

● Read each pair of sentences below.

Teddy read a news <u>story</u> to Juan.
Then Juan read <u>it</u> to Carol.
Paula gave some <u>presents</u> to Patti.
Patti showed <u>them</u> to Joan.

The pronouns and the nouns they replace are underlined.

An object pronoun can also replace a noun and a pronoun.

● Read the following pair of sentences.

The children taught Maggie and me about interviews.
Then the teacher taught us about newspapers.

In the second sentence the pronoun *us* replaces the noun *Maggie* and the pronoun *me.*

Talk About It

Read each pair of sentences. In the second sentence of each pair, some words are underlined. Tell which object pronouns can be used in place of the underlined words.

1. Pat Brown's father works for a movie company.
   One day Pat and Joey visited <u>Pat's father</u> at work.

2. The company just finished a movie.
   The company completed <u>the movie</u> in two months.

3. Pat and Joey looked all around the movie lot.
   Mr. Brown took <u>Pat and Joey</u> to every location.

Skills Practice

Read each pair of sentences. In the second sentence of each pair, some nouns are underlined. Write the second sentence. Use the correct object pronoun in place of the underlined words.

1. Gino Palma listens to the radio a lot.
   Gino plays the <u>radio</u> early in the morning.

2. Gino's mother bought a clock radio.
   Gino thanked <u>Gino's mother</u>.

3. Gino listens to the sports report.
   The report gives <u>Gino</u> facts about the city teams.

4. Gino and I heard that the Bullets won the basketball game.
   This news pleased <u>Gino and me</u>.

5. Gino listens to the weather report in the morning.
   The report tells <u>Gino</u> about today's weather.

6. Today Gino bought a CB radio.
   Gino put <u>the CB radio</u> in the car.

Sample Answer 1. Gino plays it early in the morning.

Using Subject and Object Pronouns

A *subject pronoun* is a pronoun that is used as the subject of a sentence. It tells who or what does the action. An *object pronoun* is a pronoun that is used as the object of a verb. It comes after an action verb.

It is important to know when to use a subject pronoun and when to use an object pronoun.

●Read the pair of sentences below. Which pronoun would you use to fill in the blank space?

> Benny ordered a sports magazine.
> ___ ordered the magazine by mail.   (He, Him)

Ask yourself whether the pronoun is in the subject part of the sentence or whether it is the object of the verb. In the second sentence above, the pronoun is in the subject part of the sentence. It tells who is doing the action. The subject pronoun *He* must be used.

●Now read the pair of sentences below. Which pronoun would you choose this time?

> Benny called Karen on the phone.
> Benny called ___ twice a day.   (she, her)

In the second sentence above, the pronoun comes after the action verb. It is the object of the verb. The object pronoun *her* must be used here.

●Read this list. It tells you the subject and object pronouns.

Subject Pronouns		Object Pronouns	
I	we	me	us
you		you	
she, he, it	they	her, him, it	them

Talk About It

Read each sentence. Name the pronoun that belongs in each blank space. Explain your answers.

1. Mrs. Wilson said, "Sometimes ___ speak without words."
   (I, me)
2. Then Mrs. Wilson showed ___ how. (we, us)
3. ___ walked over to Kenny. (She, Her)
4. Mrs. Wilson patted ___ on the shoulder. (he, him)
5. ___ smiled at Kenny, too. (She, Her)

Skills Practice

Read each sentence. Write the pronoun that belongs in each blank space.

1. "___ just spoke to Kenny," Mrs. Wilson said. (I, Me)
2. Kenny said, "___ heard nothing at all." (I, Me)
3. Mrs. Wilson explained, "___ smiled at Kenny." (I, Me)
4. "My smile tells ___ about my feelings." (he, him)
5. "A pat on the shoulder tells ___ the same thing."
   (he, him)
6. "___ used a silent language called body language." (I, Me)
7. "People tell ___ about their feelings with body language."
   (we, us)
8. "___ show feeling with body language." (They, Them)

Writing Sentences

You can use parts of your body other than your voice to say something. You raise your eyebrows to show surprise. You shrug your shoulders when you don't know. You nod your head when you agree. This is called *body language*.

Write three sentences. Describe a different example of body language in each sentence. Tell what each kind of body language is saying. Use subject and object pronouns.

Sample Answer 1. I

Skills Review

Read each pair of sentences. The second sentence in each pair has one or more pronouns. Write each pronoun. Then write the noun or nouns each pronoun replaces.

1. Paula reads a sports magazine.
   It tells her about the players.

2. Paula reads about basketball.
   She likes it better than baseball.

3. Paula reads about some new basketball shots.
   She tries them with friends.

4. The magazine has many ads.
   Paula reads them carefully.

5. Paula sees an ad for special sneakers.
   She orders them by mail.

Read each pair of sentences. Write the subject pronoun that can be used in place of the underlined words.

6. Esther wrote a report.
   The report told about fish.

7. First Esther read lots of articles.
   Esther found the articles in the library.

8. Jimmy found some facts for Esther.
   Jimmy discovered the facts in a nature magazine.

9. Mr. Carbera, our teacher, read the report.
   Mr. Carbera gave the report an *A*.

Read each pair of sentences. In the second sentence some words are underlined. Write the object pronoun that can be used in place of the underlined words.

10. The children made a simple telephone.
    The children made the telephone from cups and wire.

11. Paul found two good paper cups.
    Paul tied <u>the cups</u> to a long wire.

12. Anne talked softly into one cup.
    Paul heard <u>Anne</u> through the other cup.

13. Then Paul answered Anne.
    Anne heard <u>Paul</u> very clearly.

Read each pair of sentences. Write the pronoun that belongs in each blank space.

14. Dave sent a telegram to Mary.
    Dave sent ___ for Mary's birthday.   (her, it)

15. Dave used only a few words in the telegram.
    Dave chose ___ carefully.   (they, them)

16. Mary enjoyed Dave's telegram.
    Mary called ___ on the telephone.   (he, him)

17. Mary spoke to Dave.
    Mary thanked ___ for the nice birthday message.   (he, him)

The pronoun *you* once had a close relative. This word was *thou*. *Thou* had the same meaning as *you*. *Thou* was used for talking with friends and family. Now *thou* has disappeared from our language. Think of other words that have disappeared.

HOW ART THOU?

Exploring Language

Possessive Pronouns

You have learned that possessive nouns show who or what has something. Words like *Emma's* or *boys'* are possessive nouns. Special pronouns are also used to show who or what has something. They are called *possessive pronouns*.

> A **possessive pronoun** is a pronoun that names who or what has something.

There are two kinds of possessive pronouns. The first kind must be used in front of nouns. These pronouns are *my, your, his, her, its, our,* and *their*. They take the place of the name of the person or thing that has something.

●Look at this example.

> Rita's ads have words and pictures.
> <u>Her</u> ads appear in several newspapers.

Rita is one female. The possessive pronoun that takes the place of one female is *her. Her* tells what Rita has.

The second kind of possessive pronoun is not used in front of nouns. These pronouns stand alone in a sentence. They are *mine, yours, his, hers, ours,* and *theirs*. Notice that *his* is used both ways.

●Now look at this example.

> Karen writes articles about birds.
> The articles in this magazine are <u>hers</u>.

In the second sentence above, the possessive pronoun *hers* takes the place of *Karen's articles*.

●Look at each possessive pronoun in these sentences. Is it used in front of a noun or does it stand alone?

What noun does each possessive pronoun replace?

> Joel finished <u>his</u> report in two hours.
> The report on the table is <u>his</u>.

In the first sentence above, *his* is used in front of the noun *report*. *His* takes the place of *Joel's*. In the second sentence, *his* stands alone. *His* takes the place of *Joel's report*.

Talk About It

Read each sentence. Tell the possessive pronoun that fits in each blank space. Explain your choice.

1. ___ sister writes magazine ads.   (My, Mine)
2. ___ ads appear in many magazines.   (Her, Hers)
3. All of the ads on the wall are ___.   (her, hers)
4. One of ___ school reports hangs on the wall.   (my, mine)
5. The report near the door is ___.   (my, mine)

Skills Practice

Write each sentence. Use the correct possessive pronoun for each blank space.

1. Ed and Pam write articles for ___ newspaper.   (their, theirs)
2. Most of the sports articles are ___.   (their, theirs)
3. Some of ___ articles appear in the newspaper.   (our, ours)
4. Some of the nature articles are ___.   (our, ours)
5. Some of the nature articles are ___.   (your, yours)
6. One of ___ articles tells about snakes.   (your, yours)
7. The article tells about ___ unusual habits.   (their, theirs)

Sample Answer 1. Ed and Pam write articles for their newspaper.

Using Pronouns

Every sentence has a subject part and a predicate part. The subject part has a noun or a pronoun. The predicate part has a verb. You know that subject nouns must work together with verbs in a sentence. The subject noun and the verb *agree*.

● Read these sentences.

> Debbie writes science articles.
> Other girls write science articles, too.

In the first sentence the verb *writes* agrees with the subject noun *Debbie*. In the second sentence the verb *write* agrees with the subject noun *girls*. In both sentences the verbs agree with the subject nouns. *Write* and *writes* are verbs in the present tense. Verbs in the present tense tell what is happening *now*.

A subject pronoun can take the place of one or more nouns in a sentence. The pronouns *I, you, he, she, it, we* and *they* are subject pronouns. Verbs must agree with subject pronouns, too.

● Look at the following sentences.

> He watches television each night.
> She listens to the radio.
> It plays for hours.

Notice that the verb changes to agree with the subject. The verbs end in *s* or *es*.

● Look at the following sentences.

I read the newspaper each day.   We study science articles.
You like magazines better.   They tell interesting facts.

The verbs in the sentences above do not change. No *s* or *es* is added to the verbs when the subject is *I, you, we,* or *they*.

Remember these rules when you are adding endings for agreement to verbs in the present tense. Add *es* to verbs that end in *s, ss, ch, sh* or *x*. Add *s* to most other verbs.

Talk About It

Read each pair of sentences. Tell the correct form of the verb in the present tense that belongs in each blank space.

1. Nan makes movies.
   She ___ movies for television. (make)

2. Nan uses a movie camera.
   It ___ good pictures. (take)

3. Nan's movies tell about many different things.
   She ___ for interesting subjects. (watch)

Skills Practice

Read each pair of sentences. Write the second sentence. Use the correct form of the verb in the present tense.

1. Ricardo often helps Nan.
   He ___ to foreign lands. (travel)

2. Ricardo films unusual people.
   He ___ the people by surprise. (catch)

3. Nan and Ricardo often plan films together.
   First they ___ down some ideas. (write)

4. Nan's brain works hard.
   It ___ of new ideas. (think)

5. Ricardo's brain works hard, too.
   It ___ of foreign lands. (dream)

6. Nan films people from Europe.
   She ___ for interesting faces. (look)

Sample Answer 1. He travels to foreign lands.

Spelling Sound-Alikes

Some possessive pronouns sound exactly like other words. Although they sound alike, they are different in other ways.

- Read the following sentences.

> Jane and Eddie wrote their report.
> Now they're finished with the typing.
> The children put the report over there.

How are the underlined words different? *Their, they're* and *there* are different in two ways. They have different spellings and different meanings.

> Their shows what two people have. It is a possessive pronoun.
> They're is a short way of writing they are.
> There means in that place.
> Words like their, they're, and there are homonyms.

Homonyms are words that sound alike but have different spellings and different meanings.

- Read the following sentences.

> Is this your magazine?
> You're welcome to read it.

Do the sentences give you a clue to their meanings? *Your* shows what you have. It is a possessive pronoun. *You're* is a short way of writing *you are*.

- Now read these sentences.

> This television has its own antenna.
> But it's broken.

In the first sentence above, *its* means *belonging to it*. In the second sentence *it's* is a short way of writing *it is*.

Talk About It

Complete each sentence with the correct word for each blank space. Explain your answers.

1. The magazine is on the table over ___.   (their, there, they're)
2. ___ welcome to look at it.   (Your, You're)
3. Look at ___ table of contents.   (its, it's)
4. ___ full of articles about sports.   (It's, Its)
5. Reading will increase ___ word power.   (your, you're)

Skills Practice

Write each sentence. Use the correct word for each blank space.

1. ___ friends read many magazines.   (Your, You're)
2. Magazines have ads throughout ___ pages.   (there, their, they're)
3. ___ filled with items for sale.   (There, They're, Their)
4. "___ easy to order by mail," Bonnie says.   (It's Its)
5. Soon, ___ packages arrived in the mail.   (their, they're, there)
6. "___ poorly wrapped," says Bonnie.   (There, Their, They're)
7. "___ address label has been lost."   (It's, Its)
8. "I'll put it over ___," says Bonnie.   (there, their, they're)
9. "This is not ___ book."   (your, you're)

Sample Answer 1. Your friends read many magazines.

Skills Review

Read each sentence. Write the correct possessive pronoun for each blank space.

1. Many people understand ___ pets.   (theirs, their)
2. Gloria talks with ___ all the time.   (her, hers)
3. She understands ___ special language.   (their, theirs)
4. I understand ___ cat very clearly.   (my, mine)
5. Sarah understands ___ cat, too.   (her, hers)
6. Sarah's cat often plays with ___.   (my, mine)
7. Perhaps they talk about ___ owners.   (their, theirs)
8. Do you understand ___ pets?   (your, yours)

Read each pair of sentences. Write the correct form of the present tense of the verb.

9. Brian and Alice work for a newspaper.
   They ___ articles.   (write)

10. Alice writes sports articles.
    She ___ many games.   (attend)

11. Alice likes hockey games best.
    She ___ the players very carefully.   (watch)

12. The players move easily across the ice.
    They ___ very well.   (skate)

13. Brian writes human interest stories.
    They ___ about people's lives.   (tell)

14. Brian tells about helpful people.
    He ___ brave people, too.   (describe)

15. Brian waits for unusual happenings.
    He ___ for interesting events.   (wish)

16. One woman calls on the telephone.
    She ___ about an unusual event.   (whisper)

17. Brian finds people all over.
    He ___ here and there.   (rush)
18. Brian leaves in a hurry.
    He ___ off here and there.   (dash)

Read each sentence. Write the correct word for each blank space.

19. "Are those ___ magazines?" asked Maggie.   (your, you're)
20. "No," answered Ricky. "The magazines over ___ belong to Lenny and John."   (there, their, they're)
21. "___ reading the magazines for your report?"   (Your, You're)
22. "Yes, ___ for my report."   (their, there, they're)
23. "Many of ___ articles describe, plants."   (their, there, they're)
24. "___ is an article about house plants."   (Their, There)
25. "___ filled with wonderful information."   (Its, It's)
26. "May I look through ___ table of contents?"   (its, it's)

Have you ever wondered how words are made? New words come into our language every day. At the same time, other words disappear. Many words you now use, like *skateboard*, would have puzzled your grandparents when they were your age.

Try your hand at making up new words. Pick two words from the list. Put them together. Then write your meaning for the new word.

For example: *blueface*—to turn blue from being out in the cold too long. When I started to blueface, I came inside.

blue	red	face	ache	pond
arm	boat	baby	bossy	bald
bumpy	fuzzy	best	top	turn
fog	fan	bird	chocolate	scent

Exploring
Language

Parts of a Newspaper

Almost every city or town has at least one newspaper. All newspapers try to give information to their readers. They also have many parts in common.

Newspapers usually contain news articles. *News articles* give information. Some tell about world events, national events, or local events. Other articles deal with sports, business, or entertainment. A news article usually starts with a headline. A *headline* is printed in bigger, darker type. It often states the main idea of a news article.

THE GAZETTE
TOWN WINS AWARD

The mayor of Auburn happily accepted the award on Tuesday night for the cleanest city in the entire United States.

NEWS ARTICLE

● Look at these other parts of a newspaper. What kind of information would you find in each part?

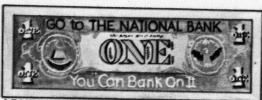

ADVERTISEMENTS

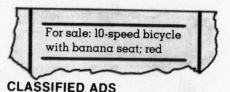

CLASSIFIED ADS

ENTERTAINMENT

WEATHER REPORTS

CARTOON/COMICS

Often editors of newspapers write about certain subjects. Their written opinions are called *editorials*. They express the point of view of the editorial board of the newspaper. Editorials usually appear on the editorial page. Sometimes readers write letters giving their opinions. Most newspapers publish some of these letters under the title of "Letters to the Editor."

THE EDITOR SPEAKS

This newspaper thinks the city park needs new tennis courts.

EDITORIAL

Talk About It

Look at the newspaper parts again. Tell which part would help you answer the following questions.

1. Which part would tell you if it will be cold tomorrow?
2. Which part would help you plan your evening?
3. Which part could make you laugh?
4. Which part would help you choose a bank?
5. Which part tries to sell you something?
6. Which section is your favorite part of the newspaper?

Skills Practice

Look at the parts of a newspaper again. Write in which part you would find the following information.

1. Vote for a new school building
2. For rent: 5 rm. apt. Near park
3. President visits Mexico City
4. Temperature drops 5°. Rain
5. Daffy Dill buys a Duckmobile
6. News about the governor's visit
7. The time a TV show begins
8. Reasons to vote for a new pool
9. An ad for a summer job
10. Weather for the weekend

Sample Answer 1. Editorial

Fact and Opinion

News articles report the facts in a newspaper. Opinions are given in editorials or letters to the editor. You will find facts and opinions in many places besides newspapers. It is important to learn the difference between a fact and an opinion.

A fact is a statement which can be checked to find out if it is true. For example, the following statement is a fact:

A new school gym was built last year on Ridge Road.

You can check this fact by looking at records, newspaper articles, or by checking the area yourself.

An opinion is what a person believes or thinks is true. For example, the following statement is an opinion:

The Rocky Mountains are the most beautiful in the world.

There are many mountains in the world that people might think are beautiful. It is an opinion that the Rocky Mountains are the *most* beautiful.

People often mix facts with opinions when they talk about various subjects. You form many of your opinions from the ideas of others. If you are able to recognize the difference between fact and opinion, you can form your own opinions in a careful and fair way.

●Decide which of the following are facts and which are opinions. How do you know the difference?

Summer is the best season of the year.
The swimming pool opened last week.
Swimming is lots of fun.

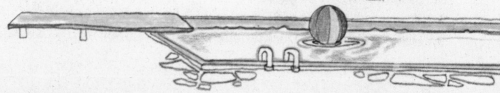

Talk About It

Tell which of the following sentences are facts and which are opinions.

1. George Washington was the first president of the United States.
2. He was the best president, too.
3. His picture is in many schools and office buildings.
4. A president today should look good on television.
5. A president should write all of his or her own speeches.

Skills Practice

Read each of the following sentences. Write *fact* for those that state facts. Be sure that they can be checked. Write *opinion* for those that give opinions.

1. Most schools in the United States close in the summer.
2. Schools should stay open all year round.
3. Some schools offer summer programs.
4. Some students go to summer camps.
5. All summer camps are about the same.

Read each of these sentences. Write F for fact and O for opinion.

6. Last Tuesday was very warm.
7. I hope tomorrow will be a beautiful day, too.
8. The robin I saw this morning pulled a fat worm from the ground.
9. It may rain next week.
10. I like rainy days best.
11. My sister likes sunny days best.
12. This morning it was 65° Fahrenheit.

Sample Answer 1. Fact

Reasons in Paragraphs

Thinking About Paragraphs

You know how to write a paragraph that uses facts in the detail sentences. But that is not the only way to use facts in a paragraph. Suppose, for example, you wrote a topic sentence that stated a point of view or an opinion:

Our school needs a media center.

A fact is a statement which can be checked to find out if it is true. An opinion is what a person believes or thinks is true. The topic sentence above states an opinion. An opinion should have facts to support it. In a paragraph you would use facts in your detail sentences. The facts are the reasons for the opinion.

●Read this paragraph. Look for reasons that support the topic sentence.

Our school needs a media center. We use media such as books, newspapers, tapes, and records every day. We also use film strips, films, and television. Next year students will use computers for individual study. This material is now kept in different classrooms. Such media would be easier to use if they were all in one place. We should change our library into a media center for the whole school.

Talking About Paragraphs

Look for facts and reasons in the detail sentences.

1. How many reasons does the writer give to support the topic sentence? Are the reasons based on facts? How could you find out?
2. Which one do you think is the strongest reason? Where does it come in the paragraph?

3. Can you think of other reasons why a school would need a media center? Can you think of any reasons not to do as the writer suggests?

Writing a Paragraph

Each topic sentence below states an opinion. Write a paragraph about one of the following opinions. Give three reasons in your detail sentences to support the topic sentence.

a. Our school needs more after-school activities.

b. I would like to have an unusual pet.

c. All team sports should be made up of girls and boys.

An Editorial

Thinking About Editorials

A newspaper has many parts. You can read news articles about world events, sports, business, or entertainment. All news articles must have facts. You can also read a special report called an editorial. It is written by the editor of the newspaper and gives an opinion about important news events. Newspaper readers can also write letters to the newspaper about what they think about certain news events. The letters and the editorial appear on the *editorial page*.

School newspapers may also have editorials. Read the following letter the fifth grade class wrote to their school newspaper:

SPRING FIELD DAY

The students in the fifth grade believe that a spring field day is important. No field days have been held for the last three years. A spring field day would give all the students a chance to show their skills in games and contests. The parents of all students would be invited. A spring field day would help the students, parents, and teachers to know each other better.

Remember that news articles can also be read to you on radio or television. A television news broadcast often has spoken editorials. When the news announcer gives an editorial, a sign will appear at the bottom of the picture saying "editorial," or "commentary." This sign is important so that you know the announcer is giving an opinion about a subject. Opinions must be supported by facts. You must have reasons for saying what you believe.

Talking About Editorials

Look at the editorial about the spring field day. The students might picture their spring day as in the drawing below.

● Read the editorial again.

1. What is the topic sentence of the news article?
2. Is the topic sentence an opinion or a fact? How can you tell?
3. What do students do on a spring field day?
4. Read this sentence. No field days have been held for the last three years. Why is it an important reason?
5. What reason do they give for wanting to play games?
6. What fact is given about parents?
7. What is the strongest reason given? Notice that it is the last reason so that you remember it best.

Your Own Editorial

Thinking About Your Editorial

Imagine that you are a television news announcer. You have been asked to write an editorial for television. Remember that an editorial states an opinion supported by reasons.

You are going to write an editorial about city parks. A park can be fun for children and adults. Think about all the things you can do in a park. If you have a dog, it might also like to play in a park. When many people use a park, it can get very dirty. Look what happened to the City Park in the picture below.

Word Bank

litter
flowers
bench
grass
mow
sign

Writing Your Editorial

1. Write this topic sentence: *Our city park needs to be cleaned.*
2. Write three or four detail sentences that give reasons for your opinion. Look at the picture again. What could be done to clean that park?
3. Use the Work Bank to help you spell words that you might like to use.
4. Read your paragraph aloud as if you were a television news announcer.

Edit Your Editorial

Read your editorial. Check it carefully with the following editing questions. Remember the two editing symbols. Use the *caret* (ʌ) and *spelling sign* (sp) if you need them.

1. Did your topic sentence tell your opinion?
2. Did your detail sentences state reasons based on facts?
3. Did each sentence state a complete idea?
4. Did you indent the first word?
5. Did you capitalize the first word in a sentence?
6. Did you end each sentence with the correct punctuation?
7. Did you check your spelling?

Careers

A person who has a job writing about the news is called a *journalist.* Journalists work on newspapers and magazines or at radio and television stations. Some journalists have college degrees. Others receive their experience by working at a newspaper office or at a television station. Some journalists write stories about news events that happen anywhere in the world. Others write about sports, entertainment, or business. Journalists must first find the facts before they write news articles. To gather their facts they ask people questions, use reference works, and observe news stories as they happen. Almost all journalists think that students should work on school newspapers if they are interested in a career in journalism.

Paul Conklin from Monkmeyer Press Photo Service

Checking Skills

Read each pair of sentences. In the second sentence some of the nouns are underlined. Write the subject pronoun that can be used in place of the underlined nouns. *pages 114–115*

1. Many people make long distance phone calls.
   <u>People</u> call friends in other countries.

2. Most places have an area code.
   <u>The area code</u> connects the phone call to another place.

Read each pair of sentences. In the second sentence some nouns are underlined. Write the object pronoun that can be used in place of the underlined nouns. *pages 116–117*

3. Peggy called Paul in Puerto Rico.
   Peggy called <u>Paul</u> on Sunday.

4. Peggy spoke to Paul for only three minutes.
   Paul heard <u>Peggy</u> very clearly.

Read each sentence. Write the correct pronoun. *pages 118–119*

5. Karen beat ___ at tennis. (I, me)
6. Then ___ beat Kevin. (I, me)
7. I beat ___ two times. (he, him)

Read each sentence. Write the correct possessive pronoun. *pages 122–123*

8. Gina and Judy write articles for ___ nature club.
   (their, theirs)
9. The nature article in last week's newspaper is ___ .
   (their, theirs)
10. The article describes how a queen bee lives ___ life.
    (her, hers)

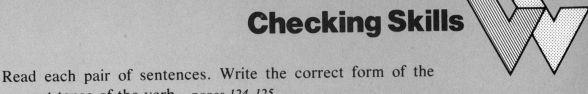

Read each pair of sentences. Write the correct form of the present tense of the verb. *pages 124–125*

11. David delivers the mail in all kinds of weather.
    He ___ the mail by truck.   (deliver)

12. David delivers the mail quickly.
    He ___ from mailbox to mailbox.   (rush)

Read each sentence. Write the correct word.   *pages 126–127*

13. "Is ___ science report ready?"   (you're, your)
14. "Yes, ___ all finished."   (its, it's)
15. "I hope ___ not late with it."   (you're, your)
16. "Joe and Sam finished ___ report very quickly."   (their, there)
17. "Leave the report over ___ ."   (there, they're)

Here is the topic sentence for a paragraph of reasons: *Our school needs to build a new gymnasium.* Below are ten sentences. Decide which seven sentences belong in the paragraph. Write the topic sentence and the detail sentences that you have chosen. Write the paragraph. *pages 134–139*

a. The walls of the old gym are cracking.
b. The floor of the old gym is sinking in certain spots.
c. Our basketball court isn't big enough to hold the crowds.
d. Basketball is an exciting sport to watch.
e. The old ceiling leaks in several places.
f. The paint is peeling off the walls of the shower room.
g. It is fun to swim during the summer.
h. I got two new bathing suits last week.
i. Half the showers in the old shower room are broken.
j. The electrical wiring in our old gym is not safe.

A Photo Essay

There is a popular saying, "One picture is worth a thousand words." It means that sometimes you can learn as much from a picture as you can from writing. In pictures you can see the expressions and emotions of people. Some reporters also use pictures or photographs when they present an article. Their work is called a *photo essay*. A photo essay is a group of pictures that tells a story or explains facts. There may also be a short paragraph that tells about the pictures. A photo essay is helpful when the reader has never seen what the reporter is telling about in the article.

Photo by Lawrence Zeleny National Geographic Society

The next selection is about the birth of bluebirds. The person who did the essay thought most readers had never seen this event. She presented a photo essay of four pictures and a paragraph of explanation. Look at the material carefully. Do the pictures help you to understand the topic of the essay?

From National Geographic Society photo by Michael L. Smith

A mother bluebird sits on her nest.
She covers her eggs and keeps them warm.
When the eggs hatch,
The baby birds cannot stand or open their eyes.
They just chirp and wait for food.
The parents are busy catching insects for them to eat.
They eat and eat all day long, and they grow very fast.
In a few days, the little birds are covered
with soft feathers. And their eyes are open.

Kathleen Costello Beer

Activities

1. Look again at the photo essay about bluebirds. Suppose you did not have the paragraph to accompany the photos. How would you explain to someone what was happening in each picture?

2. Prepare a photo essay on the life of a human being. Find the photographs in magazines. You will need five pictures. Start with a picture of a baby. Then find three other pictures that show a person growing older. The last picture could be a picture of a person about eighty years old. The five people in your pictures should look as much alike as possible. Under each picture write one sentence that tells about the person in that photo.

3. Make your own travel brochure. Think of a place you have visited or would like to visit. Find pictures, photographs, or draw your own pictures. Write a sentence or two for each picture. Your brochure might look like this one:

VISIT San Antonio

SEE The Alamo

TAKE A Walk by The River

EAT Interesting Food

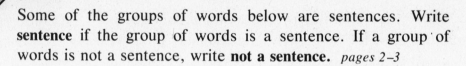

Looking Back

Some of the groups of words below are sentences. Write **sentence** if the group of words is a sentence. If a group of words is not a sentence, write **not a sentence.** *pages 2–3*

1. A shadow.
2. A candle burned in the dark.
3. Opened a squeaky door.
4. A dog howled.
5. A detective.
6. The moonless night.

Write whether each sentence is **declarative,** a **question,** a **command,** or an **exclamation.** *pages 4–5*

7. What a scary place this is!
8. Did you see a shadow at the window?
9. My friend and I look at each other.
10. Blow out the candle.

Write each of these sentences. Begin each sentence with a capital letter. End each sentence with the correct punctuation mark. *pages 6–7*

11. a fierce wind blew open a squeaky door
12. is someone hiding behind the curtain
13. get a flashlight
14. how frightening this is
15. who will help us

Write each sentence below. Draw a line between the subject part and the predicate part. Draw one line under the subject part. Draw two lines under the predicate part. *pages 10–11*

16. The dog crawled under the bed.
17. Joe hid in a closet.
18. Two young detectives searched for clues.
19. Rita found footprints in the wet grass.

Write each noun in each sentence. After each noun, write whether it names a **person, place, thing,** or **idea.** *pages 38–39*

20. Joel walked by a stream in the mountains.
21. Lana loved the quiet of the river.
22. Jeff listened to the wind in the trees.
23. Diane photographed a wildflower beside a rock.

Write the plural form of each noun. *pages 40–43*

24. class	27. loaf	30. dish	33. leaf
25. toy	28. box	31. tree	34. roof
26. sky	29. mess	32. woman	35. child

Write each noun. Write whether it is common or proper. *pages 48–49*

36. The train arrived in Chicago.
37. Mrs. Ruiz was the engineer for the train.
38. The conductor collected a ticket from Dr. Geer.

Write each underlined word as an abbreviation. *pages 50–51*

39. <u>Monday</u>, <u>August</u> 23   40. Oak <u>Street</u>   41. <u>Mister</u> Lee

Write each compound noun. Draw a line between the two words. Then write what each compound means. *pages 44–45*

42. The townspeople enjoy camping in the woods.
43. They sing songs around a campfire.
44. They get up at daybreak.

Change the word at the end of the sentence to make a possessive noun. Write the possessive noun. *pages 52–53*

45. The ___ bark woke the children.   (dog)
46. The ___ cat ran away.   (woman)
47. Many ___ children joined the search.   (neighbors)

Looking Back

Write each action verb. Then write the object of the verb. *pages 72–75*

48. Santos played a game.
49. Henry lost his cap.
50. Mike pitched the ball.

51. Santos swung the bat.
52. Henry finished the game.
53. The coach thanked the team.

Write each sentence. Use the correct form of the verb in the present tense. *pages 76–77*

54. A sick player ___ home. (stay)
55. Carlos ___ the ball. (carry)
56. Mary ___ the exercise. (finish)
57. Many fans ___ to the game. (hurry)

Read each sentence. Then write the verb in the past tense.
    pages 78–79, 86–87

58. Jon plays tennis.
59. Joanna gives tennis lessons.
60. The members practice many hours.

61. The players drink water.
62. They stop for lunch.
63. The rain begins again.

Read each sentence. Write the correct form of the verb *have*. *pages 82–83*

64. She ___ new tennis shoes. (present)
65. They ___ new uniforms. (present)
66. You ___ a new tennis racket. (present)
67. You ___ an old tennis racket. (past)
68. They ___ ragged uniforms. (past)

Write the correct past tense form of each verb in parentheses. *pages 84–86*

69. They have ___ hard. (practice)
70. She has ___ in many races. (run)
71. The boys have ___ the race. (lose)

72. She has ___ before. (race)
73. It has ___ dark. (grow)
74. The bus has ___ . (return)

Read each pair of sentences. In the second sentence some words are underlined. Write the pronoun that can be used in place of the underlined words. *pages 112–113*

75. Alicia gave her article to Ivan.
Ivan sent <u>the article</u> to a newspaper.
76. The article taught Jules and me many things.
The article taught <u>Jules and me</u> how to care for animals.
77. Alicia bought two new plants.
<u>Alicia</u> put the new plants in her office.

Read each pair of sentences. Write the pronoun that belongs in each blank. Write whether it is a subject or object pronoun. *pages 114–119*

78. Jeff sent a cable to Alicia in London.
___ sent the cable yesterday.   (He, They)
79. Jeff congratulated Alicia on her latest article.
Jeff congratulated ___ on her fine work.   (her, hers)
80. Alicia wrote a thank-you letter to Jeff.
Alicia thanked ___ for his kind words.   (he, him)

Write the correct possessive pronoun for each blank. *pages 122–123*

81. Carol writes articles about pets.
The articles on the desk are ___.   (her, hers)
82. You have two pets.
Those two puppies are ___.   (your, yours)
83. Carol and Karl have a canary.
The canary is ___ pet.   (their, theirs)
84. Ivan and I have two beautiful horses.
The horses are ___.   (our, ours)
85. I bought a mule.
The brown mule is ___.   (my, mine)
86. Josie likes hamsters.
___ hamster was a present.   (Her, Hers)

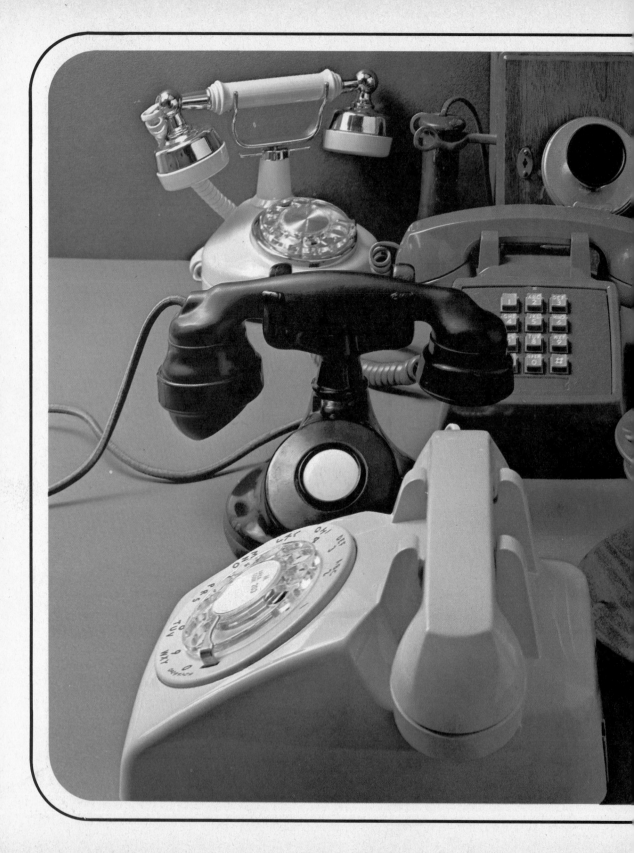

Grammar and Related Language Skills

Reviewing Sentences
Simple Subjects and Predicates
Compound Subjects and Predicates
Using Commas in Writing

Practical Communication

Using the Dictionary
Writing a Conversation

Creative Expression

A Play

151

Reviewing Sentences

A sentence is a group of words that states a complete idea. Every sentence has a subject part and a predicate part. Remember:

The **subject part** of a sentence names whom or what the sentence is about. The subject part may have one word or more than one word.

The **predicate part** of a sentence tells what action the subject part does. The predicate part may have one word or more than one word.

• Look at the sentences below.

An Indian chief invented potato chips in 1853.

His tall cap fell on the floor.

In the first sentence *An Indian chief* is the subject part. These words tell *whom* the sentence is about. The predicate part of this sentence is *invented potato chips in 1853*. These words tell what action the subject did. In the second sentence

His tall cap is the subject part. These words tell *what* the sentence is about. The predicate part of this sentence is *fell on the floor*. These words tell what action the subject did.

Talk About It

Tell what the subject part and predicate part are in each of these sentences.

1. Chief George Crum cooked at a hotel in New York.
2. A visitor came from Paris.
3. The visitor ordered French fried potatoes.
4. Chief Crum prepared them in the kitchen.
5. The visitor saw the potatoes.
6. The visitor sent a message to the cook.
7. This impossible man wanted thinner potatoes.

Skills Practice

Write the subject part of each of the following sentences.

1. The chief cut the potatoes thinner.
2. The unhappy visitor looked at them.
3. This impatient person sent another message to the chief.
4. The visitor wanted even thinner potatoes.
5. Chief Crum checked his knife.

Write the predicate part of each of the following sentences.

6. The chief cut the potatoes into very thin pieces.
7. The angry cook dipped the pieces quickly into hot fat.
8. The brown pieces of potato curled up.
9. Cook Crum put salt on them.
10. The Indian chief marched into the dining room.
11. The visitor enjoyed the potatoes very much.
12. The happy cook smiled at his new invention.

Sample Answers 1. The chief 6. cut the potatoes into very thin pieces.

Simple Subjects

The *subject part* of a sentence names whom or what the sentence is about. The subject part may have one word or more than one word.

● Look at these sentences.

Some girls invented a weather machine.

Girls in our class invented a weather machine.

Two girls in our class invented a weather machine.

In each sentence the subject part is in a blue box. However there is one word in each subject part that is more important than the other words. That word is *girls*. The word *girls* is called the *simple subject*.

The **simple subject** of a sentence is the main word in the subject part.

● Read each sentence below. The subject part is in a blue box. The simple subject, *machine,* is the main word of the subject part. The word *machine* is more important than the other words in the subject part.

The machine tells the weather.

The large machine tells the weather.

The large blue machine tells the weather.

Talk About It

Find the subject part of each sentence below. Then find the simple subject. Explain your answer.

1. Our science teacher taught the class about the weather.
2. Two girls found an idea in a book.
3. The eager girls built a special machine.
4. This amazing machine records the weather each day.
5. The two inventors entered the machine in the science fair.

Skills Practice

Write the subject part of each of the following sentences. Draw one line under the simple subject.

1. The large machine has an arrow in the middle.
2. The long arrow points to different boxes.
3. Each box names a certain kind of weather.
4. The girls show their invention.
5. The judges gather around the machine.
6. The judges at the fair watch the machine.
7. The sharp arrow points to "Snowy."
8. One judge looks out the window.
9. The bright sun shines in the sky.
10. The unhappy judge sees no snow.
11. The other judges look out the window.
12. These people see no snow on the ground.
13. The sad inventors take their machine home.
14. Our friends help the inventors repair the machine.
15. The machine stands in the corner.
16. The busy inventors work all night.

Sample Answer 1. The large machine

Simple Predicates

The *predicate part* of a sentence tells what action the subject part does. The predicate part may have one word or more than one word.

● Look at these sentences.

Elisha Otis worked.

Elisha Otis worked hard.

Elisha Otis worked hard every day.

In each sentence the predicate part is in a red box. However there is one word in each predicate part that is the most important because it names the action. The word is *worked*. The word *worked* is called the verb or *simple predicate*.

> The **simple predicate** is the main word or group of the words in the predicate part.

● Read each sentence below.

Otis invented.

Otis invented the elevator.

Otis invented the elevator in 1852.

In each sentence the predicate part is in a red box. The simple predicate, *invented,* is the main word of the predicate part. The word *invented* is the most important word because it names the action.

Talk About It

Find the predicate part of each sentence below. Then find the simple predicate. Explain your answer.

1. People used platforms for years.
2. Platforms lifted things to high places.
3. Sometimes the platforms crashed to the ground.
4. Elisha Otis built safe platforms.

Skills Practice

Write the predicate part of each of the following sentences. Draw one line under the simple predicate.

1. Otis worked his platform carefully.
2. The inventor raised beds on the platform.
3. Otis showed his elevator to many people.
4. Otis rode to the top floor.
5. Other people used the elevator too.
6. Hotel owners bought the elevator.
7. People built many skyscrapers.
8. Many people moved to big cities.
9. The Otis sons made more and more elevators.
10. Many buildings have Otis elevators.

Writing Sentences

What do you think is the best thing ever invented?

1. Write one sentence that tells about the invention.
2. Write another sentence that tells about the inventor.

Sample Answer 1. worked his platform carefully.

Words That Look Alike

Did you ever see twin brothers or sisters who dressed alike? They look the same, but the two people are still different in many ways. Words can also look alike and still be different. Sometimes two words can be spelled the same way, but the words have different meanings. Sometimes these words even have different pronunciations. They are called *homographs*.

●Read the sentences below. Notice the underlined words.

> The scientist took a <u>rose</u> from the garden.
> She <u>rose</u> from her chair and left.

Both sentences use the word *rose*. The words are spelled and pronounced the same way, but they have different meanings. In the first sentence *rose* means *a flower*. In the second sentence *rose* means *stood up*. You need to read the whole sentence to know which meaning is used.

●Now look at these sentences. Notice the underlined words.

> A strong <u>wind</u> blew out the fire.
> It is time for me to <u>wind</u> my watch.

Both sentences use the word *wind*. The words are spelled alike, but they are pronounced differently. They also have different meanings. *Wind* in the first sentence rhymes with *pinned*. It means *air that is moving*. *Wind* in the second sentence rhymes with *find*. It means *tighten the spring of*.

Talk About It_____

Read each sentence. Tell your answer to the questions that
follow it.

1. The scientist turned on the **light** and lifted a **light** box.
   Which word means *not heavy*?
   Which word means *something that lets you see*?
2. Dr. Forbes will **lead** me to a piece of **lead**.
   Which word sounds like *need*? Which word sounds like *bed*?

Skills Practice_____

Two sentences with underlined words are followed by two
meanings. Write the letter of the correct meaning next to
each number.

1. Dr. Forbes lost her <u>left</u> shoe.   2. The scientist <u>left</u> the room.
   a. went out of   **b.** the opposite of right
3. A lamp stood <u>close</u> to the door.   4. Please <u>close</u> the door.
   a. shut   **b.** near
5. The child opened a <u>chest</u>.   6. I put an apron over my <u>chest</u>.
   a. trunk   **b.** part of body

Read the sentences. Next to the number of each sentence,
write the letter of the rhyme that matches the underlined
word.

7. A <u>live</u> rabbit hopped from the chest.   8. A box is a funny place to <u>live</u>.
   a. sounds like dive   **b.** sounds like give
9. The rabbit made a <u>tear</u> in my coat.   10. A <u>tear</u> ran from my eye.
   a. sounds like near   **b.** sounds like care
11. The scientist put a <u>bow</u> on the rabbit.
12. The scientist tried to <u>bow</u> very low.
    a. sounds like go   **b.** sounds like now

Sample Answers **1.** b **7.** a

Skills Review

Write the subject part of each of the following sentences.

1. Many people invent unusual things.
2. Samuel Applegate made a different kind of clock.
3. This alarm clock has special parts.
4. The parts fall on a person's face at wake-up time.
5. The person sits up in bed.
6. The clock's parts do a good job.

Write the predicate part of each of the following sentences.

7. A man from Chicago made another kind of alarm clock.
8. The person fills a cup of water at night.
9. The alarm clock pushes the cup over.
10. Water spills on the person's face.
11. Many people buy alarm clocks with bells.

Write the subject part in each of the following sentences. Draw a line under the simple subject.

12. Thomas Jefferson invented many things.
13. Most people do not know this.
14. President Jefferson invented a turning chair.
15. Many office workers sit on turning chairs today.
16. Mr. Jefferson made a seven-day alarm clock.

Write the predicate part in each of the following sentences. Draw a line under the simple predicate.

17. Mr. Jefferson put the clock in his home.
18. Thomas Jefferson made other machines, too.
19. This scientist tried all kinds of experiments.
20. Mr. Jefferson planted one of the finest gardens.
21. He helped many farmers.

Skills Review

Two sentences with underlined words are followed by two meanings. Write the letter of the correct meaning next to each number.

22. The inventor could not <u>bear</u> our picnic.   23. A <u>bear</u> ate our lunch.
    a. a large animal   **b.** put up with
24. A <u>spoke</u> on my bicycle broke.   25. The inventor <u>spoke</u> angrily.
    a. part of a wheel   **b.** talked
26. A <u>bat</u> flew into our cave.   27. My <u>bat</u> hit the ball.
    a. baseball stick   **b.** animal
28. The <u>date</u> was June 26.   29. The baker put a <u>date</u> in the dough.
    a. fruit   **b.** time
30. The dog with us was <u>mine</u>. ₂31. The dog visited an old gold <u>mine</u>.
    a. belongs to me   **b.** place where gold is found
32. The brown <u>bark</u> fell off.   ₐ33. Dogs <u>bark</u> all day.
    a. dog noises   **b.** tree covering
34. The weather was <u>fair</u>.   35. Later our group went to a <u>fair</u>.
    a. kind of market   **b.** nice

Some words in the English language come from the names of inventors. For example:

Antoine Joseph Sax worked for his father in a music store in Brussels. He invented the *saxophone*. (The suffix *phone* means *making sound*.)

Louis Braille lost his sight in an accident at the age of three. He invented a special way for people without sight to read. They run their fingers over raised dots on paper. This kind of raised printing is called *braille*.

Exploring Language

Compound Subjects

The *simple subject* of a sentence is the most important word in the subject part. It names whom or what the sentence is about. Sometimes there are two important words in the subject part.

● Look at the following sentences.

Jan built a robot.   Jan and Molly built a robot.

The robot walked.   The robot and Molly walked.

The lights worked.   The bright lights and bells worked.

In each sentence on the left, the subject part has only one important word. That word is the simple subject. In each sentence on the right, the subject part has two simple subjects that are joined by *and*. Both simple subjects have the same predicate. The sentences on the right have *compound subjects*.

> A **compound subject** has two or more simple subjects that have the same predicate. The subjects are joined by **and**.

● Now look at these sentences.

She and Molly tested the robot.   Consuelo and I watched.

Each of these sentences has a pronoun in the subject part. The pronouns that may appear in the subject part are *I, you,*

he, she, it, we, and *they.* When the pronoun *I* is part of a compound subject, it always comes last in the subject.

Talk About It

Name the subject part in each sentence. Tell which sentences have compound subjects.

1. Jan and Molly finished their robot.
2. The giant robot has four arms.
3. Batteries and electric power move the robot.
4. Its arms and legs move in all directions.
5. The robot cleaned Molly's room this morning.
6. Her mother and father know nothing about the robot.
7. They thanked Molly for her work.
8. Molly and the robot winked at each other.

Skills Practice

Read each of the following sentences. Write the subject part of the sentence. If the subject is compound, write **compound.**

1. Jan and her sister played with the robot.
2. The robot brought them breakfast in bed.
3. Glasses and bowls rested on two arms.
4. The robot held the forks on the other two arms.
5. The girls and the robot ate breakfast together.
6. Jan thought of other jobs for the robot.
7. She and Carmen rode to school on the robot.
8. Teachers and friends stared at the invention.
9. Many boys and girls ran away.
10. The robot went to classes with Jan.
11. It took a test in science class.
12. Jan and the robot finished the test.

Sample Answer 1. Jan and her sister, compound

Compound Predicates

The *predicate part* of a sentence tells what action the subject part does. The *simple predicate* is the main word or group of words in the predicate part. Sometimes the predicate part names more than one action.

Benjamin Franklin <u>flew</u> a kite.
Benjamin Franklin <u>flew</u> a kite and <u>learned</u> about lightning.

- Look at the first sentence under the picture. The predicate part has only *one* verb. That verb is the simple predicate.

- Now look at the second sentence under the picture. The predicate part has *two* verbs. They are joined by the word *and*. The second sentence has a *compound predicate*.

> A **compound predicate** is a predicate that has two or more verbs that have the same subject. The verbs are joined by **and**.

- Now look at these sentences.

RIGHT: Franklin <u>flies</u> a kite and <u>learns</u> about lightning.
WRONG: Franklin <u>flew</u> a kite and <u>learns</u> about lightning.

In the first sentence both verbs in the compound predicate are in the present tense. They both name an action that happens now. This sentence is right because both verbs in the compound predicate must be in the same tense. In the second sentence *flew* is in the past tense and *learns* is in the present tense. This sentence is wrong because the verbs in the compound predicate are not in the same tense.

Talk About It

Name the predicate part in each sentence. Tell which sentences have compound predicates.

1. Franklin studied and experimented with lightning.
2. Franklin made a kite and used some string.
3. He found a key and tied it to the string.
4. Franklin flew the kite on a stormy night.
5. A bolt of lightning hit the key.
6. The key jumped and shook.

Skills Practice

Read each of the following sentences. Write the predicate part of the sentence. If the predicate is compound, write **compound**.

1. Benjamin Franklin invented and discovered many things.
2. He invented a special pair of glasses.
3. People look through one part and see things nearby.
4. They look through another part and see things far away.
5. Franklin invented and built a new kind of stove.
6. He invented lightning rods.
7. They carry lightning away and protect buildings.
8. He made a special stick.
9. People lift things and put things on high shelves with it.
10. Benjamin Franklin shared his ideas with the world.

Sample Answer 1. invented and discovered many things, compound

Agreement of Verbs with Compound Subjects

The simple subject in a sentence works together with the verb. In other words they agree with each other. Here are two examples.

invent | The girls invent things at home.   Plural subject
invent | Sara invents things at home.   Singular subject

When the subject is plural, the main verb does not change. When the subject is singular, an *s* is usually added to the main verb.

In a sentence with a compound subject, the verb must also agree with the subject. A compound subject with *and* names two or more people or things. It is like a plural subject. Here are two examples.

invent | Sara and Lenore invent things at home.
draw | Lenore and her brothers draw pictures of the things.

The verbs *invent* and *draw* agree with the compound subjects.

●Find the compound subjects in these examples. Check to see that the verbs agree.

Peter and his friends buy old bicycle parts.
Roy and Jennifer put the parts together.
Kathy and Todd sell the parts from their garage.

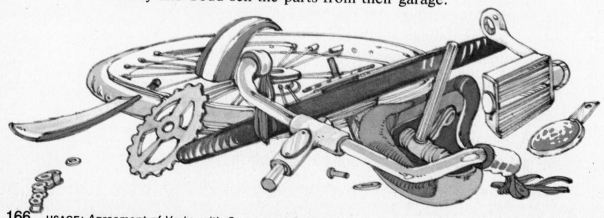

Talk About It

Complete each sentence. Use the correct form of each verb in the present tense.

1. Anthony ____ tree houses. (make)
2. Ruth ____ tree houses. (make)
3. Anthony and Ruth ____ tree houses. (make)
4. Joel ____ dog houses. (build)
5. His sisters ____ dog houses. (build)
6. Joel and his sisters ____ dog houses. (build)

Skills Practice

Write each sentence. Use the correct form of the verb in the present tense.

1. Juan ____ the dog houses. (paint)s
2. Cindy ____ the dog houses. (paint)s
3. Juan and Cindy ____ the dog houses. (paint)
4. The twins ____ the neighbors. (call)
5. Barbara ____ the neighbors, too. (call)s
6. Barbara and the twins ____ the neighbors. (call)
7. The neighbors ____ dog houses. (buy)
8. The relatives ____ dog houses. (buy)
9. The neighbors and the relatives ____ dog houses. (buy)

Writing Sentences

Imagine that you and your best friend are inventors who have made something new. Write about your invention.

1. Write one sentence with a compound subject.
2. Write one sentence with a compound predicate.

Sample Answer 1. Juan paints the dog houses.

Using Commas in Writing

You are already familiar with some punctuation marks that are used in writing. A period shows that a statement has ended. A question mark tells that something is being asked. An exclamation mark shows strong feelings.

Another sign often used in writing is the *comma*. It tells the reader when to pause in a sentence.

● Read this sentence.

George Washington Carver worked as a cook, a farmer, a scientist, and an inventor.

The commas tell the reader to pause after each word. The sentence makes sense if you pause.

> Use a **comma** to separate each noun in a series of three or more nouns.

● Read this sentence.

Carver worked, tested, and experimented.

Again, the commas tell you to pause when you read.

> Use a **comma** to separate each verb in a series of three or more verbs.

Talk About It

Decide which of these sentences need commas. Tell where they should go.

1. Life was hard for Carver and his brother.
2. Carver worked struggled and traveled for his schooling.
3. He worked in school to pay for his room food and books.
4. Carver cooked farmed and painted in his youth.
5. He won prizes for his paintings.

Skills Practice

Write the following sentences. Add commas where they are needed.

1. Carver studied tested and experimented with peanuts in the late 1800's.
2. He used peanuts to make oil milk and other foods.
3. He also made cream coffee and rubber from peanuts.
4. Many other scientists thanked honored and rewarded Carver for his work.
5. Carver made many things from sweet potatoes.
6. The inventor made candy flour and shoe polish.
7. He made paint from clay.
8. He studied plants rocks and foods.
9. He was called "the plant doctor."

Writing Sentences

1. Write one sentence with a list of three or more nouns telling about your favorite food.
2. Write another sentence with a list of three or more verbs telling how you eat your favorite food.

Sample Answer 1. Carver studied, tested, and experimented with peanuts in the late 1800's.

Skills Review

Read each of the following sentences. Write the subject part of the sentence. If the subject is compound, write **compound**.

1. The Wright brothers invented the airplane.
2. Orville and Wilbur lived in North Carolina.
3. Orville and his brother built their own flying machine.
4. It had a small engine.
5. Many men and women laughed at the Wright brothers.
6. Their first trip and second trip lasted thirty seconds.
7. Scientists and engineers worked on the airplane later.
8. Many people fly in airplanes and helicopters today.
9. Wilbur invented a flying doll, too
10. My class and I studied about the Wright brothers in school.

Read each of the following sentences. Write the predicate part of the sentence. If the predicate is compound, write **compound** after the predicate.

11. Some people invent and make clever things.
12. Eoina Nudelman made and sold "Hungry Piggy."
13. A toy pig sat at the breakfast table.
14. It hooked on a plate and opened its mouth.
15. A child ate one bite of food and gave one bite to the pig.
16. The pig's food slipped back and returned to the plate.
17. Children ate most of their food this way.
18. Thomas Zelenka invented a machine for babies.
19. It fit over the bed.
20. A hand moved and patted the baby.
21. The baby felt it and slept.

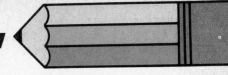
Write each sentence. Use the correct form of each verb in the present tense.

22. Wilma ___ papers every morning.   (deliver)
23. Judy ___ papers every morning.   (deliver)
24. Wilma and Judy ___ papers every morning.   (deliver)
25. Dan ___ lawns in the summer.   (mow)
26. His brothers ___ lawns in the summer.   (mow)
27. Dan and his brothers ___ lawns in the summer.   (mow)
28. Irene and Sue ___ garages.   (clean)
29. Gail and Doug ___ dogs.   (walk)

Write each sentence. Add commas where they are needed.

30. My whole family likes basketball baseball and football.
31. My brother sister and mother invented a new ball.
32. You hit kick and throw the ball during a game.
33. Black smoke comes from the ball.
34. My father brother and sister tried out the new ball.
35. It works on sand grass and water.

You have already learned about words that come from names of inventors. Here are some more:

Rudolf Diesel was a German engineer who invented a special engine that runs on a kind of oil. It is called the *diesel engine.*

Joseph Montagu, the fourth Earl of Sandwich, liked to take a piece of meat and put it between two pieces of bread. Today we call this invention a *sandwich.*

Exploring Language

Using the Dictionary

You may often use the dictionary to find the meaning of a word. You may be surprised to find that there is other information in a dictionary.

- Look at the sample dictionary page below.

---

bleak/bouquet

bleak(blēk) *adj.* **1.** open and exposed to the wind; bare: *a bleak, barren, desert.* **2.** cold; chilling: *a bleak December day.* **3.** not cheerful or hopeful; gloomy: *Our team's prospects for winning were bleak.* — **bleak·ly,** *adv.* —**bleak·ness,** *n.*
bot·a·ny (bot'ən ē) *n.* the science or study of plants

bough(bou) *n.* a branch of a tree, especially a large or main branch.
bou·quet (bō kā, 'bōō kā') *n.*
1. a bunch of flowers; especially one arranged and fastened together.
2. fragrance or aroma.

---

at; āpe; cär; end; mē; it; īce; hot; ōld; fôrk; wood; fōōl; oil; out; up; turn; sing; thin; this; **hw** in **white; zh** in treasure

The symbol ə stands for the sound of **a** in about; **e** in taken, **i** in pencil, **o** in lemon, and **u** in circus.

Notice that the following information is given in a dictionary.

1. Each word in the dictionary is called an *entry word.* The words are arranged alphabetically.
2. You can find the entry words by looking for *guide words* at the top of the page. On the sample page the guide words are **bleak** and **bouquet.**
3. Notice that the entry words are divided into *syllables.* The syllables are usually separated by dots, dashes, or spaces. The word **bouquet** is divided in two syllables: **bou · quet.**
4. Letters and symbols in parentheses follow the entry word. The marks show the *pronunciation* of the word. A pronunciation key shows you what the marks mean. Look at the pronunciation key on the sample page. It tells you to pronounce the vowels in **botany**: *o* as the *o* in *hot;* ə as the *a* in *about;* ē as the *e* in *me.*

5. After the parentheses the *parts of speech* are shown by an abbreviation which is the first letter or letters of the word. These are the most common abbreviations: *n.* noun *v.* verb *adv.* adverb *adj.* adjective

6. The *meaning* of the word follows all the above information. Remember that there can be one meaning for a word, two or more related meanings, or two or more unrelated meanings. Sometimes a part of a sentence or a sample sentence will be given to show how the word is used in a sentence.

Talk About It_____

Use the sample dictionary page to answer these questions.

1. Which entry words have two or more syllables?
2. What entry word has two pronunciations?
3. Which word has the most related meanings?
4. What sentence tells how the word **bleak** is used when it means "gloomy"?
5. What part of speech is **bough**?
6. What part of speech is **botany**?

Skills Practice_____

1. Use the pronunciation key to help you say this sentence.
   (mī) (nā′bərz) (hav) (hyo͞oj) (rōz′əz) (in) (ther) (yärd)

Look at the sample dictionary page.

2. How many related meanings does the word **bouquet** have?
3. **Bleak** can have <u>three</u> forms. What are they?
4. Write a sentence using the word **bough**.
5. Write a sentence using the first meaning of the word **bouquet**.
6. Write a sentence using the first meaning of the word **bleak**.

Sample Answer 1. My neighbors

Listening Skills

Everyday you receive a great deal of information by listening. You may even start your day by listening to the radio. Listening to directions and reports are part of your daily school work.

● Think why you should listen carefully in each of the following situations.

> Someone is telling you how to walk to his or her house.
> The coach is telling you how to play soccer.
> Your teacher is telling you what you should do in case of fire.

You may be surprised to learn that listening skills are very much like reading skills. When you listen to a talk or speech, you listen for the main idea. You also listen for important details that tell about or explain the main idea. You must practice to become a good listener just as you practice to become a good reader.

Here are some rules to help you become a good listener.

1. Look directly at the speaker.
2. Do not talk to others while you are listening.
3. Try to think only about what the speaker is saying.
4. Listen for the main idea. The speaker usually states the subject at the beginning of the speech.
5. Try to remember at least two important details that the speaker gives.
6. When the speaker is finished, take notes by writing the main idea and details immediately.
7. Ask questions about what you can't remember or don't understand.

Talk About It

Tell which of the following will help you become a good listener.

1. Whispering to your friends during a speech.
3. Looking at the speaker.
3. Looking out the window.
4. Thinking only about what the speaker is saying.

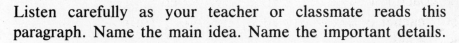

Listen carefully as your teacher or classmate reads this paragraph. Name the main idea. Name the important details.

A bloodhound is a kind of hunting dog. It hunts by scent alone. It can even follow scent when there are not any tracks. Many police departments use bloodhounds to track down criminals.

Skills Practice

Listen carefully as your teacher or classmate reads these two paragraphs. After you have listened to each paragraph, write a sentence telling the main idea. Write one or more sentences which tell about important details. Now close your book and listen carefully.

1. Camels are good desert animals. Their bodies can store food and water. They can store food in their humps. Their stomachs have many pouches. Camels store water in each pouch. When a camel needs water it releases water from one of these pouches.

2. There are several different kinds of bear. Many bears belong to a group called brown bears. The American grizzly bear is a brown bear. It is very large and powerful. The American grizzly bear lives in the West.

Conversation

Thinking About Conversation

Think about the stories you like to read. One important way to make a story lively and fun to read is to use conversation or dialogue. Writers use conversation in a story to make the characters seem real to the reader. Instead of talking about the conversation in the story, the people actually speak for themselves. In 1877 Thomas Edison and a worker in his shop might have had this conversation.

> The worker asked, "Mr. Edison, what is this thing?"
> "This machine is going to talk," Mr. Edison said. He spoke loudly into a special opening.
> "Mary had a little lamb," he shouted. He played with the machine for a moment.
> The machine said, "Mary had a little lamb."
> "I don't believe it," the worker whispered. Mr. Edison had invented the phonograph or record player.

● Read the conversation carefully.
1. Punctuation marks named quotation marks show the exact words that a person speaks. They are used to show *where* the conversation starts and where it stops.
   "This machine is going to talk," Mr. Edison said.
2. You know who is speaking because the name or title of the person follows or comes before the spoken words. Then you know *how* the person is speaking by conversation words such as asked, shouted, and cried. Whenever a

conversation begins with a new speaker, you must indent the first word.

"This machine is going to talk," Mr. Edison said.

3. A comma is used to divide the spoken words from the person who is saying them. It always comes *before* the quotation marks.

"This machine is going to talk," Mr Edison said.

4. If the speaker asks a question, a question mark is used instead of a comma before the end quotation marks.

"Mr. Edison, what is this thing?" the worker asked.

5. You capitalize the first word of the quotation as you do in any sentence.

"Mary had a little lamb," he shouted.

6. Sometimes the conversation words and the speaker's name *follow* the quotation. The first word after the quotation is *not* capitalized. Proper nouns are always capitalized.

"Mary had a little lamb," he shouted.

7. A period is placed at the end of the complete quotation or sentence.

"Mary had a little lamb," he shouted.

Talking About Conversation

Look at the conversation again.

1. What are the first spoken words? Who says it? What conversation word tells *how* it is said? What is the end mark punctuation?

2. Who answers the first speaker? Do the conversation words come before or after the spoken words? How could you tell immediately that there was a new speaker?

3. How did Mr. Edison talk into the machine? What action word told how the worker's last words were said?

4. Why is "Mr. Edison" capitalized when following the quotation and "he" is not?

A Class Conversation

Thinking About Your Conversation

Your class is going to write a conversation together. The pictures below will help you. It will be about an invention.

There have been many inventions in the 20th century. How many can you name? Television, automobiles, and refrigerators are very important to us. But there have been inventions made by people for thousands of years. Think about what some early inventions might have been. Someone had to invent the first candle or sheet of paper.

People have always tried to invent things to make traveling easier. First they walked and carried their belongings on their backs, and then they used animals. Next someone had animals pull a sled that would slide on the ground. But it made the animals tired, and the sled was a problem over rocky ground. Someone else invented the first wheel to make traveling easier. That may seem like a simple invention, but remember no one had ever seen a wheel before.

● Look at the pictures below. What are Ogg and Blogg inventing?

A
B
C
D

Writing Your Conversation

Think about the conversation that the cavepeople might be having. Ogg is the caveman with the long hair, sitting on the ground. Blogg is his wife, and the cave is their home. Blogg is watching Ogg invent the first wheel. In the first picture they might be having this conversation:

"What are you doing?" asked Blogg.
"I am inventing a wheel for the wagon," answered Ogg.

1. Think about what conversation might be taking place in the second picture. Blogg could say something about how she feels about the new wheel. Ogg could answer her. Write all the sentences on the board. Check to be sure you use the correct punctuation marks and capitals in the conversation.
2. Think about the conversation in the third picture. Suggest two sentences that describe their conversation. Blogg could ask Ogg a question. Ogg could say how he feels about the wheel.
3. Think of two sentences that describe the conversation in the last picture.
4. Together all the sentences make a long conversation. Check the board to be sure that you have used the correct capitals and punctuation marks in the conversation.

Writing Your Own Conversation

Thinking About Your Conversation

Now you are ready to write your own conversation. The pictures will help you. The Word Bank shows you how to spell some of the words you may want to use.

Gayle is a school safety guard. She has many conversations with her friends as she gives them directions about crossing the street. Look at the pictures below. Think about the conversation Gayle could be having with her friend Marilyn. In a drawing a conversation balloon above a character's head is used to show who is speaking.

Writing Your Own Conversation

Look at the conversation between Gayle and Marilyn again.

1. Your conversation between Gayle and Marilyn will start with the first picture. Write it like this:

   "Good morning, Gayle," said Marilyn happily.

2. Look at the other five pictures. The conversation balloon above a head means that is the person who is speaking. A question mark in the balloon means a question is being asked.

3. Write in order what each girl might be saying to the other in the five pictures. Remember to indent the words of each new speaker and to follow all the rules for punctuation and capitals in a conversation. Try to use conversation words other than "said" to show how the words are spoken.

4. Use the Word Bank to help you spell your words.

Word Bank

cross
wait
bicycle
monkey
riding
sign

Edit Your Conversation

Read your conversation between Gayle and Marilyn. Check it carefully with the following editing questions. Remember the two editing symbols. Use the *caret* (‸) and *spelling sign* (sp) if you make those mistakes.

1. Did you use good conversation words to show how a person was speaking?
2. Did you put quotation marks around a person's exact words?
3. Did you indent the first word in the quotation?
4. Did you capitalize the first word in the quotation?
5. Did you use the correct punctuation marks in a quotation and at the end of the sentence?
6. Did you check your spelling?

Checking Skills

Write the subject part of each of the following sentences.
Draw a line under the simple subject. *pages 154–155*

1. Leonardo da Vinci lived in Italy long ago.
2. This famous man kept many notebooks.
3. We read Leonardo's ideas in these notebooks.
4. This man covered page after page with drawings.
5. The drawings show many inventions.

Write the predicate part of each of the following sentences.
Draw a line under the simple predicate. *pages 156–157*

6. Leonardo painted pictures.
7. His paintings hang in museums all over the world.
8. We see drawings of airplanes in his notebooks.
9. Leonardo watched birds during the day.
10. He had ideas for helicopters.

Two sentences with underlined words are followed by two
meanings. Write the letter of the correct meaning. *pages 158–159*

11. Leonardo worked <u>fast</u>.   12. On Sundays there was a <u>fast</u>.
   (a) quickly   (b) time without food

13. The duke's <u>page</u> wore a cap.   14. Leonardo drew on each <u>page</u>.
   (a) part of a notebook   (b) helper to carry messages

Read each sentence. Write the subject part of the sentence.
If the subject is compound, write **compound**. *pages 162–163*

15. Leonardo da Vinci and the Duke of Milan lived in Italy.
16. Leonardo worked for the Duke.
17. He painted pictures and designed costumes.
18. The Duke and his friends listened to Leonardo sing.
19. This famous inventor moved to France in 1516.

Read each sentence. Write the predicate part of the sentence.
If the predicate is compound, write **compound.** *pages 164–165*

20. Leonardo drew and painted.

21. He invented things and tested them.

22. Da Vinci wrote with both hands.

23. He read his notes in a mirror.

Write the correct form of each verb in the present tense. *pages 166–167*

24. Scientists and teachers still ___ Leonardo's notebooks. (study)

25. Lili ___ and ___ his notebooks. (read) (enjoy)

26. Inventors and engineers ___ from his work. (learn)

Write the following sentences. Add commas where they are needed.

pages 168–169

27. Leonardo enjoyed his work.

28. He drew painted and invented.

29. He drew planes helicopters and guns.

The following conversation does not have the correct
capitalization and punctuation marks. Read the conversation.
Write it correctly on your paper. Put in the correct capital
letters, quotation marks, commas, and end punctuation. *pages 176–181*

the teacher looked up when robert entered the classroom

where were you all last week the teacher asked

robert replied I was not able to come to school because my
friend accidentally broke a toe

the teacher sighed but why did that keep *you* out

because it was *my* toe robert laughed

A Play

Plays are fun to read, to watch, to act in, and to write. Plays tell stories by having the characters speak to each other. This speech is called *dialogue*. You learn about the characters by the way that they talk to each other. Besides dialogue a play has *stage directions*. These directions are written in parentheses. Sometimes they tell the actors and actresses where to move on stage. The characters do not read these stage directions aloud. They just do what the directions say to do.

Now you are going to read a play called *Mr. Maybe*. You might read the dialogue aloud with other classmates. Also read the stage directions to yourself. Think about how the characters would talk and act. How would they be dressed? Would their voices sound different? Why do you think the characters acted as they did?

Mr. Maybe

PLAYERS:

Mr. Maybe
Mike
Farmer
Old Woman
Old Man
Little Girl

Mr. Maybe: Come, Mike!

Mike: Where are we going, Father?

Mr. Maybe: We are going to walk our donkey to town to sell him.

(They go down the road till they meet a farmer.)

Farmer: Look at you!
You have a donkey to ride,
but both of you are walking!
Why not let the boy get on
the donkey's back and ride?

Mr. Maybe: Maybe you are right.
Get on, Mike.

(Mike gets on the donkey and they go down the road till they meet an old woman.)

Old Woman: Look at that lazy boy!
He rides the donkey
and his old father walks!
The boy should be the one
to walk!

Mr. Maybe: Maybe you are right.
Get off the donkey, Mike.

*(Mr. Maybe gets on the donkey
and they go down the road
till they meet an old man.)*

Old Man: Look at that lazy father!
He takes a ride, but his poor boy
has to walk!

Mr. Maybe: Oh, my!
Here, Mike, you get on the
donkey with me.
Then everyone will be pleased.

*(They both ride the donkey down
the road till they meet
a little girl.)*

Little Girl: Oh, look!
That poor donkey!
He looks so tired!
He should have the ride,
not that man and his boy.

Mr. Maybe: Maybe she is right.
Here, Mike, we will give
the donkey a ride.

*(It is hard to do,
but they lift the donkey up.
They come to a little bridge.)*

Mike: Look out, Father!

Mr. Maybe: Help! I am falling!

Mike: So am I!

(Splash! Mr. Maybe, Mike, and the donkey all fall in the water.)

Mike: Father, let's just walk the donkey into town the way you wanted to when we started out. I don't think we can please everyone.

Mr. Maybe: Maybe you are right. After this we will do things our own way.

Sally Jarvis

Activities

1. Perform the play *Mr. Maybe* for your class or for other classes. You will need seven people in your group. There are six players, and one person will play the donkey. Decide which part each person will take. Practice reading your lines. You do not have to memorize them, but you should be able to read them well. Also practice where you will move on stage. Decide what costumes each character will wear. Your group can also paint scenery on large sheets of paper and hang them on the wall. Practice the play several times before performing it for a group.

2. Write your own play. Think about a main event that could involve two or more characters. Write a beginning, middle, and ending about that event. A friend could help you with the dialogue. Remember to include stage directions. It would be fun to perform your own play with costumes and scenery.

3. Think of a good joke that you know. It should involve two people in a conversation. On your paper write the lines that each person says to the other one in the joke. Practice the joke with a friend. Here is an example:

Meg: Hey Jane, I had a strange dream last night.
Jane: What did you dream?
Meg: I dreamed that I ate a giant marshmallow.
Jane: What is so strange about that?
Meg: When I woke up, my pillow was missing!

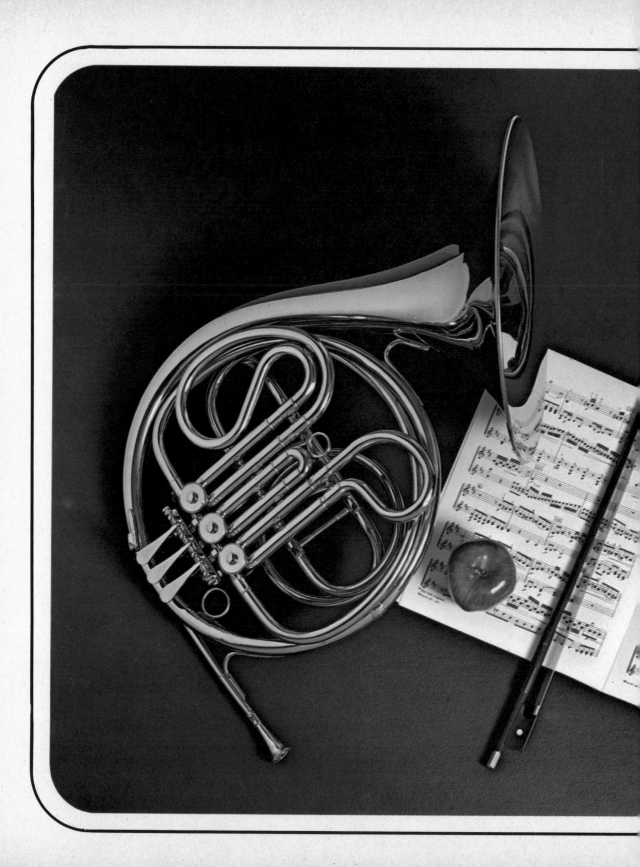

Grammar and Related Language Skills

Learning About Adjectives
Adjectives That Compare
Endings of Adjectives
Prefixes and Suffixes

Practical Communication

Using Reference Works
Writing a Summary Paragraph

Creative Expression

A Biography

Adjectives

Take a look around you. Suppose you were asked to tell about everything you see. You would need to use words that describe people, places, and things. You would need to use *adjectives*. Adjectives describe in two ways. They can tell *how many* or *what kind*.

● Look at these three sentences that tell about the picture.

<u>Three</u> children play in a band.
The leader holds a <u>red</u> stick.
The children sing a <u>pretty</u> song.

In the first sentence the word *three* describes *children*. It tells how many children. In the second sentence the word *red* describes *stick*. It tells what kind of stick. In the third sentence the word *pretty* describes *song*. It tells what kind of song. *Three, red,* and *pretty* are adjectives.

An **adjective** is a word that describes
a noun or a pronoun.

Talk About It

Read each sentence. Then look at each underlined adjective.
Tell what noun it describes.

1. The small band practices for two hours.
2. A white dog with black spots makes funny faces.
3. The happy musicians sit on the hard chairs.
4. The band gives a beautiful concert.

Skills Practice

Write each adjective that appears in each sentence. After
each adjective, write the noun it describes.

1. Large crowds of people drive to the park.
2. They spread colorful blankets on the green grass.
3. The musicians walk onto the high stage.
4. Tiny bugs crawl on the bright lights.
5. The tall leader turns to the quiet audience.
6. She has a deep voice and a serious look.
7. She lifts her wooden stick.
8. The three musicians take a deep breath.
9. Heavy rain falls from the dark sky.
10. The happy musicians smile at the beautiful rain.

Writing Sentences

Think about a concert or a movie you have gone to. Write
three sentences about it. Use three of these adjectives in your
sentences.

long	two
beautiful	happy

Sample Answer 1. Large, crowds

Adjectives That Compare

Adjectives are words that describe. One way to describe a thing is by comparing it to something else. Adjectives that compare often end in *er* or *est*.

Toby plays a **long** horn.

*Carla's horn is a **longer** horn than Toby's.*

*José's horn is the **longest** horn of all.*

- Look at the picture on the left. What adjective describes the horn?

- Now look at the picture in the middle. Two horns are compared. What adjective describes Carla's horn?

- Look at the picture on the right. Three horns are compared. What adjective describes José's horn?

An adjective ending in **er** compares two nouns. An adjective ending in **est** compares more than two nouns.

●Note how the form of the adjective changes in each of these groups of words.

bright	cool	neat
brighter	cooler	neater
brightest	coolest	neatest

●Notice how the form changes in these adjectives.

large	pale	safe
larger	paler	safer
largest	palest	safest

> If an adjective ends in **e,** drop the **e** and add **er** or **est** to make the correct form of the adjective.

Talk About It

Tell what form of the adjective goes in each sentence.

1. Myra is the ___ player in the whole band.   (loud)
2. Her horn is ___ than mine.   (large)
3. She plays a ___ note than I can.   (high)

Skills Practice

Write each sentence with the correct form of the adjective.

1. The ___ member of the band plays the drum.   (short)
2. His drum makes a ___ sound than my horn.   (dull)
3. The flute player is the ___ person of all.   (smart)
4. Her flute is ___ than my horn.   (light)
5. It is also a ___ instrument than mine.   (simple)
6. It makes ___ music than the horn.   (soft)
7. She even plays on the ___ day of the year.   (cold)

Sample Answer 1. The shortest member of the band plays the drum.

Adjectives That End in Y

You already know that *er* or *est* is added to an adjective when two or more things are compared. Sometimes you must change the spelling of the adjective before adding *er* or *est*.

> If an adjective ends with a **consonant** and **y,** change the **y** to **i** and add **er** or **est** to make the correct form of the adjective.

heavy——→heav**y** + er = heavier
    i
A piano is <u>heavier</u> than a violin.

heavy——→heav**y** + est = heaviest
    i
A piano is the <u>heaviest</u> instrument in a band.

Talk About It

Spell each of these words with an **er** ending.

1. happy   **2.** gloomy   **3.** juicy

Spell each of these words with an **est** ending.

4. mushy   **5.** noisy   **6.** roomy

Skills Practice

Write each of these adjectives with an **er** ending and then with an **est** ending.

1. pretty	**4.** salty	**7.** windy	**10.** funny
2. rosy	**5.** tiny	**8.** busy	**11.** lazy
3. snowy	**6.** tasty	**9.** angry	**12.** greedy

Sample Answer **1.** prettier, prettiest

More About Endings of Adjectives

Some adjectives change in another way before *er* or *est* is added to them.

> If a one-syllable adjective ends with consonant, vowel, consonant, double the last consonant and add **er** or **est** to make the correct form of the adjective.

Adjectives that end in *w, x,* or *y* are exceptions to this rule.

big——→big + g + er = bigger
She plays a <u>bigger</u> drum than I do.

big——→big + g + est = biggest
He plays the <u>biggest</u> drum of all in the band.

Talk About It

Spell each word with an **er** ending and then with an **est** ending.

1. fat   **2.** hot   **3.** glad   **4.** thin

Skills Practice

Write each word with an **er** ending and then with an **est** ending.

1. mad   3. dim   5. snug   7. wet
2. flat   4. red   6. slim   8. grim

Writing Sentences

Imagine you are comparing two or more instruments in a band. Write three sentences in which you add *er* or *est* to three of these adjectives: happy, pretty, dim, flat.

Sample Answer 1. madder, maddest

Skills Review

Write each adjective that appears in each sentence. After each adjective, write the noun it describes.

1. The three musicians play on a new stage.
2. The new place has many seats.
3. Many people buy tickets.
4. A clear sky covers the entire city.
5. Happy people arrive at the large building.
6. The nervous leader peeks through the gold curtain.
7. People rush to the empty seats.
8. The unhappy musicians give the leader a late message.
9. They forgot the new instruments.
10. The sad leader has a pale face.
11. She walks on the wide stage.
12. She faces the bright lights.

Read each sentence. Write the correct form of the adjective.

13. It is the ___ audience of all.   (large)
14. She has a ___ face than she did five minutes ago.   (pale)
15. She speaks in a ___ voice than last time.   (soft)
16. This is the ___ problem she has ever had.   (great)
17. It seems like the ___ moment in her life.   (long)
18. Then the ___ voice of all shouts, "Come outside for free food!"   (loud)
19. They leave the ___ way they can.   (quick)
20. The musicians are the ___ runners of all.   (fast)
21. People exit in a ___ time than last time.   (short)
22. The musicians can not think of a ___ thing.   (sweet)

Write each of these adjectives with an **er** ending and then with an **est** ending.

23. ripe   24. tasty   25. windy

26. tiny	**32.** busy	**38.** high
27. snowy	**33.** dusty	**39.** speedy
28. angry	**34.** dizzy	**40.** sticky
29. noisy	**35.** funny	**41.** sleepy
30. deep	**36.** little	**42.** waxy
31. salty	**37.** rusty	**43.** small

Write each word with an **er** ending and then with an **est** ending.

44. sad	**47.** fat	**50.** red
45. thin	**48.** big	**51.** hot
46. wet	**49.** slim	**52.** flat

SMiLES

Have you ever wondered what the longest and shortest words are in the English language? The shortest words, of course, are *a* and *I*. They have only one letter each.

The longest word, believe it or not, has 3,600 letters! It is the name of a certain chemical. (Would you like that word on your next spelling test?)

A long word is called a *sesquiped* (ses'kwi ped'). Here are two sesquipeds and their meanings: **abecedarian** (ā'bē sē der'ē ən), simple, elementary. **triskaidekaphobia** (tris'kī dek' ə fo' bē ə), fear of the number 13.

Some people say the longest word is *smiles*, because there is a *mile* between the first and last letters.

Exploring Language

Using More and Most to Compare

Many adjectives have an *er* or *est* ending when they compare two or more things. However some adjectives do not use the *er* or *est* ending. Instead these adjectives have a different form for comparing.

Carmen is a <u>more interesting</u> musician than Paul.

Susan is the <u>most interesting</u> musician of all.

- Look at the sentence under the picture on the left. The word *interesting* describes *musician*. Since two people are compared, the form of the adjective is **more interesting.**

- Now look at the sentence under the picture on the right. In this case, more than two people are compared. Therefore the form of the adjective is **most interesting.**

> Use **more** before some adjectives when comparing two nouns.
>
> Use **most** before some adjectives when comparing more than two nouns.

Do not use *more* or *most* before adjectives that already have *er* or *est* added to them.

WRONG: Carmen plays a more louder horn than Paul.
RIGHT: Carmen plays a louder horn than Paul.

WRONG: Susan plays the most loudest horn of all.
RIGHT: Susan plays the loudest horn of all.

Talk About It

Tell which form of the adjective goes in each sentence.

1. Carmen plays ___ music than Paul.
   (more beautiful, most beautiful)
2. Susan is the ___ player in the group.
   (more careful, most careful)
3. She has the ___ job of all.   (more difficult, most difficult)

Skills Practice

Write each sentence. Use the correct form of the adjective that goes in each sentence.

1. Susan is the ___ person in the whole band.
   (more wonderful, most wonderful)
2. She makes a ___ sound than Paul does.
   (more powerful, most powerful)
3. Martha plays the ___ music of all.
   (more beautiful, most beautiful)
4. She is also a ___ person than Paul is.
   (more polite, most polite)
5. Carmen is the ___ musician I know.
   (more nervous, most nervous)
6. Bob is a ___ player than Susan.
   (more patient, most patient)
7. He is a ___ musician than I am.
   (more serious, most serious)
8. He is the ___ musician of all our friends.
   (more exciting, most exciting)

Sample Answer 1. Susan is the most wonderful person in the whole band.

Prefixes and Suffixes

Sometimes new words are made by adding groups of letters to words.

> A **prefix** is one or more letters added to the beginning of a word.

> A **suffix** is one or more letters added to the end of a word.

- Look at these sentences.

Ira plays an <u>unusual</u> instrument. Ira is <u>unaware</u> of the noise.

The prefix *un* before an adjective means *not*. *Unusual* means *not usual*. What does *unaware* mean?

- Now look at these sentences.

Rose is a <u>thirsty</u> girl. She drinks the <u>chilly</u> water.

The suffix *y* means *having*. *Thirsty* means *having a thirst*. What does *chilly* mean?

- Read these two sentences.

Ira is a <u>careful</u> musician. Ira has played a <u>cheerful</u> song.

The suffix *ful* means *full of*. *Careful* means *full of care*. What does *cheerful* mean?

- Now read these sentences.

Rose played a <u>harmless</u> joke. She wouldn't hurt a <u>helpless</u> person.

The suffix *less* means *without*. *Harmless* means *without harm*. What does *helpless* mean?

		Meaning	Example
Prefix	un	not	unusual (not usual)
Suffix	y ful less	having full of without	thirsty (having thirst) careful (full of care) harmless (without harm)

Talk About It

Tell what each underlined word means.

1. You must be a <u>skillful</u> musician to play the bottles.
2. Most musicians use <u>colorless</u> bottles.
3. Fill the bottles with <u>unequal</u> amounts of water.
4. Make sure you do not have any <u>leaky</u> bottles.

Skills Practice

Write each underlined word. Then write the meaning of the word.

1. Take an <u>unbroken</u> pencil or a spoon.
2. Give a <u>powerful</u> tap on each bottle.
3. A <u>lucky</u> person will not break the bottles.
4. A <u>careless</u> musician spills the bottles.
5. We enjoy this <u>noisy</u> music.
6. The musicians are <u>hopeful</u> about the music.

Write one word to replace each group of underlined words.

7. It is <u>not wise</u> to hit the bottles too hard.
8. A player who is <u>having luck</u> hits each note correctly.
9. Bottle music can be <u>full of joy</u>.
10. A player who is <u>without thought</u> hits the wrong notes.
11. That kind of music is <u>not bearable</u>.

Sample Answers 1. unbroken, not broken. 7. unwise.

Adjectives That Mean the Same Thing

Suppose everyone in your class were asked to describe the same person, place, or thing. All the students probably would not use the same adjectives. There are many adjectives that have similar meanings.

A **synonym** is a word that has nearly the same meaning as another word.

- Look at the instrument on the left side of the picture. You might describe it as *small* instrument. But *small* is not the only adjective you can use. Here are five synonyms for the word *small*:

little   tiny   short   thin   narrow

Any of these words can also be used to describe the instrument on the left.

- Now look at the instrument on the right. You can describe it as a *big* instrument. But *big* is not the only adjective you can use. Here are five synonyms for the word *big*:

huge   enormous   giant   grand   large

Any of these words can also be used to describe the instrument on the right.

Talk About It

Read each sentence. Read the words after each sentence. Which of these words is a synonym for the underlined word?

1. It was a peaceful night.   (calm, dark, cold)
2. A happy audience filled the hall.   (brave, large, cheerful)
3. They came to hear pleasant music.   (costly, lovely, loud)

Skills Practice

Read each sentence. Read the words after each sentence. Write the word that is a synonym for the underlined word.

1. The nervous musicians waited.   (bitter, scared, eager)
2. They had done a silly thing.   (different, old, foolish)
3. They had brought the wrong music.   (sad, true, incorrect)
4. The noisy crowd became silent.   (anxious, loud, angry)
5. The lights went out in the whole room.   (crowded, entire, dark)

Replace each underlined word with a synonym. Write the sentence with the word you have chosen.

6. The cautious audience walked in the darkness.
7. They looked for a fast way to leave the room.
8. The musician walked through the long hall.
9. The unhappy people went home without a concert.

Writing Sentences

1. Write two sentences that describe music you like. Use synonyms for these words in your sentences.
   a. great   b. nice
2. Write two sentences that describe music you don't like. Use synonyms for these words in your sentences.
   a. silly   b. loud

Sample Answers 1. scared **6.** The careful audience walked in the darkness.

Skills Review

Read each sentence. Write the correct form of the adjective that goes in each sentence.

1. Which instrument makes the ___ music in the world?
   (more beautiful, most beautiful)
2. Some people think a violin makes the ___ sound of all.
   (more delicate, most delicate)
3. The violin is the ___ instrument in the band.
   (more common, most common)
4. A piano is ___ than a violin to move.
   (more difficult, most difficult)
5. I think a flute has a ___ sound than a piano.
   (more exciting, most exciting)
6. A drum has the ___ sound I can think of.
   (more powerful, most powerful)
7. A horn is the ___ instrument I know.
   (more joyful, most joyful)
8. Some people say it is the ___ instrument of all to play.
   (more difficult, most difficult)

Write each underlined word. Then write the meaning of the word.

9. I am <u>unable</u> to carry a tune.
10. My singing is <u>hopeless</u>.
11. My friend has a <u>powerful</u> voice.
12. She can break a <u>frosty</u> glass with her high notes.

Write one word to replace each group of underlined words.

13. I once had singing lessons that were <u>not pleasant</u>.
14. I was <u>full of hope</u> that voice lessons would improve my singing.
15. When I sang, my teacher was <u>without speech</u>.
16. I was <u>having luck</u> to have such a good teacher.

Skills Review

Read each sentence. Read the words after each sentence.
Write the word that is a synonym for the underlined word.

17. The musicians prepared for a <u>final</u> concert.   (best, last, single)
18. They brought the <u>entire</u> music.   (right, proper, complete)
19. They remembered their <u>usual</u> instruments.   (regular, odd, old)
20. The <u>frightened</u> musicians appeared.   (sleepy, nervous, angry)
21. Their leader entered the <u>large</u> hall.   (enormous, crowded, new)
22. The musicians played a <u>difficult</u> song.   (long, familiar, hard)
23. They did a <u>perfect</u> job.   (fair, excellent, awful)
24. The <u>cheerful</u> audience clapped at the end.   (sad, happy, dull)
25. The <u>astonished</u> musicians fainted from surprise.
    (red, amazed, tired)

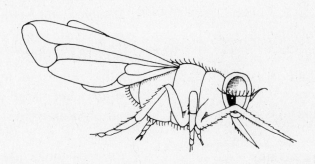

Have you ever played "Think Pink?" All you have to do is think of an adjective and a noun that rhyme. Then make up a question for someone else to answer. For example:
—What do you call a sneaky insect?   (a sly fly)
You also can play the game with two-syllable words.
—What do you call an empty gulp?
(a hollow swallow)
How many "Think Pinks" can you make up?

Using Reference Works

You know that a library is a place where you can borrow books on many subjects. A card catalog can help you find the books you need. Remember that there are three cards you can use: the author card, title card, and subject card.

Reference works in a library can help you with reports.

WORLD ATLAS

ROAD MAP

RELIEF MAP

1. The *encyclopedia* gives information about many subjects.
2. The *almanac* gives the latest facts and figures.
3. An *atlas* is a book of maps. It has a table of contents and an index to help you find the map you need. The most complete kind of atlas is a *world atlas* that contains maps of separate countries and the world. There are also other kinds of maps. A *road map* can help you plan an automobile trip. A *relief map* shows you what the land in an area looks like with mountains, valleys, and bodies of water.
4. *Periodicals* are magazines or newspapers that are published at certain periods of time. Most magazines are printed weekly or monthly. You can find magazines about hobbies, news, and many other subjects.

● Look at the chart on the next page. It shows you how most libraries are organized.

LIBRARY ORGANIZATION	
1. Fiction books (books of stories)	Arranged alphabetically by the authors' last name.
2. Nonfiction books (books about subjects based on fact)	Arranged alphabetically by subject
3. Reference works (encyclopedia, almanac, atlas)	Arranged in a reference section
4. Magazines, newspapers, records	Arranged in a special section
5. Children's books	Arranged in a special room.

Talk About It

Tell where you would find the following information in a library. Use the library organization chart above.

1. A book on American history
2. A book of children's poems
3. A detective story for an adult
4. A map of China
5. A children's book of stories
6. An encyclopedia article on Africa.

Skills Practice

Write whether you would use an encyclopedia, almanac, atlas, newspaper, or magazine to find information about each of the following.

1. The lowest temperature recorded in Texas
2. Road maps of the Western states
3. Facts about Mexico
4. Last week's baseball scores
5. Information about Native Americans.

Write one sentence about what you might look for in each of the following reference works.

6. An encyclopedia 7. An atlas 8. An almanac 9. A magazine

Sample Answer 1. Almanac

Reviewing Paragraphs

Thinking About Paragraphs

You have learned that most paragraphs have two types of sentences. The topic sentence states the main idea of the paragraph. Detail sentences give more information about the main idea or topic sentence.

You have learned how to write four different types of paragraphs, depending on the kind of detail sentences you want to use. These are the different types of detail sentences.

1. time order   **2.** description   **3.** facts   **4.** reasons

The kind of paragraphs you use depends on what you are writing. For example, you would put your details in *time order* if you write to a friend about an exciting trip you took. But you would use details that *describe* if you write about the view from a mountaintop in Vermont. You will need *facts* to explain your topic sentences when you write a report in school. And you will need *reasons* for your opinions when you write to convince people of your point of view.

Ray Manley from Shostal Associates

Talking About Paragraphs

Read these paragraphs. What type of paragraph is each of the following? Give reasons for your answers. Remember that there are four types of paragraphs.

1. The concert was about to begin. First the lights grew dim. Next the audience grew quiet. Then the conductor stepped on stage. She turned to the musicians. At last she lowered her baton.
2. Our band needs uniforms. Band members would have more pride if they wore uniforms. Other bands wear coats or sweaters with their school colors. We need uniforms to wear at band contests.
3. The concert was held outdoors high on a hill. The setting sun turned the river far below a fiery orange. Stars soon crowded the sky as though they, too, had come to listen. Music filled the sky.
4. Our marching band won the state contest last year. We have 70 members, and we practice every day after school. The school bought us new uniforms for the contest. We are putting the prize in the front hall.

Writing Paragraphs

Notice the kind of paragraph that would be written. Write two detail sentences for each of the topic sentences below. Be sure that you write complete sentences.

1. Our band is raising money for a trip to Mexico. Write a paragraph using facts.
2. My sister's rock band practices in our basement. Write a paragraph that uses words that describe.
3. Music is a language everyone in the world loves and understands. Write an opinion paragraph with reasons.
4. We left for the spring concert an hour early. Write a time order paragraph about the trip.

Interviews

Thinking About Interviews

You remember that the first step in writing any type of paragraph is to think of an idea. Then you must look for information to help explain your idea more clearly. You already know you can find information in reference works in the library. Another good way to gather information is to interview a person who knows something about the idea.

There are two parts to interviewing. First you must get ready for the interview. Second you must actually interview the person. Here are some steps to follow in interviewing.

Getting Ready for Your Interview	Doing Your Interview
1. Read about your idea. If you know something about your idea, you can ask better questions.	1. Arrive on time and have your pen and pencil for notes.
2. Find out about the person you are going to interview. Try to find out about the person's home, work, and hobbies.	2. Be a good listener. The answers you hear may give you ideas for other questions.
3. Decide what questions you will ask and write them in your notebook.	3. Ask the person to repeat or to explain an answer if you do not understand it.
4. Call or write to ask for a date and time for the interview. Remember to write it in a notebook so you will not forget it.	4. Thank the person when you have finished.
	5. Reread what you have written and correct any mistakes while the interview is still clear in your mind.

Read this interview with a school guidance counselor.

Interview Questions

1. What does a guidance counselor do?
2. How could you help a fifth grade student?
3. Why do you give tests?

Interview Notes

Marcia Gerdes. October 30, 19__
A counselor helps people make decisions about their lives. She could help a student who is having problems in school, or she could help a person decide what after-school activities to choose. She gives tests to get more information about students so she can better help them.

Talking About Interviews

Look at the interview again.

1. What information is found in the first line of the notes? Why?
2. Why are the notes taken in the order of the questions?
3. How would the interviewer know to ask a counselor the question about tests?
4. Can you think of other questions you would ask a counselor?

Doing an Interview

Now you are ready to try an interview. First choose a partner. Decide who should be interviewed first and who should ask the questions. Then switch parts. Imagine that you are one of the following people being interviewed:

1. A character in one of your favorite books
2. A character in a television series
3. A sports hero

Before you begin, think about what information you want to know. Then write your questions. Remember to take notes on your partner's answers. Save your notes for the next lesson.

A Summary Paragraph

Thinking About Paragraphs

You have learned about many types of paragraphs. Another important type is called a summary paragraph. This type of paragraph does just what its name suggests. It summarizes or briefly states only the most important facts or ideas you have learned. A summary paragraph has a topic sentence and detail sentences like other paragraphs.

Suppose you have a great deal of information about a subject. When you write a summary paragraph, you must ask yourself some questions about your information.

1. What facts are the most important?
2. What facts could be combined or put together?
3. What facts are interesting but are not about the main idea?

Review all your information and ask yourself these questions. Then you are ready to write a summary paragraph.

●Read the information below. It was gathered from an interview with a man who lived in a desert.

Interview Questions

1. What desert animals have you seen?
2. Where do they live?
3. How do they get water?

Interview Notes

Robert Knoll. March 3, 19___.
He has seen kangaroo rats and gila monsters. Most animals go without water for days. They live under stones or dig in the sand. The gila monster gets water by eating other animals. The kangaroo rat eats plants to get water. They also eat seeds. They have small bodies.

Think about how the interview notes could be arranged into a summary paragraph. Read the paragraph below.

Many animals live in the desert. Some desert animals are gila monsters and kangaroo rats. They stay out of the sun by living under stones or by digging a hole in the sand. Most desert animals can go without water for days. The gila monster gets water by eating other animals. The kangaroo rat gets water from plants and seeds.

Writing Your Paragraph

Now it is your turn to write a summary paragraph. Read the interview notes you made when you interviewed your partner in the last lesson.

1. Think about the main idea you want to use for your topic sentence.
2. Study your interview notes and questions.
   a. Choose the most important facts to be in the summary.
   b. Put together or combine facts about the same subject.
   c. Do not use any information that is not about the main idea stated in your topic sentence.
3. Write your topic sentence. Use your facts to write the detail sentences.

Edit Your Paragraph

Read your summary paragraph again. Check it with the following questions. Remember to use the two editing symbols.

1. Are all the facts in the paragraph about the main idea?
2. Did you write only the most important facts?
3. Did you use punctuation marks and capital letters correctly?
4. Did you spell your words correctly?

Checking Skills

Write each adjective that appears in each sentence. After each adjective write the noun it describes. *pages 192–193*

1. The ten children wait to go to the concert.
2. The anxious friends talk about the concert.
3. One boy talks about the lively songs.
4. The boy with the green cap talks about his favorite song.

Write the correct form of the adjective for each sentence. *pages 194–195*

5. The ___ girl in the class leads the group.   (tall)
6. The theater is the ___ of all.   (large)
7. The music sounds ___ than last week's music.   (soft)

Write each of these adjectives with an **er** ending and then with an **est** ending. *pages 194–197*

8. sad
9. muddy
10. crazy
11. cloudy
12. wide
13. short

Read each sentence. Write the correct form of the adjective that goes in each sentence. *pages 200–201*

14. The band plays the ___ music of any band.
    (more lively, most lively)
15. Josie plays the ___ guitar music of anyone I know.
    (more beautiful, most beautiful)
16. I think Donald is the ___ musician in our school.
    (more famous, most famous)
17. I think a guitar makes ___ music than a drum.
    (more interesting, most interesting)
18. I am ___ in the piano than the guitar.
    (more interested, most interested)

Write each underlined word. Write the meaning of the word. *pages 202–203*

19. Tina has a <u>healthy</u> voice.
20. I was <u>unaware</u> of her desire to be a singer.
21. I hope her efforts are not <u>hopeless</u>.
22. Singing lessons are a <u>wonderful</u> idea.
23. Tina might make a <u>delightful</u> entertainer.

Read each sentence. Read the words after each sentence. Write the word that is a synonym for the underlined word. *pages 204–205*

24. I sang a <u>jolly</u> song at the party. (quiet, happy, sad)
25. Friends were amazed by my <u>lovely</u> voice. (pretty, loud, slow)
26. I sang a <u>lively</u> song. (slow, fast, funny)

Read the four paragraphs below. Each paragraph either gives directions in time order, describes something, explains facts, or states reasons. Label your paper from a to d. Write the kind of paragraph that each represents. *pages 210–215*

a. Bill cleaned his clothes today. First he put them in the washer. Next he added soap. Later he placed the clothes in the dryer. Then he folded them.

b. All drivers of cars should wear seat belts. Seat belts make driving much safer. They have saved many people's lives. The seat belts are easy to fasten and to remove.

c. The card catalog in a library helps you find books. Each card has the author and title of a book. It also has a special number that tells where the book is located.

d. I have a pet rabbit. Her ears are white. Her eyes are red. She hops around all day and makes a funny sound when eating. Her fur is soft.

A Biography

A *biography* is a story of someone's life. It tells about the events in that person's life. Marian Anderson is a famous black singer who worked very hard in her life to reach her goals. The following selection about her early life is from a biography about Marian Anderson.

Courtesy of Hurok Attractions

Marian Anderson

In a small house in Philadelphia a three-year-old girl was singing. She sat at a little table that she liked to make believe was her piano. The walls of the room were covered with flowered paper. The child thought she saw friendly faces in the flowers, looking down at her as she played and sang. The child's name was Marian Anderson. When she grew up, she became one of the world's best-loved singers.

Marian was born on February 27, 1903. Her father, John Anderson, worked long hours delivering coal and ice. Her mother, Anna Anderson, had been a schoolteacher once. Now she was busy keeping the house comfortable for her husband and their three daughters: Marian, Alyce, and Ethel. The Anderson family did not have much money, but they cared about each other and had many happy times together.

As Marian grew older, her father took her to church with him every Sunday. The Union Baptist Church was important to the people in Marian's neighborhood. Often their lives were unhappy. Many of them were poor. Some of them had trouble getting jobs. In church they heard words and music that said to them: "Yes, you have troubles. We know that life can be hard. We must hope for good things to come."

Marian joined the children's choir of the church. As she sang with this group, the choirmaster noticed her beautiful voice. He asked her to practice a duet with her best friend, Viola Johnson. The next Sunday the two girls stood up to sing for the whole congregation. It was Marian's first public performance. She was six years old.

Marian was finding out about music in other ways, too. When she was eight, her father bought an old piano. But there was no money for music lessons. After weeks of trying, Marian taught herself to play simple tunes. She wished she could learn more.

Then one day she saw a used violin in a store window. She went in and asked the man how much it cost. "Three dollars and ninety-five cents," he said. "Is it a good violin?" Marian asked. She knew how hard it would be for her to get that much money. "Oh, it's a very fine instrument," the storekeeper said.

Marian went to work after school. She scrubbed steps for her neighbors and ran their errands. If someone gave her a few cents for candy, she put the money carefully away. At last she earned and saved enough nickels and pennies. Proudly she went back to the store and bought the violin. A friend of the family taught her to tune it and to play a few notes. But before long the strings snapped and the wood of the violin cracked. It was no good at all. Marian was sad and disappointed. She wanted so much to make music well.

Still she was never downhearted for long. She loved singing in the choir. Her full, rich voice poured through the church. The sound she made was so loud the choirmaster sometimes laughed and said, "Hold back a little there, Marian. We want

to hear the other singers, too." Friends and neighbors in the congregation, though, had nothing but praise for Marian.

Her voice was deep and velvety, the kind musicians called contralto. But she could reach up to the high soprano notes, too, and even down to the low music of the baritone. When the choir prepared a new song, Marian learned all the different parts, high and low, not just her own. Then, if a singer could not come to church on Sunday, she helped out by singing in his place. It made her happy to know the choir needed her, and she learned a lot about music this way. Secretly she dreamed of being a singer when she grew up.

But when Marian was twelve, her father died. Life changed then. Harder times began. Marian's mother had to go out to work. She got a job cleaning other people's houses and bringing their laundry home to wash and iron. Mrs. Anderson was a frail, gentle woman, but she had great spirit. She never complained and somehow she found the extra strength to make a good home for her children.

As the years went by, Marian began to realize how hard her mother worked to provide for her family. "I'm getting old enough now," she thought, "I must do something, too." When she entered high school she tried to study useful subjects, like typing. But all the time her heart was really set on singing.

If only she could earn enough money at it, she could make singing her life's work. Of course she was not paid for singing

in church. Ever since she was eight, though, she had been invited to sing in other churches, too. People all over Philadelphia got to know about her splendid voice. They began asking her to perform at their parties and club meetings. By the time Marian was in high school, she was getting $5.00 every time she sang at one of these gatherings.

This seemed like a lot of money to her. Yet she knew she was still a long way from being a professional singer. She had been born with a fine voice and she sang with deep feeling. But Marian saw how much she still had to learn. The best way, she decided, would be to have lessons, at a music school.

Early one morning she took the trolley car to a well-known school in uptown Philadelphia. She went into the building and got in line with a group of girls who were waiting to apply. When Marian's turn came, the pretty, blue-eyed woman in charge paid no attention to her. Marian stepped aside. After everyone else had been taken care of, the woman said, "What do *you* want?" in a sharp voice. "I'd like to arrange for lessons, please—" Marian began politely. "We don't take colored," said the woman coldly, and turned away.

Marion felt hurt and confused. She had often heard that white people sometimes behaved in this cruel, thoughtless way toward Negroes. But it had never really happened to her before. In her neighborhood black people and white people lived side by side. Most of the time they were comfortable and friendly with each other. True enough, their skins were different, Marian thought, but not their feelings.

Sadly she went home to tell her mother what happened at the school. "The way that woman spoke," she cried, "it bit into my soul." Was she wrong to think a Negro girl could become a singer? Marian asked.

Mrs. Anderson thought for a while. Then, in her calm, sure way, she said, "Of course you can become a singer, Marian. You must have faith. There will be another way for you to learn what you need to know."

And there was another way. The people at the Union Baptist Church believed in Marian's talent. These friends and neighbors planned a concert to help her. Every bit of money they got from the tickets was set aside to pay for private singing lessons for Marian.

Marian performed at the concert herself, but the main star was Roland Hayes. Mr. Hayes was the first Negro singer to become famous in the concert halls of America and Europe.

He sang the spirituals Marian and her people knew so well. These were powerful songs of sorrow, of joy, and of hope that the Negroes made up when they were slaves. Mr. Hayes also sang lieder, poems set to music by the great European composers. Marian could not understand the French or German languages they were sung in. Still she was quick to hear the beauty of the music. She longed to learn such songs herself.

Then, as she listened to Mr. Hayes's pure tenor voice, she suddenly realized, "His skin is dark, like mine. And he has gone so far. They say he has even sung for kings and queens. If he can, perhaps I can too." Slowly, from this time on, Marian's pride began to grow. It was never an angry pride, but full of faith and hope. Throughout her life, no matter what happened, it kept her strong.

Tobi Tobias

Activities

1. Imagine that you were given the chance to interview Marian Anderson. What questions would you ask? How would she answer them? Here is one possible question and answer:
   YOU: What did you dream of when you were a child?
   MARIAN: I secretly dreamed of becoming a singer.
   Write four more questions that you would ask Marian Anderson. Also write her answers based on the information in her biography.
2. Imagine that someone wanted to write your biography. Think of the events in your life that would be most interesting or unusual. For example, did you ever move from another town? Did you ever get lost or lose something important? Have you ever won an award? Write three sentences that tell about three important events in your life.

Grammar and Related Language Skills

Learning About Linking Verbs

Nouns and Adjectives After Linking Verbs

Linking Verbs in Present and Past Tense

Apostrophes in Possessives and Contractions

Practical Communication

Using Note-Taking Skills

Writing a Two-Paragraph Report

Creative Expression

A Ballad

225

Linking Verbs

Every sentence has a verb. Some verbs name an action. Other verbs do not name an action, but they still help to make a statement.

> An **action verb** is a word that names an action.

> A **linking verb** is a verb that connects the subject part with a noun or adjective in the predicate part. It tells what the subject is or is like.

The most common linking verb is *be*. The chart shows the forms of *be* in the present tense and the past tense.

Present	Past
I am She He } is It You We } are They	I She He } was It You We } were They

● Look at these two sentences.

Tracy <u>works</u> in a circus.   She <u>is</u> a clown.

The verb *works* names an action. The verb *is* does not name an action, but it still helps to make a statement. *Is* is a linking verb.

● Now look at these two sentences.

Tracy <u>went</u> to a clown school.   She <u>was</u> a student for two years.

The verb *went* names an action. Does the verb *was* name an action, or is it a *linking verb*?

Howard Brainen c 1977

Talk About It

Tell whether each underlined verb is an action verb or a linking verb.

1. Tracy <u>prepares</u> for the show.
2. Her job <u>is</u> unusual.
3. She <u>is</u> a clown.
4. Her costume <u>is</u> colorful.
5. The buttons <u>are</u> special.
6. They <u>spray</u> people with water.

Skills Practice

Write the verb in each sentence. If the verb names an action, write **action verb** after the verb. If the verb is a linking verb, write **linking verb** after the verb.

1. Tracy studied in a clown school.
2. Her teachers were clowns.
3. They taught her about makeup.
4. She paints her face blue today.
5. Her face was yellow yesterday.
6. Her nose is round and red.
7. Her shoes are very large.
8. Tracy chases other clowns.
9. The audience is happy.
10. I am happy, too.
11. Tracy travels with the circus.
12. She was sick.
13. Now she is well.
14. Clowns are cheerful.

Sample Answer 1. studied, **action verb**

Nouns and Adjectives After Linking Verbs

You know that a linking verb helps to make a statement without naming an action. Sometimes a linking verb is followed by a noun or an adjective.

A **noun** is a word that names a person, place, thing, or idea.
An **adjective** is a word that describes a noun or pronoun.

A linking verb connects, or *links*, the noun or adjective that follows it with another word in the sentence.

● Read the sentences below.

Roberta is a shepherd.   Her great-grandfather was a rancher.

In the first sentence the verb *is* links the noun *shepherd* with *Roberta*. (Do not count words such as *a, an, the, her, his,* or *their.*) *Shepherd* and *Roberta* are the same person. In the second sentence the verb *was* links the noun *rancher* with *great-grandfather*. *Rancher* and *great-grandfather* are the same person.

•Now look at these sentences.

Roberta is busy.   The sheep are restless.

In the first sentence the verb *is* links the adjective *busy* to *Roberta*. *Busy* describes *Roberta*. In the second sentence the verb *are* links the adjective *restless* to *sheep*. *Restless* describes *sheep*.

Talk About It

Tell whether a noun or an adjective follows each linking verb. Then tell the word to which the noun or adjective is linked.

1. Some jobs are difficult.
2. Roberto's job is unusual.
3. He is a shepherd.
4. His sheep are young.

5. His hours are long.
6. Roberto is sleepy.
7. His feet are sore.
8. His father is a farmer.

Skills Practice

Read each sentence. Write the word that follows the linking verb. (Do not count words such as *a, an, the, his, her,* or *their.*) If the word is a noun, write **noun.** If the word is an adjective, write **adjective.** Then write the word to which the noun or adjective is linked.

1. His boss is a rancher.
2. Shepherds are busy.
3. Their work is hard.
4. Coyotes are dangerous.
5. Roberto is careful.
6. The dog is a companion.
7. The sheep are noisy.
8. Their home is the pasture.

9. Some girls are shepherds.
10. The job is fun.
11. The life is different.
12. I am curious.
13. My dog is a shepherd.
14. She is tan.
15. She is lazy.
16. She is a pet.

Sample Answer 1. rancher, **noun,** boss

Using Linking Verbs in the Present Tense

The subject of a sentence tells whom or what the sentence is about. The subject may be singular or plural.

● Notice how the subjects and the verbs work together.

I <u>am</u> a reporter.	Gary <u>is</u> a lawyer. He <u>is</u> a friend of Sue. She <u>is</u> a judge. The courtroom <u>is</u> huge. It <u>is</u> old.	You <u>are</u> innocent. We <u>are</u> happy. John and Ed <u>are</u> sad. They <u>are</u> angry. Our friends <u>are</u> joyful.

Each column shows a different form of the linking verb *be* in the present tense. Remember, use *am* when the subject is *I*. Use *is* when the subject is *she, he, it,* or a singular noun. Use *are* when the subject is *you, we, they,* a plural noun, or a compound subject.

Talk About It

Read each sentence. Tell which linking verb to use.

1. Ed ___ angry.   (is, are)
2. He and John ___ upset.   (is, are)
3. The coins ___ old.   (is, are)
4. Ed's face ___ sad.   (is, are)
5. The coins ___ rare.   (is, are)
6. John ___ furious.   (is, are)

Skills Practice

Write each sentence. Use the correct form of the linking verb.

1. The judge ___ wise.   (is, are)
2. I ___ nervous.   (is, am)
3. John ___ calm.   (is, are)
4. The coins ___ old.   (is, are)
5. The judge ___ smart.   (is, are)
6. Her mind ___ quick.   (is, are)
7. I ___ curious.   (is, am)
8. The case ___ clear.   (is, are)

Sample Answer 1. is

Using Linking Verbs in the Past Tense

In the present tense the linking verb in a sentence must agree with the subject part. The same is true of linking verbs in the past tense.

●Notice how the subjects and verbs work together.

I <u>was</u> a cook.	You <u>were</u> hungry.
Sam <u>was</u> a cook.	We <u>were</u> busy.
He <u>was</u> quick.	The children <u>were</u> happy.
Joyce <u>was</u> a customer.	They <u>were</u> playful.
She <u>was</u> hungry for lunch.	Toni and Sue <u>were</u> thirsty.

Each column shows a different form of the linking verb *be*. Use *was* when the subject is *I, she, he, it,* or a singular noun. Use *were* when the subject is *you, we, they,* a plural noun, or a compound subject.

Talk About It

Read each sentence. Tell which linking verb to use.

1. The day ___ hot. (was, were)
2. We ___ thirsty. (was, were)
3. Our mouths ___ dry (was, were)
4. Sam ___ busy. (was, were)
5. We ___ hungry. (was, were)
6. The meal ___ good. (was, were)

Skills Practice

Write each sentence. Use the correct form of the linking verb.

1. The day ___ strange. (was, were)
2. Sam ___ nervous. (was, were)
3. His hands ___ damp. (was, were)
4. His boss ___ angry. (was, were)
5. You ___ curious. (was, were)
6. The eggs ___ bad. (was, were)
7. We ___ angry. (was, were)
8. I ___ sick. (was, were)

Sample Answer 1. The day was strange.

Antonyms

Some words have opposite meanings. These words are called *antonyms*.

Daniel <u>enters</u> his shop.   Daniel <u>leaves</u> his shop.

●Look at the two sentences that describe the pictures. The verb in the first sentence is *enters*. The verb in the second sentence is *leaves*. *Leaves* means the opposite of *enters*. The words *enter* and *leave* are antonyms.

> An **antonym** is a word that means the opposite of another word.

●Look at the words in the boxes. The two words in each box are antonyms.

| win lose | | live die | | succeed fail |

Not every word has an antonym. For example, the word *yawn* can be a verb, but there is not a verb that means the opposite of *yawn*. There is not a word that means the opposite of *tickle* or of *rhyme*. These words do not have antonyms.

Talk About It

Read each sentence. Tell which word is an antonym for the underlined word.

1. Daniel opens his barber shop.   (designs, closes, measures)
2. He stands all day.   (sits, cuts, plays)
3. A customer arrives early.   (applies, leaves, smiles)
4. Daniel grins at him.   (frowns, smiles, looks)

Skills Practice

Read each sentence. Write the word that is an antonym for the underlined word.

1. The customer raises his chin.   (lowers, rests, lifts)
2. He begins telling a story.   (relates, finishes, starts)
3. The story bores Daniel.   (interests, surprises, bothers)
4. He forgets his work.   (speaks, outlines, remembers)
5. Daniel removes too much hair.   (clips, replaces, brushes)
6. This upsets the customer.   (calms, angers, awakens)
7. He yells at Daniel.   (screams, whispers, sings)
8. Daniel watches the customer.   (calms, ignores, scares)
9. Daniel dislikes his job sometimes. (enjoys, lives, succeeds)

Writing Sentences

So far in this unit you have read about a clown, a shepherd, a judge, a cook, and a barber. Now think of a different type of worker. Tell about him or her in your sentences.

1. Write two sentences with action verbs that are antonyms. For example, you might write: I like barbers. I hate barbers.
2. Write two sentences with linking verbs.

Sample Answer 1. lowers

Skills Review

Write the verb in each sentence. If the verb names an action, write **action verb.** If the verb is a linking verb, write **linking verb.**

1. Ruth works in an unusual job.
2. She is a chimney cleaner.
3. She sweeps chimneys.
4. Her uniforms are always dirty.
5. She wears a special suit.
6. The color is black.
7. Her hat is also black.
8. Her boots are gray.
9. She uses brooms and brushes.
10. The equipment is important.
11. Ruth cleaned a chimney today.
12. Dust was heavy.
13. Dirt was grimy.
14. Ruth climbed the chimney.
15. Bats were black.
16. Ruth was calm.
17. They flew away.
18. Ruth watched from the roof.
19. Ruth's job is different.
20. I am curious about her job.

Write the word that follows the linking verb. (Do not count words such as *a, an,* or *the*.) If the word is a noun, write **noun.** If the word is an adjective, write **adjective.** Then write the word to which the noun or adjective is linked.

21. Consuelo is a banker.
22. Her work is pleasant.
23. The job is fun.
24. Friends are customers.
25. They are neighbors.
26. Consuelo is friendly.
27. She is helpful.
28. The customers are thankful.
29. I am happy.
30. The job was easy.
31. Consuelo was busy.
32. Two customers were nervous.
33. They were strangers.
34. The strangers were thieves.
35. Consuelo was alert.
36. The alarm was loud.
37. The police were quick.
38. Both strangers were sorry.

Read each sentence. Write the correct form of the linking verb.

39. Kay ___ a ranger. (is, are)
40. Her work ___ fun. (is, are)
41. She and Vi ___ busy. (is, are)
42. They ___ foresters. (is, are)
43. The area ___ clean. (is, are)
44. Fires ___ common. (is, are)

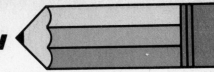
45. I ___ warm. (is, am)
46. We ___ curious. (was, were)
47. Smoke ___ heavy. (was, were)
48. The fire ___ small. (was, were)
49. It ___ strange. (was, were)
50. Vi ___ grateful. (was, were)

Write the word that is an antonym for the underlined word.

51. Otto <u>repaired</u> a watch in his shop.   (studied, broke, lifted)
52. He <u>scattered</u> the parts on a table.   (gathered, emptied, lost)
53. Then he <u>lowered</u> a bright lamp.   (switched, clicked, raised)
54. Otto <u>bent</u> a piece of metal.   (hammered, folded, straightened)
55. He <u>hooked</u> two springs.   (unfastened, locked, tied)
56. The watch <u>stopped</u> ticking.   (ended, began, decided)
57. The angry owner <u>left</u>.   (arrived, ran, stepped)
58. Otto <u>lost</u> another customer.   (pleased, bothered, found)

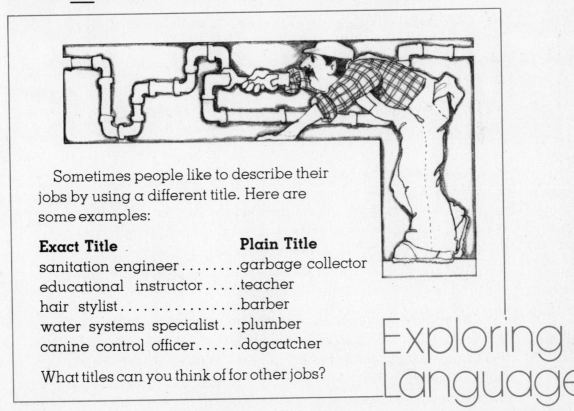

Sometimes people like to describe their jobs by using a different title. Here are some examples:

Exact Title   **Plain Title**
sanitation engineer........garbage collector
educational instructor.....teacher
hair stylist...............barber
water systems specialist...plumber
canine control officer.....dogcatcher

What titles can you think of for other jobs?

Exploring Language

Verbs Ending in ing

The form of a verb tells the time of the action. The *present tense* of a verb names an action that happens now. The *past tense* of a verb names an action that already happened. There is another form that tells when something happens. It tells that the action continues.

Jesse <u>was</u> <u>selling</u> ice before.   Jesse <u>is</u> <u>selling</u> water now.

● Look at the sentence under the picture on the left. *Was selling* is the entire verb. *Was* is a helping verb. It tells you that the action happened in the past. *Selling* is the main verb. It has an *ing* ending. The verb *was selling* shows action that began in the past and continued for a time.

● Now look at the sentence under the picture on the right. *Is selling* is the entire verb. *Is* is a helping verb. It tells you that the action is happening in the present. *Selling* is the main verb. It has an *ing* ending. The verb *is selling* shows action that continues in the present.

When a verb ends in *ing,* the helping verb is a form of *be.* Remember the forms of *be* in present tense and past tense.

Present I **am** she, he, it **is**   You, we, they **are**
Past   I, she, he, it **was**   You, we, they **were**

Now you know other ways to talk about the present and the past. The present tense of the helping verb *be* (*am, is, are*) and a main verb ending with *ing* name an action that continues in the present. The past tense of the helping verb *be* (*was, were*) and a main verb ending with *ing* name an action that began in the past and continued for a time.

Talk About It

Read each sentence. Decide if each verb should be in the present or past tense. Tell the correct form of the verb *be.*

1. Jesse ___ selling ice on the street before.   (was, is)
2. Many people ___ buying it three hours ago.   (were, are)
3. The sun ___ melting all his ice now.   (was, is)
4. Now people ___ going away.   (is, are)

Skills Practice

Write each sentence. Decide if each verb should be in the present or past tense. Use the correct form of the verb *be.*

1. I ___ watching Jesse before.   (am, was)
2. He ___ doing very well a while ago.   (was, is)
3. His customers ___ asking for lots of ice before.   (were, are)
4. They ___ calling for ice yesterday, too.   (are, were)
5. Now the heat ___ hurting his business.   (is, was)
6. The ice ___ turning into water now.   (was, is)
7. I ___ helping Jesse at this moment.   (am, was)
8. His customers ___ buying cold water now.   (are, were)

Sample Answer **1.** I was watching Jesse before.

Using Apostrophes in Possessives

The English language has many marks and symbols that are used in writing. Some of these are the period, the comma, the question mark, and the exclamation mark. Another symbol is the *apostrophe*.

●Look at these sentences.

The hobby of Walter is fun.   Walter's hobby is fun.

Both sentences tell whose hobby is fun. In the second sentence an apostrophe (') and an *s* are added to *Walter* to show possession.

> Add an **apostrophe** and **s ('s)** to form the possessive of most singular nouns.

●Look at these sentences.

The voices of the boys are good.   The boys' voices are good.

In the second sentence an apostrophe (') is added after the *s* of *boys* to show possession.

> Add an **apostrophe (')** to form the possessive of a plural noun that ends with **s.**

●Look at these sentences.

The boys sing the words of people.   The boys sing people's words.

The word *people* is a plural noun that does not end in *s*. In the second sentence an apostrophe (') and *s* are added to *people* to show possession.

> Add an **apostrophe** and **s ('s)** to form the possessive of a plural noun that does not end with **s.**

Talk About It

Each underlined noun has an apostrophe to show possession. Tell whether the noun is singular or plural.

1. The <u>boys'</u> songs are interesting.
2. <u>Walter's</u> parents like the music.
3. His <u>friends'</u> parents also like the music.
4. He sings often at <u>children's</u> parties.
5. He is singing at a <u>child's</u> party today.

Skills Practice

Read each sentence. Write the noun in each sentence that shows possession. If the noun is singular, write **singular.** If the noun is plural, write **plural.**

1. Our neighbors' friend went on a vacation last week.
2. We drove him to the airport in his brother's car.
3. We parked in a friend's parking space.
4. All the passengers' families were saying good-bye.
5. Suddenly I heard Walter's voice.
6. He was singing the man's favorite good-bye song.

Change each group of underlined words to a possessive form of the noun. Write each new sentence.

7. The job <u>of Walter</u> takes him many places.
8. Yesterday he went to the hospital <u>of a friend</u>.
9. A helper <u>of the director</u> called him.
10. Walter reported to the office <u>of the directors</u>.
11. They took him to the rooms <u>of the patients</u>.
12. The smiles <u>of the people</u> showed their pleasure.
13. The eyes <u>of one person</u> were full of tears.

Sample Answers **1.** neighbors', plural **7.** Walter's job takes him many places.

Using Apostrophes in Contractions

You know that an apostrophe is used to show possession by a noun. An apostrophe is also used to join two words together to make one word. The new word with the apostrophe is called a *contraction*.

> A **contraction** is a word made up of two words. The words are joined together to make one word.

The chart on the left shows contractions of pronouns with the present tense of *be*. The middle chart shows contractions of pronouns with *have* and *has*. The chart on the right shows contractions of pronouns with *had*.

Contraction	Short For	Contraction	Short For	Contraction	Short For
I'm	I am	I've	I have	I'd	I had
you're	you are	you've	you have	you'd	you had
he's	he is	he's	he has	he'd	he had
she's	she is	she's	she has	she'd	she had
it's	it is	it's	it has	it'd	it had
we're	we are	we've	we have	we'd	we had
they're	they are	they've	they have	they'd	they had

Some contractions are often confused with other words that sound the same. Be careful when using these words.

you're	*You're* a window washer. (*You are* a window washer.)
your	*Your* job is hard.
it's	*It's* a big window. (*It is* a big window.)
its	*Its* glass is dirty.
they're	*They're* washing it. (*They are* washing it.)
their	*Their* job is done.
there	*There* is a clean window.

Talk About It

Tell how you would write each group of underlined words as a contraction.

1. <u>She is</u> a window washer.
2. <u>It is</u> dangerous work.
3. <u>You are</u> high in the air.
4. <u>We had</u> done it last year.
5. <u>I have</u> tried it again.
6. <u>They have</u> also tried it.

Skills Practice

Read each sentence. Write the underlined words as contractions.

1. <u>We have</u> brought a bucket.
2. <u>It is</u> full of water.
3. <u>I am</u> ready to wash.
4. <u>He has</u> dropped the rags.
5. <u>You had</u> given him too many.
6. <u>They are</u> waiting for us.
7. <u>We are</u> worried.
8. <u>I am</u> losing my balance.
9. <u>She is</u> hanging on.
10. <u>She had</u> spilled the water.
11. <u>You are</u> a good worker.
12. <u>It is</u> time to dry the glass.
13. <u>We have</u> finished.
14. <u>She has</u> broken a window.
15. <u>It is</u> not my fault.
16. <u>They are</u> leaving us.

Writing Sentences

Think about what you would like to do for a living. Tell about the job in the sentences you write.

1. Write one sentence that uses a contraction of a pronoun and the present tense of <u>be</u>.
2. Write one sentence that uses a contraction of a pronoun and <u>have</u>.
3. Write one sentence that uses a contraction of a pronoun and <u>had</u>.

Sample Answer 1. We've

Skills Review

Write each sentence. Decide if each verb should be in the present or past tense. Use the form of the verb *be*.

1. Rick ___ working for the post office last week.   (is, was)
2. Now he ___ resting from his accident.   (was, is)
3. Last Friday we ___ waiting for our mail.   (are, were)
4. That morning our cousin ___ visiting us.   (was, is)
5. Her two dogs ___ running in our yard then.   (were, are)
6. Rick ___ carrying a large sack of mail that time.   (is, was)
7. The dogs ___ chasing him for an hour that day.   (were, are)
8. I ___ delivering mail for Rick now.   (am, was)
9. The dogs ___ playing at their own home now.   (were, are)

Write the noun in each sentence that shows possession. If the noun is singular, write **singular.** If the noun is plural, write **plural.**

10. Paul works as a cook's helper.
11. He fills the children's plates.
12. Someone shouts the customers' orders.
13. Paul takes a woman's order.
14. The pay is good for students' work.

Change each group of underlined words to a possessive form of the noun. Write each new sentence.

15. The hair of Paul falls in his eyes.
16. He bumps into the arm of a waiter.
17. The tray of the man flies through the door.
18. A salad bowl lands on the head of the owner.
19. The eyes of a child open wide.
20. The laughter of the people is loud.
21. The dinner of our friends was late.
22. The soup of the boys was cold.

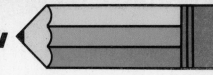

Read each sentence. Write the underlined words as contractions.

23. I am a librarian.
24. It is a nice job.
25. I have watched that boy.
26. He is noisy.
27. He had arrived quietly.
28. He has dropped his books.
29. We are returning books.

30. They are late.
31. I had forgotten about them.
32. She has lost a book.
33. It has fallen into water.
34. You are crying.
35. We had better pay for it.
36. You had better take a vacation.

Language often tells us something about the way people live. For example, for a long time in the United States, few jobs were held by women. Many jobs even had male titles such as *policeman*, *fireman*, and *chairman*.

Times are changing and the language is changing, too. As more women enter the work world, job titles are changing. *Policeman* has become *police officer*, *fireman* is now *firefighter*, and *chairman* is *chairperson* or *chair*.

What other job titles are changing with the times?

Exploring Language

Using Note-Taking Skills

To prepare a report, you gather information from different places. It is helpful to take notes on the important facts. Careful notes will help you write a well-organized report.

These steps are helpful to follow when taking notes.

1. Know the main subject of your report.
2. Think about the kinds of information in the library.
3. Read the information carefully.
4. Decide what facts are most important.
5. Write your notes in sentences or in groups of words called phrases.
6. Reread your notes and compare them with the sources. Make sure you have chosen the most important facts.

● Look at these examples of taking notes from a reference source.

There are many kinds of ants. *Carpenter ants* chew holes in wood to make homes. *Army ants* make no nests at all but travel in large groups. *Pharaoh's ants* are smaller than this letter **a**. *Honey ants* live on sweet juices from flowers. *Amazon ants* capture ants from different groups to work for them.

Sentence Notes	Phrase Notes
Many types of ants exist.	—types of ants
Carpenter ants live in wood.	—*carpenter ants* (wood)
Army ants travel and have no home.	—*army ants* (travel)
Pharaoh's ants are tiny.	—*Pharaoh's ants* (tiny)
Honey ants collect juices.	—*honey ants* (juices)
Amazon ants have slaves.	—*Amazon ants* (slaves)

Talk About It

Look at the selection and notes about ants again.

1. What is the main idea of the selection?
2. What is the difference between the sentence notes and the selection?
3. What is the major difference between the two kinds of notes?
4. When would you want to use phrase notes rather than sentence notes?

Skills Practice

Review how to take notes. Take sentence notes on the first paragraph. Take phrase notes on the second paragraph.

1.   Many people do not know that backgammon is a very old game. It was developed by the Persians long ago. The ancient Greeks and Romans played backgammon. Native Americans also played backgammon. Backgammon has become popular again.

2.   The most important part of making bread is kneading the dough. To knead dough, first fold the dough toward you. Next, press the dough with the heel of your hands. Then turn it a little bit. Fold it and press it again. Keep kneading the dough until it is smooth.

Sample Answer 1. Backgammon is a very old game.

Writing Two-Paragraph Reports

Thinking About Paragraphs

You have been learning how to write different types of paragraphs. Now you are going to use your skills to write a longer report. A two-paragraph report must have a main idea. Both paragraphs in the report should be about that main idea. Usually the first paragraph introduces the idea and tells about it in a general way. The second paragraph then uses more details and tells about the idea in a more specific way. Sometimes the report has a title. The title briefly states the main idea.

You can use any of the types of paragraphs you have learned to write in a two-paragraph report. The report could contain two paragraphs with facts or two paragraphs that describe. You can also mix the two paragraphs. The first paragraph could be an opinion paragraph with reasons that introduce the main idea. The second paragraph could use facts to prove the main idea.

● Read the two-paragraph report below that uses facts.

Oceanography

Oceanography is the study of the ocean or sea. The ocean needs to be studied because it covers over 70 per cent of the earth. Plants and fish may someday increase our food supply. Also oil and natural gas can be found in rocks under the ocean bottom.

An oceanographer can study the sea in many different ways. Some oceanographers draw the plants and animals for reports. Others study only certain parts of the sea such as rocks or shellfish. All oceanographers should be good sailors because they must study the sea on stormy as well as on calm days.

Talking About Paragraphs

Look at the report about oceanography.

1. What is the main idea of this two-paragraph report?
2. What kind of paragraphs are they?
3. What is the topic sentence of the first paragraph?
4. What is the topic sentence of the second paragraph?
5. What words are similar in each topic sentence?
6. How is the second paragraph different from the first?
7. What is the title of the report?

Writing Paragraphs

You are going to write a two-paragraph report based on the following topic sentences and detail sentences. Follow these directions carefully.

1. Use this topic sentence for the first paragraph: *Veterinary medicine is an interesting career.*
2. Use this topic sentence for the second paragraph: *A veterinarian is an animal doctor.*
3. Read the following detail sentences. Some of these detail sentences go with the first topic sentence, and some go with the second topic sentence. Decide which ones support the first topic sentence. Choose the ones that support the second topic sentence.
   a. It deals with the health and care of animals.
   b. In cities veterinarians take care of people's pets.
   c. In the country they take care of farm animals.
   d. People in veterinary medicine must like to work with animals.
   e. There are hospitals for animals that have the same equipment that is used with human beings in hospitals.
   f. Veterinarians also test meat and milk for diseases.
4. Write the report using the topic and detail sentences.
5. Write a title for the report.

Writing a Class Report

Thinking About a Report

Your class can write a two-paragraph report together. Remember that the first step in preparing for report writing is to decide upon your main idea. Then you must gather information about the idea. You can use a card catalog in a library to find the reference works you need. Besides books you can use magazines to find the most up-to-date information. You can also use nonprint materials such as records, films, and filmstrips.

The main idea of your report will be clowns. Besides going to the library, you can also use notes from interviews. Imagine that you are going to interview a clown.

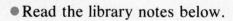

- Read the library notes below.

Library Notes

1. Clowns used to be called jesters.

2. Modern circuses started in England two hundred years ago.

3. Clowns have always been an important part of the circus.

4. Clowns make people laugh after scary acts like the high wire or trapeze artists.

5. Every clown has a special costume and make-up.

Next you would need to think of questions to ask the clown. Then you would use your library notes and the questions to do the actual interview with the clown.

Interview Questions	Interview Notes
1. What is your real name?	Jolly the Clown. August 4, 19__.
2. Why did you become a clown?	Her real name is Lisa Dunne.
3. How did you become a clown?	She likes to make people laugh.
4. How do you like the circus?	She went to a special clown school. She learned to walk on stilts there. She finds circus work hard but fun.

Writing a Report

Now you are ready to write the class report.

1. Choose one of the two topic sentences below for the beginning of the first paragraph. Remember that the first paragraph usually introduces the main idea in a general way.
   a. Circuses have changed over the years.
   b. Clowns have been entertaining people for hundreds of years.
2. Now choose a topic sentence for the second paragraph of your class report from the two sentences below. The second paragraph tells more about the main idea of the report. It usually has more specific information than in the the first paragraph.
   a. A circus clown has to learn many things.
   b. A clown needs to know how to walk on stilts.
3. Write your report on the board.
4. Write the topic sentence of the first paragraph.
5. Use the library and interview notes for information. Write the detail sentences for the first paragraph.
6. Write the topic sentence for the second paragraph. Then write the detail sentences.
7. Read the two paragraphs aloud. Check that all the sentences are about the main idea of clowns.
8. Write a title for the report.

Writing Your Own
Two-Paragraph Report

Thinking About Your Report

Now you are ready to write your own two-paragraph report. Imagine that a Navy pilot came to speak at a school assembly. He is training to be an astronaut. You are to write a report for the school newspaper.

● Read these library notes about astronauts.

Library Notes

1. Astronauts are pilots or scientists.
2. They spend two or more years in training.
3. Much time is spent in classroom work.
4. They learn how rockets work.
5. They study many different sciences.
6. There are many tests for the body and the mind.

● Read the interview notes taken with the Navy pilot.

Interview Questions

1. How did you learn to fly?
2. Where do you live now?
3. What do you want to do?
4. Do you have any hobbies?

Interview Notes

John Knight. April, 19___.
He served on an aircraft carrier. He was a test pilot, also. He now lives at The Space Center, Houston, Texas. He wants to explore other planets. His hobby is science fiction.

Writing Your Own Report

1. Write a topic sentence for the first paragraph. The sentence should tell that U.S. astronauts usually must be either pilots or scientists.
2. Use the library notes to write detail sentences for the first paragraph. These sentences should tell how astronauts are trained.
3. Write a topic sentence for the second paragraph. The sentence should tell about the interview with astronaut John Knight at your school.
4. Use your interview notes to write detail sentences for the second paragraph.
5. Write a title for your report.

Edit Your Report

Good writers always edit their work. Use the check list to edit your two-paragraph report. Remember to use the two editing symbols if you make those mistakes.

1. Do both paragraphs tell about the main idea of the report?
2. Do the topic sentences state the main idea of each paragraph?
3. Do the detail sentences tell about each topic sentence?
4. Did you indent the first sentence of each paragraph?
5. Does each sentence start with a capital and end with the correct punctuation mark?
6. Did you use correct punctuation for dates and names of places?
7. Did you spell your words correctly?

NASA Photo

COMPOSITION: *Two-Paragraph Report* 251

Checking Skills

Write the verb in each sentence. If the verb names an action, write **action verb** after the verb. If the verb is a linking verb, write **linking verb** after the verb. *pages 226–227*

1. Gina works in a factory.
2. She is an operator.
3. She twisted the dough.
4. It was sticky.

Read each sentence. Write the word that follows the linking verb. (Do not count words such as *a, an, the, his, her,* or *their.*) If the word is a noun, write **noun.** If the word is an adjective, write **adjective.** Then write the word to which the noun or adjective is linked. *pages 228–229*

5. Bob is a secretary.
6. He is a typist.
7. Bob was busy.
8. The others were loud.

Write the correct form of the linking verb for each sentence. *page 230*

9. Lee ___ a fashion designer.   (is, are)
10. His customers ___ women.   (is, are)
11. The clothes ___ expensive.   (is, are)

Write the word that is an antonym for the underlined word. *pages 232–233*

12. Carmen placed a sign in her window.   (removed, repaired, put)
13. She lowered the curtains.   (raised, shut, closed)
14. Then she locked all the doors.   (turned, opened, checked)

Read each sentence in the story below. Decide if the verb should be in the present or past tense. Write the form of the verb **be** that belongs in each blank. *pages 236–237*

15. Bill ___ working as a page-turner now.   (is, was)
16. He ___ washing dishes before.   (is, was)
17. Bill ___ enjoying his new job now.   (is, was)

Write the noun in each sentence that shows possession. If the noun is singular, write **singular.** If the noun is plural, write **plural.** *pages 238–239*

18. Rae directs the city's traffic.
19. Rae's job helps.
20. The people's cars stop.

Change each group of underlined words to a possessive noun. *pages 238–239*

21. The job of <u>Rae</u> gets hectic.
22. The driver <u>of the car</u> calls for help.

Read each sentence. Write the underlined words as contractions. *pages 240–241*

23. <u>She is</u> an interpreter.
24. <u>It is</u> an interesting job.
26. <u>They are</u> very interesting.
25. <u>I have</u> learned a lot.

Write a two-paragraph report from the following topic sentences. *pages 246–251*

The topic sentence of the <u>first</u> paragraph: *My friends like to read different kinds of stories.*
The topic sentence of the <u>second</u> paragraph: *It is important to be able to read.*
Read these detail sentences. Decide which ones support the first topic sentence. Decide which support the second. Write both paragraphs, using the topic and detail sentences you chose.

a. You may read an encyclopedia to learn different facts.
b. Four friends told me that they like books about animals.
c. Two friends like to read sports stories.
d. In a restaurant you need to read the menu.
e. One friend said he likes to read ghost stories.
f. Reading a newspaper tells you about world events.

A Ballad

One of the oldest forms of poetry is a ballad. A *ballad* is any story told in song. In the Middle Ages there were many poets who wandered through castles and villages singing ballads. Ballads usually introduce characters who are part of a situation. Often there is a problem to solve or some danger from which to escape. Because ballads tell a story and usually have a particular rhythm, they are also called *narrative poems*.

One of the most famous American ballads is *Casey Jones*. It tells the story of a man who made a brave sacrifice for others. The ballad was written in memory of a railroad engineer named John Luther Jones, better know as Casey Jones. In the spring of the year 1900, Casey saw that his mail train, called the *Cannonball*, was going to crash into two freight trains. He stayed on board to slow down the train. He gave his life to save the lives of his passengers.

Read the ballad about this brave man. Do you know the tune that goes with the poem?

Come all you rounders if you want to hear
The story of a brave engineer;
Casey Jones was the hogger's name,
On a big eight-wheeler, boys, he won his fame.
Caller called Casey at half-past four,
He kissed his wife at the station door,
Mounted to the cabin with orders in his hand,
And took his farewell trip to the promised land.

   Casey Jones, he mounted to the cabin,
   Casey Jones, with his orders in his hand!
   Casey Jones, he mounted to the cabin,
   Took his farewell trip into the promised land.

"Put in your water and shovel in your coal,
Put your head out the window, watch the drivers roll,
I'll run her till she leaves the rail,
'Cause we're eight hours late with the Western Mail!"
He looked at his watch and his watch was slow,
Looked at the water and the water was low,
Turned to his fireboy and said,
"We'll get to 'Frisco, but we'll all be dead!"

   Casey Jones, he mounted to the cabin,
   Casey Jones, with his orders in his hand!
   Casey Jones, he mounted to the cabin,
   Took his farewell trip into the promised land.

Casey pulled up Reno Hill,
Tooted for the crossing with an awful shrill,
Snakes all knew by the engine's moans
That the hogger at the throttle was Casey Jones.
He pulled up short two miles from the place,
Number Four stared him right in the face,
Turned to his fireboy, said, "You'd better jump,
'Cause there's two locomotives that's going to bump."

Casey Jones, he mounted to the cabin,
Casey Jones, with his orders in his hand,
Casey Jones, he mounted to the cabin,
Took his farewell trip into the promised land.

Activities

1. Imagine that you are a TV newscaster or a newspaper reporter. You are reporting the story of Casey Jones. Your report might start like this:

   > Yesterday near San Francisco tragedy struck on the railroad. John Luther Jones, better known as "Casey" to his friends, died in a train accident.

   Continue the rest of the news article. Add about six more sentences. Tell when, where, and how the accident occurred. Use the content of the ballad as information for your article. When you are finished, read the article to the class.

2. Read *Casey Jones* aloud as a choral reading. Three different class members can read the stanzas of eight lines each. The whole class can chant the refrain. The refrain is a group of lines that are repeated. Think about which lines could be read fast and which ones slower. Also think about which words should be read softly, and which ones should be read more forcefully.

3. Go to a library and find other ballads to read. *The Adventures of Robin Hood* is a famous ballad. You could also listen to ballads sung as songs on a record.

4. Choose a famous event from history. You might choose the discovery of America, the walk on the moon, or an historical character such as Joan of Arc. Thing about who took part in the event. Also think about when, where, and how it happened. Try writing a ballad that tells the story. Introduce the characters and mention the most important details of the story. Later you can try to set your poem to music.

Grammar and
Related Language Skills

Learning About Adverbs
Using Adverbs to Compare
Forming Adverbs from Adjectives
Reviewing Capital Letters

Practical Communication

Developing an Outline
Writing a News Story

Creative Expression

A True Story

Adverbs

Suppose someone asked you to tell about the things you do each day. You would need to use verbs to name the actions. You would also use words that describe the actions.

> An **adverb** is a word that describes an action.

An adverb may tell *how, when, where,* or *how often* an action is done.

● Look at these sentences.

James worked quickly.   The visitors walked slowly.

In the first sentence *quickly* describes the action verb *worked.* In the second sentence *slowly* describes the action verb *walked.* *Quickly* and *slowly* are adverbs. They tell how the action is done.

● Now read these sentences.

David Weng arrived early.   The children came later.

In the first sentence *early* describes the action verb *arrived.* In the second sentence *later* describes the action verb *came.* *Early* and *later* are adverbs. They tell when the action is done.

• Read these sentences.

The children played outdoors.   Some adults walked nearby.

In the first sentence *outdoors* describes the action verb *played*. In the second sentence *nearby* describes *walked*. *Outdoors* and *nearby* are adverbs and tell where the action is done.

• Now read these sentences.

The children shouted frequently.   The adults laughed once.

In the first sentence *frequently* describes *shouted*. In the second sentence *once* describes *laughed*. *Frequently* and *once* tell how often the action is done. Both are adverbs.

Notice that many of the adverbs in the examples end in *ly*. Look at the examples again. Which adverbs end in *ly*?

Talk About It

What is the adverb in each sentence? Tell the word it describes.

1. Weng disappeared quietly.
2. The family clapped merrily.
3. The visitors talked excitedly.
4. They looked indoors.
5. They searched everywhere.
6. Weng performs often.

Skills Practice

Write the adverb in each sentence. Then write the word it describes.

1. Neighbors came quickly.
2. They searched carefully.
3. Mr. Weng spoke then.
4. A bell rang next.
5. Everyone listened curiously.
6. Children played nearby.
7. They called loudly.
8. A voice answered suddenly.
9. He laughed happily.
10. The family called again.
11. Weng returned immediately.
12. He showed his trick later.

Sample Answer 1. quickly, came

Using Adverbs to Compare

Sometimes you may describe an action by comparing it to another action. When you do, the adverb has a special form.

● Look at these sentences.

> Eddie walked <u>fast</u>.
> Susan walked <u>faster</u> than Eddie.
> Their mother walked <u>fastest</u> of all.

Add *er* to some adverbs when comparing two actions. Add *est* to some adverbs when comparing more than two actions.

● Look at these sentences.

> Eddie May ran <u>quickly</u> to the window.
> His sister ran <u>more quickly</u> than Eddie.
> Mrs. May ran <u>most quickly</u> of all.

In each sentence, *quickly* is an adverb describing the verb *ran*. The second sentence uses *more quickly* because two actions are compared. The third sentence uses *most quickly* because more than two actions are compared. Use *more* before most adverbs ending in *ly* when comparing two actions. Use *most* before most adverbs ending in *ly* when comparing more than two actions.

You usually use *more* or *most* before an adverb when comparing. A few one-syllable adverbs add an *er* or *est* ending. If an adverb does have an *er* or *est* ending, do NOT use *more* or *most* before the adverb.

RIGHT: Eddie went *nearer* to the UFO than Susan.
WRONG: Eddie went *more nearer* to the UFO than Susan.

RIGHT: Mrs. May went *nearest* of all to the UFO.
WRONG: Mrs. May went *most nearest* of all to the UFO.

Talk About It

Read each sentence. Use **er** or **est** to make the correct form of the adverb.

1. I hid ___ in the grass than my friend. (low)
2. Purple creatures jumped out of the UFO ___ than green ones. (fast)
3. The blue creatures squealed ___ of all. (loud)

Read each sentence. Use *more* or *most* to complete the sentence.

4. The first UFO landed ___ quickly than the second.
5. The third UFO landed the ___ swiftly of all.
6. The green door opened ___ slowly than the red door.

Skills Practice

Write each sentence. Use **er** or **est** to make the correct form of the adverb.

1. The first UFO dug ___ into the ground than the second. (deep)
2. The third UFO landed ___ to us. (near)
3. It braked ___ of them all. (late)
4. The second UFO bounced ___ than the first. (high)
5. It came ___ to the tree than the second. (close)

Write each sentence. Use *more* or *most* to complete each sentence.

6. The creatures behaved ___ politely than humans.
7. The first pilot answered questions ___ completely than the second.
8. The third pilot whispered ___ softly of all.
9. She also wiggled her ears ___ rapidly.
10. The creatures spoke ___ rapidly than we did.

Sample Answers 1. The first UFO dug deeper into the ground than the second.
6. The creatures behaved more politely than humans.

Forming Adverbs from Adjectives

You know that an adjective describes a person, place, or thing. Some adjectives can be made into adverbs. The form of the adjective must be changed.

clever——→clever + ly = cleverly
Albert Ostman escaped *cleverly* from strange animals.

Add **ly** to some adjectives to form an adverb.

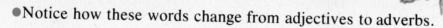

●Notice how these words change from adjectives to adverbs.

final	wild	main	thick
finally	wildly	mainly	thickly

Sometimes an adjective must be changed before *ly* is added.

busy——→busi + ly = busily
Ostman was searching *busily* for gold in Canada.

Change **y** to **i** and add **ly** to form an adverb from an adjective that ends in **y.**

●Notice how these words change from adjectives to adverbs.

happy	heavy	jerky	tricky
happily	heavily	jerkily	trickily

Talk About It

Change each adjective to an adverb. Tell how the adverb is formed.

1. Albert Ostman was hunting ___ for gold in Canada. (eager)
2. A hairy thing called Sasquatch grabbed Ostman ___ in his sleep. (sudden)
3. The large animal carried his prize ___ in a sack. (easy)
4. Ostman kicked ___, but he could not escape. (wild)

Skills Practice

Change each adjective to an adverb. Write the adverb.

1. Ostman rode ___ in the sack for a long time. (unhappy)
2. The Sasquatch ___ lowered the bag. (final)
3. Ostman looked ___ around him. (careful)
4. Four large Sasquatch stood ___ in the mountains. (excited)
5. They spoke ___ with one another. (loud)
6. Ostman searched ___ for the way out. (wild)
7. Ostman ___ found that he was trapped. (sad)
8. He lived ___ with the Sasquatch for a week. (helpless)
9. He waited ___ for a chance to escape. (patient)
10. One day they went ___ for water. (quick)
11. Ostman moved ___ from the camp. (hurried)
12. Ostman escaped ___ through the mountains. (merry)
13. Today some people search ___ for Sasquatch. (curious)

Writing Sentences

Imagine you are telling about your search for Sasquatch.

Write four sentences with adverbs ending in *ly*.

Sample Answers 1. unhappily 2. finally

Reviewing Capital Letters

Most words in your writing do not begin with a capital letter. However it is important to remember the special times when a word needs to be capitalized.

Use a **capital letter** to begin the first word of every sentence.

Have you heard about the giant animal?
Some people believe it lives in a lake.

Use a **capital letter** to begin each important word of a proper noun. A proper noun is a noun that names a special person, place, thing, or idea.

Mr. John Mackay lived on Fifth Avenue in New York City.
Mr. Mackay saw the giant animal in a large lake in Scotland.
The thing is called the Loch Ness Monster.
One was reported in the Lake of the Seven Glaciers.

Use a **capital letter** to begin the names of the months and days of the week.

John Mackay visited Scotland in May.
He camped by the lake on Monday and Tuesday.

Use a **capital letter** for each initial in a person's name. Use a **period (.)** after an initial.

Honey T. Williams read about this monster.

Use a **capital letter** to begin each important word in the title of a book. Always begin the first word of a title with a capital letter.

Louisa read a book called The Monster in the Lake.

Words in a book title should be underlined when you write them.

Talk About It

Tell each word in each sentence that should begin with a capital letter.

1. the lake in loch ness is twice as deep as the north sea.
2. a police officer says he saw the animal in 1933.
3. mr. john mackay saw it on a tuesday.
4. in july, some people from london saw the thing.

Skills Practice

Write each word in each sentence that should begin with a capital letter.

1. sir edward mountain took his camera to scotland.
2. the strange animal has been talked about often.
3. people on a bus saw the thing on a wednesday.
4. a fishing boat was crossing the lake in december.
5. in 1958, the loch ness monster made a noise.
6. a broadcasting company from britain heard it.
7. a group of scientists from japan studied the animal in 1974.
8. lieutenant commander t. r. gould thinks it is something from the early days of the world.
9. dr. m. barton wrote a book called <u>the</u> <u>monster</u> <u>of</u> <u>loch</u> <u>ness</u>.
10. dr. barton lives on first avenue.

Writing Sentences

Imagine you traveled to Scotland to find the animal at Loch Ness. Now write about your adventure there.

1. Write one sentence in which someone's name is capitalized.
2. Write one sentence in which the name of a place is capitalized.
3. Write one sentence in which a day or a month is capitalized.

Sample Answer 1: Sir Edward Mountain, Scotland

Using Language

In our language there are many ways to say the same thing. Often you choose the words you say to fit the situation. You might say to a friend:

"Want to eat chow at my house?"

Suppose you are asking your grandmother to dinner. Then you might say:

"Would you like to come to dinner at my house?"

When speaking with friends in everyday situations, you often use everyday words. At other times you choose your words more carefully.

● Look at the pictures below. Which picture shows a situation where you would use everyday language? Which picture shows a situation where you would want to choose words more carefully?

● Read the sentences below. Which pair of sentences would you use in each of the situations pictured above?

Thank you very much. This is a great honor.
Thanks a lot. These are super.

● Here are some other special kinds of situations when you may want to choose your words carefully:

> You are talking to some people at your mother's office.
> You are speaking to a judge to arrange a class visit to the city court.
> You are writing a letter to your town newspaper.
> You are applying for a job delivering newspapers.

Talk About It_____

Read the pairs of words and phrases below. Which might you hear on the school bus? Which might be used for more special situations?

Let's take off.
It's time to leave.

This is a nice surprise!
Wow! What a treat!

Have a seat.
Please sit down.

Want to tag along?
Would you like to join us?

What's the story?
What happened?

Please call me.
Give me a buzz.

Practice interviewing for a job. Choose the job you want:

newspaper delivery   salesperson   lawn mowing

Be sure to use the kind of language that will help you get the job. Which of the sentences below might you use in your speech? Which would you avoid?

My past experience qualifies me for this job.
Would you believe my experience?
I'm always right on top of things.
I have a good sense of responsibility.
Cheap rates.
My rates are reasonable.

Skills Review

Write the adverb in each sentence. Then write the word it describes.

1. The Bermuda Triangle frequently confuses people.
2. Airplanes disappear suddenly.
3. Five planes left smoothly on a trip.
4. They flew together.
5. The planes traveled quickly.
6. The pilots flew happily.
7. A strange thing happened then.
8. The head pilot called wildly.
9. His sense of direction disappeared completely.
10. The plane acted crazily.

Read each sentence. Add **er** or **est** to make the correct form of the adverb.

11. Della sang ___ than ever. (fast)
12. Her breath came ___ than before. (hard)
13. She sang the ___ of all the girls. (loud)
14. Tom sang the ___ of all the boys. (soft)
15. The girls sang ___ than the boys. (long)

Read each sentence. Use *more* or *most* to complete each sentence correctly.

16. Bob drove ___ carefully than before. (more, most)
17. Sue drove ___ carefully of all. (more, most)
18. Bob drove ___ quickly than Sue. (more, most)
19. Earl drove the ___ recklessly of all. (more, most)
20. The police stopped him ___ happily. (more, most)

Change each adjective to an adverb. Write the adverb.

21. All six planes disappeared ___. (curious)
22. This puzzle cannot be answered ___. (easy)

23. People talk ___ about planes lost in the Bermuda Triangle.   (sad)

24. They speak ___ of ships lost in these waters.   (fond)

25. Scientists are working ___ to find the reason.   (busy)

26. Is a strange animal living ___ in the waters?   (secret)

Write each word in each sentence that should begin with a capital letter.

27. mr. ramirez told us about the bermuda triangle.

28. he said there were often strong winds near florida.

29. last july mr. ramirez and dr. baker visited miami beach.

30. captain lowell talked to the visitors in august.

31. the missing planes and boats might disappear in storms.

32. captain lowell sent me a book called <u>the</u> <u>bermuda</u> <u>triangle</u>.

Have you ever written a Tom Swifty? What is it, you say? A Tom Swifty is a sentence in which the adverb makes a joke. Here are some examples:

"Where are all the sick people?" said the doctor *patiently.*
"I need to sharpen my pencil," said Linda *pointlessly.*
"Please buy me a pony," said Mary *hoarsely.*
Now try to think up your own Tom Swifties.

Exploring
Language

Developing a Two-Part Outline

A good report starts with careful planning. First you choose your main idea. Then you gather information and take notes. Finally you make an outline. The *outline* is your plan for arranging your ideas into paragraphs.

- Read this outline.

Fur Traders in America

I. Fur traders in the West
   A. Found new lands
   B. Found new routes for pioneers
II. Fur traders in the mountains
   A. Called mountain men
   B. Learned many Indian skills

- Look again at the parts of this outline.

1. The main idea is shown in the title.
2. Roman numerals identify the main headings of an outline. Develop these main headings into the topic sentences for your paragraph.

   Fur traders were the first explorers in the American West.

3. Put a period after the Roman numeral for each main heading.
4. Capital letters identify the subheadings of an outline. Develop these subheadings into the detail sentences for the paragraphs in your report.

   They found many new lands as they traveled west.

5. Put a period after the capital letter for each subheading.
6. Notice that the main headings and subheadings in this outline are written in phrases. Sentences can be used instead of phrases in an outline.

Talk About It

Read the outline again about fur traders.

1. What is the main idea of the report? How did you know?
2. What is the first heading? How are the subheadings related to the main heading?
3. What is the second heading? How are the subheadings related to the main heading?
4. Is the outline written in sentences or phrases?

Skills Practice

Read the following two-paragraph report.

The Moon

The moon is a natural satellite that travels around the earth. It has no light of its own. It seems to change as different parts are lighted by the sun. It appears to have no life.

The moon's surface is covered with craters. Scientists think there may be half a million craters that are over a mile wide. Some are called <u>ray craters</u> because they have light gray streaks known as rays. Others are called <u>secondary craters</u> because they were formed by rocks thrown out of the ray craters.

Review the parts to an outline. Write an outline for this report using the following steps:

1. Write the title of the outline.
2. Write this first heading and subheading:
   I. Travels around the earth
      A. No light of its own
3. Write two more subheadings after this first heading.
4. Write the second main heading.
5. Write two subheadings under the heading.

Outlining a Two-Paragraph Report

Thinking About Outlines

The key to writing a good report is *planning*. You prepare to write about your main idea by gathering information from reference works and from interviews. You should take notes about the important facts so that you can remember the information. Your notes should try to put the main ideas into your own words. You can use sentences or phrases. Then you can be sure that you understand the facts that you are writing.

After you have taken your notes, the next step is to write a plan for your report. The *outline* is your plan. It helps you arrange your ideas so that they make sense. When you write a two-paragraph outline, you must think about these questions:

1. What is the main idea of the two-paragraph report?
2. What are the main topics for each paragraph?
3. What information will be in the report?
4. How will you arrange that information?

● Read this outline for a report. Note that Roman numerals list the main headings, and the capital letters list the subheadings.

Unidentified Flying Object

    I. UFO's as strange sights in the sky
       A. Saucer shapes
       B. Flying patterns of UFO's
       C. Strange effects on animals
   II. Many reports on UFO's since World War II
       A. Air Force and 12,000 reports
       B. Unexplained reports
       C. Flying saucers and some groups

Talking About Outlines

Look again at the outline.

1. What is the main idea of the outline? How do you know?

2. What are the two main headings in the outline? How do you know that these are the main headings?
3. What subheadings are listed under each topic? Why are capital letters used? Why are these subheadings indented?

Using An Outline

Read the outline again. You are going to write a two-paragraph report using that outline. Read the sentences below. Match the sentences with the main heading and subheadings in the first part of the outline. Write the sentences in a paragraph.

1. UFO's are strange sights in the sky.
2. Most reports say that UFO's can fly very fast or float near the ground.
3. People claim UFO's make animals act strangely.
4. People report that they have saucer shapes and glow brightly.

Match these sentences with the main heading and subheadings in the second part of the outline. Write these sentences in a paragraph.

1. Thousands of people from many countries have reported seeing UFO's since World War II.
2. That study and others explained most, but not all, of the reports.
3. The Air Force *Project Blue Book* was a study of more than 12,000 UFO reports.
4. Some groups insist that flying saucers really exist.

Writing an Outline

Thinking About an Outline

Your class is going to write an outline together. The outline will help you to plan a two-paragraph report that will use facts. The report will be about science projects that could be shown at science fairs and school programs. First an encyclopedia will be used to research the main idea of a science project. Then a student will be interviewed about a science project. The notes from the reference work and from the interview will be used to make the outline.

● Read the notes taken in phrases about science projects.

> ### Library Notes
> - models and experiments done by students
> - planning and doing can take days or months
> - report prepared and project shown at science fair
> - report must tell what was learned and how it was done

● Read the notes taken from an interview with a science student.

> ### Interview Questions
>
> 1. What is your science project about?
> 2. What are some different types of precipitation?
> 3. What will be in your report?
>
>
> 4. What is your experiment?
>
> ### Interview Notes
> Janet Katz. December 1, 19__
> - precipitation
>
> - rain, snow, sleet, hailstones
>
>
> - chart of types of water and the temperatures needed to make them
> - to make rain inside a jar

Writing an Outline

Study the library and interview notes. Your class will use them to write a class outline. Your teacher or a student should write the headings and subheadings of the outline on the board.

1. The title of the report is "Science Projects." It is the main idea of the report. Write it at the top of the board.
2. Look at the library notes. The topic for the first main heading of your outline is: I. A science project
3. Read the library notes. Use the library notes for the subheadings in the first part of your outline. The first subheading could be: A. Activities for a science project.
4. Now your outline should look like this:

    I. A science project

       A. Activities for a science project
5. Use the library notes to write two more subheadings for this part of your outline. Remember to use only important facts and combine them when possible.
6. Look at the interview notes. The topic for the second main heading of your outline is: II. Janet Katz's science project.
7. Use the interview notes to write the subheadings in the second part of your outline. The first subheading could be: A. Topic of project.
8. Use the other interview notes to write two more subheadings. Remember to combine facts when possible.

Writing News Articles

Thinking About News Articles

A two-paragraph report must have a main idea. The paragraphs give details about the main idea. The first paragraph introduces or states the general information. The second paragraph usually gives examples. One kind of a two-paragraph report is often found in a newspaper. A news article is a report that gives information about many subjects. A news reporter follows these steps:

1. Chooses the main idea for the report
2. Gathers information from reference works and interviews
3. Takes notes
4. Makes an outline
5. Writes the report

Writing Your Own News Article

Reread the library and interview notes in the last lesson. Look at your class outline. You are ready to use it to write a two-paragraph report.

1. Write a topic sentence using the first main heading from the outline.
2. Use the subheadings under the first heading to write four detail sentences about science projects in general. You have just written the first paragraph of your news article.
3. Write a topic sentence using the second main heading from the outline.
4. Use the subheadings under the second heading to write four detail sentences about Janet Katz's specific project.

Edit Your News Article

Use these editing questions to help you check your news article. Use the two editing marks if they are needed.

1. Do all your sentences tell about the main idea?
2. Is the topic sentence in each paragraph based on the main headings in the outline?
3. Are the detail sentences in each paragraph based on the subheadings in the outline?
4. Did you indent each paragraph?
5. Did you capitalize the beginning of each sentence?
6. Did you end each sentence with the correct punctuation?
7. Did you spell your words correctly?

An Oral Report

Sometimes you may want to share a report with your class. Follow these steps in giving an oral report:

1. Write the report using your notes and outline.
2. Practice reading your report aloud in front of a mirror or read it to a friend. You could also tape-record the report.
3. Begin your report with an interesting sentence to capture the attention of your audience.
4. Use pictures, charts, or maps to add interest to your report.
5. Look directly at your audience.
6. Speak clearly and loudly enough to be heard by the audience.
7. Use your voice to make the report sound interesting.
8. End with a good last sentence.
9. Ask for questions from the audience.

Checking Skills

Write the adverb in each sentence and the word it describes. *pages 260–261*

1. Della rode slowly.
2. She sang often.
3. She laughed once.
4. She looked carefully.
5. A light shone brightly.
6. It moved closer.
7. Della stood stiffly.
8. She watched silently.
9. The light traveled smoothly.
10. It arrived soon.
11. Its beam shone everywhere.
12. People gathered around.
13. A voice spoke then.
14. It talked softly.
15. The people listened gladly.
16. Della nodded happily.

Read each sentence. Use **er** or **est** to make the correct form of the adverb. *pages 262–263*

17. Janet rode ____ than ever.   (fast)
18. Her breath came ____ than before.   (hard)
19. She sang the ____ of everyone.   (loud)
20. She stared ____ than other people.   (long)
21. Mike stared the ____ of all.   (long)

Read each sentence. Use *more* or *most* to make the correct form of the adverb. *pages 262–263*

22. Bob drove ____ carefully than Milt.
23. Greg drove the ____ carefully of all.
24. His car traveled the ____ slowly of all the cars.
25. The bus traveled ____ rapidly than Greg's car.
26. The train traveled ____ rapidly than the bus.

Change each adjective to an adverb. Write the adverb. *pages 264–265*

27. That week Della talked ____ .   (curious)
28. She ate ____ .   (light)
29. She slept ____ .   (poor)
30. She woke ____ .   (lazy)

31. From her window she watched ___ .   (secret)
32. She remembered ___ .   (easy)
33. The light shone ___ .   (perfect)
34. It arrived ___ .   (strange)
35. Its voice spoke ___ .   (nice)
36. It left ___ .   (quick)
37. Mike laughed ___ .   (happy)
38. Did Della act ___ ?   (brave)

Write each word or letter in each sentence that should begin with a capital letter. *pages 266–267*

39. della montelone and mike stevens told their story to dr. bean.
40. there was a strange light in illinois, too.
41. della spotted another light near talcott street in bloomsdale.
42. on the next monday mr. j.g. peron saw a strange ship in the air.
43. it landed on blueberry lake, near bakerville.
44. della and mike began a notebook of all these things.
45. they read a book called strange airships from outer space.

Below on the left is the outline for a two-paragraph report. On the right are sentences for the report. The sentences are not in the right order. Put them in the correct order by following the outline. Then write both paragraphs. *pages 274–279*

I. Forms of energy
   A. Gas
   B. Coal
   C. Sun
II. Uses of energy
   A. Travel
   B. Heat
   C. Light

1. It lets us travel quickly.
2. Gas is one type of energy.
3. We also depend on the sun for energy.
4. It also gives us light to see.
5. Energy comes in many forms.
6. Much of our energy is from coal.
7. Energy supplies the heat we need.
8. Energy has many valuable uses.

A True Story

Writers often try to use experiences in their personal lives as ideas for stories. This story is true. The author remembers an experience as a child in Kansas in the 1930's.

PRAIRIE BLIZZARD

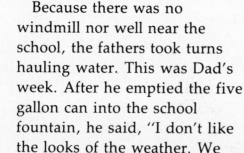

When I was a child in western Kansas, there were no school buses. On windy wintery days, if Dad didn't have to work on the farm machinery, he drove me. On other days, I walked the mile and a half to the one-room schoolhouse.

Because there was no windmill nor well near the school, the fathers took turns hauling water. This was Dad's week. After he emptied the five gallon can into the school fountain, he said, ''I don't like the looks of the weather. We may have a blizzard before dark.''

A chill ran down my backbone, as I watched Dad's car move along the flat straight road toward town.

I walked into the schoolhouse just in time to see Leroy pick up my lunch pail. Leroy was an eighth grader and the biggest boy in school. He had strong hands and a face that turned hard and ugly when he twisted someone's arms to make them do what he said. He probably wanted to hide my lunch, but when he saw me, he just grinned, said, ''Hi, Georgia,'' and set the pail on a cupboard shelf.

Miss Talcott rang the bell to call her twelve pupils in from the first recess. By this time a northwind was howling around the building. She sent Leroy and then one of the Reece boys out with a bucket to get more coal for the big round stove. And she pulled down the window shades on the north side of the room to keep out some of the cold wind. This made it darker inside.

The clouds got thicker. Soon it started to snow. It was a fine stinging snow that burned and froze my face. The snow was blowing so hard that you couldn't even see the schoolhouse. Why couldn't there be at least a few trees to break the wind?

Miss Talcott said we weren't going to have an afternoon recess. Then she looked at her watch and out into the storm in a worried way. "To make up for no recess, I'll let school out early at a quarter to four."

The fire roared, but the schoolhouse was getting cold as the storm grew worse. Suddenly there was a loud pounding on the school door. Miss Talcott jumped, and so did the rest of us. No one had heard a car outside. Maybe it was a tramp.

The bigger Reece boy went to the window and peered into the storm. He said, "There ain't no car out there."

Miss Talcott didn't even bother to correct his speech. More pounding shook the door of the dim room. She went to the stove and picked up the iron poker. Then, in a strange voice, she said, "Leroy, come with me to the door."

In the past, Leroy's swagger had always made me feel scared. But now I was glad that he looked almost as strong as a man as he stomped to the back of the room after Miss Talcott and opened the door.

Mr. Reece, whose farm was about a half mile from school, came in stamping his feet and brushing snow off his red, wind-burned face. He took a big pack from his shoulders, got out some blankets, and said, "I walked up here to tell you kids that the blizzard's getting so bad nobody can see to drive. Georgia's dad called me on the phone. He barely made it home from town. He says you kids aren't supposed to try walking home. Most of you would have to walk against the wind. I had a hard enough time getting here with the wind at my back. You'll have to stay in the schoolhouse all night."

At three in the afternoon, it was almost dark. How could a blizzard of white snow make the day black?

Mr. Reece told Leroy and his two boys to put on their coats. Leroy picked up the coal bucket, and Mr. Reece and the boys went outside. Because of the howling storm, we couldn't see what they were doing. But Mr. Reece had said they would stand at arms' length from each other so that no one would get lost between the school building and the coal shed. By passing the bucket from hand to hand, they brought in a lot of coal and dumped it beside the stove. When the snow from the coal melted, dirty blobs of inky water lay on the wood floor.

Mr. Reece said, "I'm going to take my boys home. Leroy, I want you to behave yourself and help Miss Talcott take care of the little kids. If the blizzard eases off after a while, Georgia's dad will come over on horseback and bring more blankets and something to eat."

A shaky feeling came around me when the door closed behind Mr. Reece and his two boys. I couldn't help thinking about what had happened last year along the road to town. Three children, the oldest in high school, had been driving home during a blizzard. Their car got stuck, and they tried to walk home—less than a mile. But the snow had drifted so deep and the wind blew so hard that finally they sank down exhausted.

Dad always said, "They ought to have stayed in the car. They could have sat close together to keep from freezing. Else they should have kept each other going. If you don't want to freeze to death in a blizzard, you've got to keep moving."

I squeezed closer to the big stove. My front got warm, but my back felt colder than ever.

Leroy put on his coat and said, "I'm going out and get some snow to melt, so we'll have something to drink."

He brought in a big heap of snow and put it in the pan Miss Talcott used for making her coffee at noon. The snow melted down into only a little bit of water. Leroy fought his way out into the storm and got more snow and still more. Bits of it clung to his face like soft fuzz.

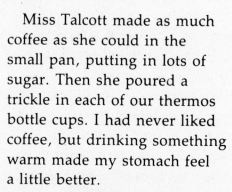

Miss Talcott made as much coffee as she could in the small pan, putting in lots of sugar. Then she poured a trickle in each of our thermos bottle cups. I had never liked coffee, but drinking something warm made my stomach feel a little better.

Soon the coffee and the sugar were used up. Nothing warm was left to drink and nothing at all to eat. The winds howled louder. Never before had there been enough time for Miss Talcott to read as much from the Tom Swift book as we wanted to hear. Tonight there was too much time.

At last Miss Talcott said, "We'll put the blankets on the floor near the stove. The littlest children can lie down on them and cover up with their coats and go to sleep."

One of the first graders cried, "I want Mamma." He cried the words over and over until I almost felt like crying too.

Miss Talcott took him on her lap and told the rest of us to sing softly together. Finally he fell asleep, and Miss Talcott put him on one of the seats. We tried lying down on the floor but were soon shivering.

Leroy pushed some desk benches toward the stove, and we used them to lie on. I knew I would never be able to fall asleep. My coat wouldn't cover my shoulders and my feet at the same time. My stomach was a big empty cave, and my bones felt as though they were pushing down through my sore skin to touch the hard bench.

After a long while, I asked Miss Talcott what time it was. "Nine o'clock," she whispered.

The wind rattled the windows fiercely. The room was completely dark except for a little glow from the stove.

Suddenly there came a loud pounding on the door. I squeezed tight against the wooden bench until I heard my father's gruff voice outside. He had come to the schoolhouse on horseback, bringing a big can of chocolate milk with marshmallows melted on top, three loaves of fresh bread, and some blankets.

Miss Talcott reheated the chocolate on the stove. Those of us who were still awake ate as much as we wanted. After that, we fell asleep.

I woke up to see sunlight streaming in the windows. I ran over and looked out. The whole country was white and wonderful, with drifts of snow glistening like silver stars all over the flat fields.

I climbed up on the horse behind Dad. We waved at Leroy and the others. Then we rode off over the fresh crunchy snow. I was so excited, I felt sure I could have walked all the way home without getting the least bit tired. Mother gave me a bearhug, and I gave Dick one. Breakfast smelled delicious. But before I sat down, I ran over to the window and looked out at the sparkling country again. Everything was so beautiful.

Louise Budde DeLaurentis

Activities

1. "Prairie Blizzard" taught you many things about life in western Kansas in the 1930's. Here is one fact that you learned from the story: Some schools used a well or windmill to get their water. Compare this fact to your life today. Divide a paper into two parts. List on one side of your chart facts about life in the 1930's. On the other side compare the facts to your life now.

2. You can learn more about life in years past by interviewing your parents, grandparents, or other adults. Ask them to describe the biggest changes that they have seen since they were children. Write or tape-record the answers you receive. Later you can present your interview to the class.

Grammar and Related Language Skills

Reviewing Compound Subjects and Predicates

Compound Sentences

Parts of Speech in Sentences

Reviewing Punctuation

Practical Communication

Reviewing Study Skills

Writing a Book Report

Creative Expression

A Short Story

Reviewing Compound Subjects and Predicates

Every sentence has a subject part and a predicate part. The *subject part* names whom or what the sentence is about. The *predicate part* tells what action the subject does. Sometimes the predicate part tells what the subject is or is like.

Some sentences have a compound subject.

• Look at each of these sentences. The subject parts are in a blue box.

Maria and Zeb liked horses.

The children got a book about two horses at the library.

Muhammed and Zarif were special horses from Germany.

The second sentence has just one important word, or *simple subject*. The first and last sentences have two simple subjects joined by the word *and*. They have *compound subjects*.

A **compound subject** has two or more simple subjects that have the same predicate. The subjects are joined by **and.**

Some sentences have more than one simple predicate, or verb. Some have *compound predicates*.

• Look at each of these sentences. The predicate parts are in red boxes.

Muhammed and Zarif solved arithmetic problems.

They could add and subtract.

The two horses amazed the public and puzzled scientists.

The first sentence has just one verb, or *simple predicate*. There is just one action in the sentence.

The second and last sentences have compound predicates. Each sentence has two verbs joined by the word *and*.

> A **compound predicate** is a predicate that has two or more verbs that have the same subject. The verbs are joined by **and.**

Talk About It

Which of these sentences have a compound subject? Which have a compound predicate?

1. The trainer and his pretty helper gave the questions.
2. Muhammed and Zarif answered with their feet.
3. The horses stamped their feet and tapped their hooves.
4. People looked for signals and watched for tricks.

Skills Practice

Read each sentence. If the predicate is compound, write **compound predicate.** If the subject is compound, write **compound subject.**

1. Kluge Hans and Berto were also smart horses.
2. Berto added numbers and gave the answers.
3. People stared and gasped in amazement.
4. Kluge Hans performed tricks and solved problems.
5. Many young people and some old people came.
6. They sat quietly and watched closely.
7. The girls and boys were thrilled.

Writing Sentences

Imagine you are at an aquarium.

1. Write two sentences with a compound subject.
2. Write two sentences with a compound predicate.

Sample Answer 1. compound subject

Compound Sentences

When you go on a trip, you pack several things together in a suitcase. The same is sometimes true when you write. You can pack two related ideas into the same sentence.

● Look at these sentences.

> Most alligators prefer fresh water.
>
> Most crocodiles like salt water.

Each of these sentences expresses one complete idea. They are simple sentences. A *simple sentence* has one subject part and one predicate part. Now read this sentence.

> Most alligators prefer fresh water, and most
> crocodiles like salt water.

This sentence expresses two complete ideas. The two ideas are joined by the word *and*. This sentence is a *compound sentence*. Notice that a comma is placed before the word *and* in a compound sentence.

> A **compound sentence** is a sentence that contains two simple sentences joined by **and.**

There is a way to check if a sentence is compound. If the sentence has the word *and,* cover it up and see if there are two complete sentences. If so, then you have a compound sentence.

● Look at this sentence.

These reptiles live in swamps and hunt for fish.

Cover up the word *and.* You are not left with two complete sentences. *Hunt for fish* is not a whole idea because there is no subject. Therefore, the sentence is not a compound sentence. It is a simple sentence with a compound predicate.

● Now look at this sentence.

Alligators are black, and crocodiles are gray-green.

Cover up the word *and.* You are left with two complete sentences. Therefore, the sentence is a compound sentence.

Talk About It

Which sentences are compound sentences? Tell why.

1. They are closely related, and they are very much alike.
2. Alligators and crocodiles are reptiles.
3. Their hides are thick, and their tails are strong.

Skills Practice

Write each compound sentence. If a sentence is not compound, write **not compound** on your paper.

1. Some alligators and crocodiles live in Florida.
2. They live in swamps and lie on river banks.
3. People fear them, and they fear people.
4. The alligators have broad heads, and their teeth are sharp.
5. Crocodiles can be vicious, and some have hurt people.

Read each pair of simple sentences. Make them into one compound sentence. Write the compound sentence.

6. Some crocodiles live in Florida. Other crocodiles live in Africa.
7. Crocodiles have narrow heads. Their teeth are long.
8. We saw some crocodiles in Florida. Jane almost stepped on one.
9. Matt yelled. Jane jumped backwards.
10. A young crocodile slept on the bank. An older one moved toward the water.
11. The older crocodile looked at us with a horrible grin. We left in a hurry.
12. I told my class about the crocodiles. My teacher showed a film about them.

Sample Answers 1. not compound; **6.** Some crocodiles live in Florida, and other crocodiles live in Africa.

Skills Review

If the subject is compound, write **compound subject.** If the subject is not compound, write **not compound.**

1. Rudy and Elsie read a book about dogs.
2. Some dogs rescue people from dangerous situations.
3. Princess was a Saint Bernard.
4. Men and women got lost in the mountains in Switzerland.
5. The snow and ice created problems for them.
6. Cold weather and strong winds were constant dangers.
7. Princess and other dogs helped the travelers.
8. They rescued the travelers in the mountains.

If the predicate is compound, write **compound predicate.** If the predicate is not compound, write **not compound.**

9. The dog Chips lived and worked during World War II.
10. The Army shipped him to Europe.
11. Chips helped the soldiers and attacked the enemy.
12. He captured one man and chased others.
13. The Army gave Chips a medal.
14. Chips left the Army in 1945 and returned to his owner.

If a sentence is compound, write **compound.** If a sentence is not compound, write **not compound.**

15. I like animals, and I love stories about them.
16. My brother and sister told me about a cat named Daisy.
17. She lived with a family, and the family had two homes.
18. Their country home was big, and it had a barn in back.
19. The family packed and returned to the city in the fall.
20. Daisy was going to have kittens, and she stayed behind.
21. Later Daisy walked to the city, and she found the family.
22. The family was surprised to see Daisy and a kitten.

23. Daisy left later and returned with another kitten.
24. She made five trips, and each time she brought a kitten.

Read each pair of simple sentences. Make them into one compound sentence. Write the compound sentence.

25. Dan bought our cat Boots at a pet store. Our home is no longer the same.
26. Boots has black fur. His feet are white.
27. We put Boots down on the living room rug. He immediately headed for the door.
28. Mom chased him into the corner. Julia grabbed him.
29. Later we fed our new cat. He purred loudly.
30. Boots loves the backyard. He watches birds by the hour.
31. Last week he caught a bird. Mother got very angry.
32. She hung the bird feeder higher. Now Boots climbs up the pole.
33. Boots likes mother's flowers. Sometimes he rolls over on them.

Sometimes when it is raining hard, people say it is "raining cats and dogs." How did this expression start?

No one knows for sure. Some say it may come from the Greek word *catadupa,* meaning "waterfall." Perhaps Greek people said *catadupa* when it rained hard. People who did not know Greek may have thought they were saying "cats and dogs."

Another reason might be this: in England many cats and dogs used to run wild in the streets. During storms many drowned. Some people may have seen the animals lying in the street. They may have imagined the storm had really "rained cats and dogs."

Exploring
Language

Parts of Speech in Sentences

Words can be divided into groups according to the role they play in a sentence. You already know five word groups: *nouns, pronouns, verbs, adjectives,* and *adverbs.* These word groups are called *parts of speech.* Some parts of speech are more important in sentences than others. You cannot make a complete sentence without a verb. Most sentences have either a noun or a pronoun.

● Look at the first two words in this sentence.

Brave sailors cheered loudly.

Brave is an adjective. *Sailors* is a noun.

> A **noun** is a word that names a person, place, thing, or idea.

> An **adjective** is a word that describes a noun or a pronoun.

Brave and *sailors* make up the subject part of the sentence. Without the word *brave,* the sentence still makes sense. *Sailors cheered loudly* is a complete thought. Without the word *sailors,* the sentence no longer makes sense. *Cheered loudly* is not a complete thought. A subject part is needed.

● Look at the last part of the sentence.

Brave sailors cheered loudly.

Cheered is a verb. *Loudly* is an adverb.

> A **verb** is a word that names an action.

> An **adverb** is a word that describes an action.

Together *cheered* and *loudly* make up the predicate part of the sentence. Without the word *loudly,* the sentence still makes sense. *Brave sailors cheered* is a complete thought.

Without *cheered,* the sentence no longer makes sense. *Brave sailors* is not a complete thought. A verb is needed.

You can see that sentences need verbs. Sentences need nouns, too, or something to take the place of a noun.

A **pronoun** is a word that takes the place
of one or more nouns.

● Look at these sentences.

Brave sailors cheered loudly.   They cheered loudly.

The word *they* is a pronoun. It takes the place of the word *sailors.* The pronoun *they* is the subject.

Talk About It

Read each sentence. Decide what part of speech each word is. Tell whether the underlined word is a **noun, pronoun, verb, adjective,** or **adverb.**

1. The sailors liked Sid the porpoise.
2. The smart porpoise lived in the ocean.
3. Sid often helped the sailors.
4. Sid swam in front of the ship.
5. He guided the sailors carefully.

Skills Practice

Write each underlined word. Write whether the word is a **noun, pronoun, verb, adjective,** or **adverb.**

1. The waves crashed fiercely.
2. The big ship tilted.
3. It missed the sharp rocks.
4. The sailors cheered loudly.
5. Many sailors cried with joy.
6. Sid leaped high in the air.
7. He helped other sailors.
8. A man hurt Sid.
9. The accident happened suddenly.
10. Sid healed quickly.

Sample Answer 1. crashed, verb; fiercely, adverb

Reviewing Punctuation for Sentences

Punctuation marks tell a reader how to read sentences. You use them within sentences and at the end of sentences.

- Read these sentences.

I know a story about a canary.   Tell it to me.

The first is a declarative sentence. A *declarative sentence* is a sentence that makes a statement or tells something. The second is a command sentence. A *command sentence* is a sentence that tells or asks someone to do something.

> Use a **period (.)** at the end of a declarative sentence.

> Use a **period (.)** at the end of a command sentence.

- Look at this sentence. It is a question sentence.

Shall I tell it now?

A *question sentence* is a sentence that asks something.

> Use a **question mark (?)** at the end of a question sentence.

- Now look at this sentence. It is an exclamation sentence.

How I love stories!

An *exclamation sentence* is a sentence that shows excitement or strong feeling. It ends with an exclamation mark.

> Use an **exclamation mark (!)** at the end of an exclamation sentence.

The *comma* separates words and ideas within a sentence.

> If a compound subject or a compound predicate has three or more parts, use a **comma** to separate them.

Stop, sit, and listen to my story.
The names, dates, and places are all real.

> Use a **comma** before the word **and** in a
> compound sentence.

This story is true, and it is amazing.

Talk About It

Tell what kind of sentence each one is. Tell the proper end punctuation.

1. The story is about a canary
2. What beautiful birds they are
3. Was it very yellow
4. Please stop interrupting

Tell where commas belong in each of these sentences.

5. The bird belonged to Tess and Tess loved it very much.
6. Tess lived in an apartment and her niece lived nearby.
7. Tess's niece stopped visited and talked with Tess almost everyday.

Skills Practice

Write each sentence with the proper end punctuation. Write whether the sentence is **declarative, question, command,** or **exclamation.**

1. Is the story over
2. Be patient
3. How touchy you are
4. Tess became ill one day
5. What noise did the niece hear
6. She went to the window

Write each sentence. Add commas where they are needed.

7. It was the canary and it was pecking at the window.
8. Tess's friends neighbors and family could not believe it.
9. That was a good story and I want another one.

Sample Answer   **1.** Is the story over?

Words with Several Meanings

Sometimes one word has several meanings. You may be familiar with some, but not all of the meanings. A dictionary can help you find all of the meanings of one word.

● Look at these two sentences.

The fish swam against a strong <u>current</u> in the water.
Barbara gave a report on a <u>current</u> event to the class.

Both sentences use the word *current*. The word does not have the same meaning both times. In the first sentence *current* means "a flow of water in a certain direction." In the second sentence, *current* means "at the present time."

● Look at these sentences.

The ram is brave and will <u>face</u> the bear.
Seth's <u>face</u> lit up when his father came home.
Kim needed a new <u>face</u> for her watch.

All three sentences use the word *face*, but the word has a different meaning each time. In the first sentence *face* means "to stand up to with courage." In the second sentence *face* means "the front of the head." In the third sentence it means "the marked surface of a watch."

Sometimes you can figure out the meaning of a word by the way it is used in a sentence. Other times you may need to use a dictionary. If the dictionary gives more than one meaning, choose the one that makes the most sense in the sentence.

Talk About It

Read each sentence and answer the questions that follow it.

1. I tried to <u>hide</u> the <u>hide</u> of the cow in my basement.
   Which word means "the skin of an animal"? Which word
   means "to keep out of sight"?
2. Erma watched a <u>school</u> of fish in the pond near <u>school</u>.
   Which word means "a place for learning"? Which word
   means "a large number of animals swimming together"?

Skills Practice

Read each sentence. Study the meanings. Write the letter of
the correct meaning next to each number on your paper.

1. <u>Duck</u> before you enter.   2. The <u>duck</u> swam in the pond.
   a. a kind of water bird   **b.** bend the head
3. The <u>fawn</u> had big eyes.   4. Some dogs <u>fawn</u> over people.
   a. show affection   **b.** a young deer
5. <u>Seal</u> the letter.   6. The <u>seal</u> balanced a ball on its nose.
   a. close completely   **b.** a sea animal
7. The fish's <u>scale</u> was thin.   8. I broke the bathroom <u>scale</u>.
   a. a balance for weighing things   **b.** outer layer of skin
9. The carpenter sharpened his <u>plane</u>.   10. I traveled by <u>plane</u>.
   a. a tool for smoothing wood   **b.** a vehicle that flies

Writing Sentences

Look up these words in a dictionary. Find two meanings for
each word. Write two sentences of your own for each word
using the different meanings.

1. cell   2. ram   3. ring

Sample Answer 1. b; 2. a

Skills Review

Write each underlined word. Then write whether the word is a **noun, pronoun, adjective, verb,** or **adverb.**

1. <u>Jumbo</u> was one of the <u>biggest</u> <u>elephants</u> ever.
2. <u>He</u> lived <u>peacefully</u> at the <u>zoo</u>.
3. <u>Children</u> and adults <u>visited</u> Jumbo.
4. Everyone loved <u>him</u> <u>dearly</u>.
5. P. T. Barnum <u>ran</u> a <u>circus</u> in <u>America</u>.
6. He <u>brought</u> Jumbo to the <u>United States</u>.
7. Crowds of <u>people</u> <u>watched</u> <u>him</u>.
8. Some <u>friends</u> and <u>I</u> read a <u>book</u> about this elephant.

Write each sentence with the proper end punctuation. Then write whether the sentence is **declarative, question, command,** or **exclamation.**

9. What an elephant he was
10. People rode on his back
11. He performed many tricks
12. Did you ever see him
13. I never did
14. Go see him now
15. We cannot visit Jumbo now
16. Why are we unable to visit him
17. He died in a train accident
18. What a terrible thing to happen
19. He was sent to a museum
20. Which one was it

Write each sentence. Add commas where they are needed.

21. Lions tigers and monkeys performed in the circus.
22. Jumbo also performed and everyone loved him.
23. He walked danced and rode in the ring.

24. People sat watched and cheered for Jumbo.
25. My grandparents saw him and they said he was a wonder.

Read each sentence. Study the meanings. Write the letter of the correct meaning next to each number on your paper.

26. The workers will <u>strike</u> tomorrow.
    a. set on fire by rubbing

27. <u>Strike</u> a match.
    b. stop working out of protest

28. Her singing voice is <u>flat</u>.
    a. a box for growing small plants

29. We planted the seeds in a <u>flat</u>.
    b. below the true pitch in music

30. Will that hammer <u>pound</u> a nail?
    a. hit with heavy blows

31. We saw a dog at the <u>pound</u>.
    b. a place for stray animals

32. <u>Race</u> me across the yard.
    a. run in a contest

33. We belong to the human <u>race</u>.
    b. a group of people

Have you ever heard the expression "to let the cat out of the bag"? It means "to let a secret be found out." How did this expression get started? It began in old England where country fairs were held. Pigs were sold in the market there, and they were often wrapped in a sack.

Some sellers tried to trick the buyers. They would not wrap a pig in the bag, but instead they would put in a cat. Usually the buyer did not find out until opening the bag at home.

Careful buyers insisted that the bag be opened at the fair. If the seller was trying to cheat, it was discovered when the buyer "let the cat out of the bag."

Exploring Language

Reviewing Study Skills

You have been practicing the skill of report writing. Study skills are helpful tools for writing good reports. Review these important steps for writing a report.

1. *Choose the subject* or main idea of your report.
2. *List all the information* you might need to research a good report. Remember that you can use books, periodicals, and people.
3. *Go to a library* to find reference works that can help you gather information on your subject. Use the card catalog to help you. The subject card would be especially useful.
4. *Take notes* about the most important ideas in the reference works and from the interviews. The notes can be written in sentences or phrases.
5. *Organize your information* into an outline. The outline is the plan for your report.
6. *Write the report* from your outline and notes.
7. *Edit your report* using the editing symbols if necessary.
8. *Copy the report*. Be sure to correct your mistakes.

Talk About It

Imagine that you are preparing a two-paragraph report about how the automobile developed. Answer each question.

1. Name a reference work that can help you find information on automobiles.
2. What subject would you look for to find a book for your report in the card catalog?
3. After you find your information, what is the next step?
4. What is usually the best way to organize the information from your notes?
5. What is the last step you do before copying the report?

Skills Practice

Imagine that you are writing a report on the history of flying. First you would gather information on your subject. Answer these questions.

1. What two reference works could help you find information?
2. How would you find books for your report?

Read the notes below about the history of flying.

Phrase Notes
—flying has been a dream for years
—Greek story about two men with wings
   of feathers and wax
—balloons of hot air in the 1700's
—planes called gliders in the 1800's
—first airplane in 1903 by Wright brothers

---

3. Use the notes to write an outline.
4. Use your outline to write a paragraph.

Using Test-Taking Skills

Most people do not really like to take tests, but tests can be a helpful measure of how well you have learned something. You can often help yourself do better on a test by following a few common-sense guidelines.

1. Follow directions carefully. This step is the first and most important guideline.
   a. Listen closely if the directions are *spoken*.
   b. Read all of the directions before you begin to answer any questions if the directions are *written*.
   c. Look for the main idea in the directions.
   d. Look also for important details.
   e. Ask your teacher about any directions you don't understand.
2. Be sure to have pens, pencils, ruler, paper, or any other materials you need for the test.
3. If the test is short, read all the questions in a section before you answer any questions. Often one question contains information that can help you answer another question.
4. First answer the questions that you know. Go back to work on the more difficult questions if you have the time.
5. Write your answers neatly and clearly. Be sure to write your answers where the directions tell you. Try not to erase or to make any extra marks on your paper.

Talk About It

Below is a test on test-taking. Review the guidelines for test-taking and take the test on your own paper.

---

1. Read items 2 through 6 before you begin to write.
2. Write your name at the top left part of your paper.
3. Write the date at the top right.
4. Number 1 to 15 on the left side of your paper.
5. Draw a line down the middle of your paper.
6. Do not write anything on your paper. Ignore items 2 through 5.

You did not follow the directions if you wrote on your paper.

Skills Practice

Read the test paper below.

Read each sentence carefully. Choose the answer that completes the sentence correctly. Fill in the circle for the correct answer in the answer column. Do not write on the test paper.	Name *April 12,19-* Date *J. C. Samuels* Answer Column
1. The correct plural for mouse is _mice_ A. mouses B. mousse C. mice D. mousies	1. A B C D ○ ● ● ○
2. The opposite of hot is _____ A. warm B. rapid C. cold D. exciting	2. A B C D ○ ○ ● ○
3. A synonym for shiny is _bright_ (A. bright) B. dull C. slow D. funny	3. A B (C) D ○ ○ ○ ○

1. What is wrong with the name and date?
2. What mistakes can you find on the answer sheet and test paper?

A Story

Thinking About a Story

Almost everyone likes stories. Before you could read, maybe someone read stories to you. Do you remember your favorite ones? Stories can be about many different subjects. Some stories may be about an animal. Others might be about life in a family. Still others could be adventure stories full of excitement.

Stories may be about different ideas, but all stories share common parts. You can use these parts to talk about stories. You can also use them to write your own story.

1. The *plot* describes the action or events of the story. Usually the plot has a beginning, a middle, and an ending.
2. The *setting* tells where and when the story takes place. The setting in a story could change if the plot moves the action from one place to another.
3. The *characters* are people or animals in the story. You find what characters are like by what they say and what they do.

●Read this story and look for the setting, characters, and plot.

Maria's Slippers

Maria was very excited. It was the morning of her tenth birthday. She wondered what her present would be. She looked in her house, but no one was inside. She looked around her yard, but no one was outside either. She wondered if her family had forgotten her birthday.

She sat on the back step feeling very sad. Then she felt something funny on her right bare foot. A little grey and white patch of fur was licking her toe. Before she could say anything, another little furball started licking her other toe. She looked as if she were wearing furry bedroom slippers.

Suddenly, she heard giggling behind her. She turned around to see her family in the doorway. She heard tiny little meows at her feet. She looked again. The little patches of fur were tiny kittens. Her family smiled and shouted "Happy Birthday."

Talking About Stories

1. What was the main character's name?
2. What else did you know about the main character?
3. What was the setting of the story?
4. What happened in the beginning of the story?
5. What happened in the middle of the story?
6. How did the story end?

Your Story

Thinking About Your Story

All authors face one problem when they want to write a story. First they must think of an idea. When they have decided on an idea, they must do some careful planning.

Follow these steps in planning your story. Take notes as you think over each step.

1. Think about the *plot*. You can use your own idea or you can use this following one. Look at the map below. You can use it to help plan your plot. The main character of

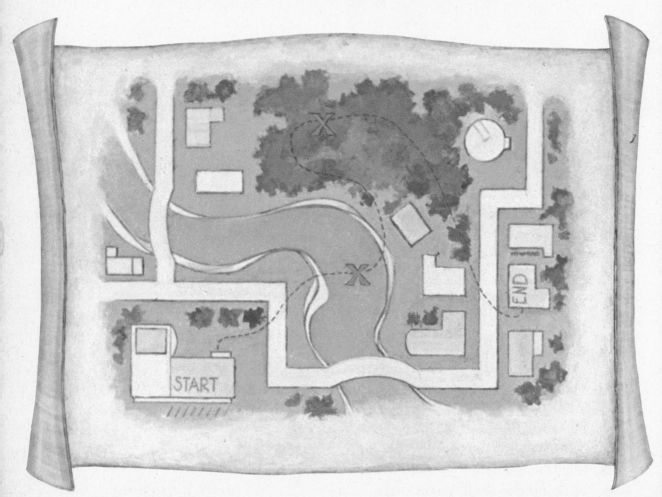

your story has an exciting, wonderful adventure on the way home from school. Follow the dotted line that shows the path that the character took home to the house marked END. What events might have happened to the character? Look at the two X's on the map. Two special events happened at these places. What could they be?

2. Where did the story take place? Think about the *setting* for your story. Describe the river, the forest, and the house.

3. Who is the *main character*? Describe the appearance of the main character. Think about the character's color of hair, eyes, and clothes. Think about how the person will act in the story. Name your main character.

Writing Your Story

Now that you have planned the plot, setting, and main character of your story, you are ready to write. Use your notes and the map to help you.

1. Write a paragraph about the main character.
2. Write a paragraph about what happened to your main character. Describe the setting.
3. Write a title for your story.

Edit Your Story

1. Did your story have a beginning, a middle, and an end?
2. Did you describe your main character clearly?
3. Did you describe the setting of the story?
4. Did you write a title for your story?
5. Did each sentence have a subject and predicate?
6. Did you choose adjectives and adverbs that clearly described your nouns and verbs?
7. Did you indent the first word in each paragraph?
8. Did you capitalize the first word in a sentence?
9. Did you use the correct end mark punctuation?
10. Did you check your spelling?

Writing Your Book Report

Thinking About Your Book Report

Stories are fun to read. They are fun to write. Stories are also fun to share with others. When you read a good book, you often want to tell your friends about its *plot, characters,* and *setting.* Those three parts helped you to read and write a story. You can also use them to *report* on a *book.* A book report helps you remember the book, lets you share it with others, and can help you learn how to express your thoughts in writing.

A *book report* tells about a story in two or three summary paragraphs. The summary tells enough about the story to interest the reader, but it doesn't give away the whole story. Follow these steps to write a book report.

1. Write the title and author of the book.
2. In the first paragraph describe the main character and tell the setting where the character lives. The summary paragraph should tell what the main character says and does, and what the author says about the character.
3. Tell one or two important events that happened in the story. This second paragraph is also a summary paragraph.

● Read the following book report.

Stuart Little

by E. B. White

Stuart Little is the second son in the Little family. Just over two inches tall, he looks like a mouse. He lives in New York City with his father and mother, his brother George, and Snowball the cat. Stuart dresses very well and often carries a cane. He even has little ice skates made from paper clips.

Stuart has many adventures. Once he was rolled up in a window shade. Another time he was almost dumped into the ocean with a load of garbage. His greatest adventure happens when he decides to go out into the world to search for his friend Margalo. Margalo had run away because of a mysterious note.

Talk About It

Read the book report again.

1. What are the title and author of the book?
2. Who is the main character? Describe him.
3. Where does the main character live?
4. What is the main character's most important adventure or event?
5. What are two other events that happen to him?

Writing a Book Report

Choose a book that you have read and liked. Take notes on the parts of the book that you will use in your book report.

1. Write the title and author of the book.
2. Write a summary paragraph that describes the main characters. Tell what the character says and does. Also tell the setting where the character lives.
3. Write a summary paragraph about the plot of the book. Tell about one or two important events that happened in the story.

Edit Your Book Report

1. Did you write the title and author of the book?
2. Did you describe the main character and the setting?
3. Did you write a summary paragraph about the plot?
4. Did you indent the first sentence of each paragraph?
5. Did you begin your sentences with a capital letter?
6. Did you end your sentences with the correct punctuation?
7. Did you spell your words correctly?

Checking Skills

Read each sentence. If the subject is compound, write **compound subject.** If the predicate is compound, write **compound predicate.** *pages 290–291*

1. The seals swam in the pool and delighted the boys.
2. The gorillas sat in the corner and ate their bananas.
3. Fifty boys and girls crowded around them.
4. Carl and his friend liked the elephants best.
5. The elephants stamped their feet and lifted their trunks.

Read each sentence. If a sentence is not compound, write **not compound.** *pages 292–293*

6. Our whole class went to the aquarium.
7. The divers were cleaning the pool, and they said to wait.
8. A big codfish bumped the diver, and another nibbled his ear.
9. The diver brushed it away and went on with his job.

Read each pair of simple sentences. Make them into one compound sentence. Write the compound sentence. *pages 292–293*

10. Thousands of pigeons live in our city. Some of them roost on our building.
11. At night I hear the pigeons outside my window. They disturb me.
12. During the day many pigeons flock to the park. Some people feed them.

Write each underlined word. Write whether the word is a **noun, pronoun, verb, adjective,** or **adverb.** *pages 296–297*

13. The <u>soldiers</u> used a <u>large</u> eagle during the war.
14. <u>They</u> used <u>it</u> to scare the <u>enemy</u>.
15. The soldiers <u>tied</u> <u>colorful</u> ribbons around its neck.
16. The bird <u>spread</u> its <u>huge</u> wings and <u>flew</u> high above them.
17. The bird <u>screamed</u> <u>loudly</u> at the enemy <u>soldiers</u>.

Checking Skills

Write each sentence with the proper end punctuation. Then write whether the sentence is **declarative, question, command,** or **exclamation.** *pages 298–299*

18. Emily was a marvelous dog
19. How old was she
20. She was fifteen years old
21. How you must miss her

Write each sentence. Add commas where they are needed. *pages 298–299*

22. Beavers are clever animals and they are useful.
23. They build repair and lengthen dams.
24. Beavers eat tree bark and they like some grasses.

Read each sentence. Study the meanings. Write the letter of the correct meaning next to each number on your paper. *pages 300–301*

25. The raccoon left the swamp.
    (a) wet, spongy land
26. Don't swamp me with work.
    (b) flood or overcome
27. The cat might desert the kitten.
    (a) dry, arid place
28. The snake lives in the desert.
    (b) leave
29. The squirrel left the cherry pit.
    (a) hard stone, seed
30. The fox hid in the pit.
    (b) hole

A story has characters, setting, and a plot. The plot has a beginning, a middle, and an ending. Write a story using your own idea, or you can use one of these topics:

      a story about a baby animal and its adventure
      a story about a character's trip to a strange place
      a story about something that happened on your vacation *pages 308–313*

a. Write a paragraph about the main characters.
b. Write a paragraph about what happened to your character. Tell about the setting.
c. Write a title for your story.

A Short Story

A *short story* has three main parts. The *plot* is the action of the story. The *setting* is the place and time of the action. And the *characters* are the people or animals in the story. Most short stories have a beginning, a middle, and an ending. You meet the characters in the beginning part. The middle tells about some problem the characters face. And the ending shows how the characters solve the problem.

The short story you will now read is from a book called *Henry and Ribsy*. The book is about a boy and his dog.

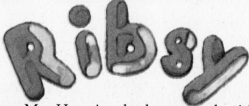

When Mr. Huggins had arranged with Al, the owner of the service station, to have the car lubricated, he turned to his son Henry and said, "I have to go to the bank and do a few errands. Are you coming with me or do you want to wait here?"

Henry looked at the car beside the grease rack and hesitated. Maybe it was a silly idea. Still, it was something he had always wanted to do. "Say . . . uh, Dad, do you suppose I could stay in the car and ride up on the grease rack?"

Mr. Huggins and Al both laughed. "You know, I always wanted to do the same thing when I was a kid," said Mr. Huggins. "It's all right with me, but maybe Al won't think it's such a good idea."

"It's O.K. with me," said Al, "but once you get up there you'll have to stay till I finish the job. It may take awhile because I have to wait on customers."

"Sure, I'll stay," agreed Henry.

"And you're not to open the car door while you're up there," cautioned Henry's father.

"I won't," promised Henry, and got back into the car. Al drove it onto the rack and then got out to fix the axle supports that held the car to the rack. He turned a handle and Henry felt the car begin to rise.

"So long, Dad," Henry called, as he and the car rose slowly into the air. He felt as if he were riding in an elevator that didn't have a building around it.

The car stopped and Henry could hear the *pish-tush, pish-tush* of the grease gun as Al worked beneath him.

"Wuf!" said Ribsy, looking anxiously up at Henry as if he could not understand what the Huggins car was doing up in the air.

"It's all right, Ribsy," said Henry. "I won't go any higher. Pretty soon, fellow," said Henry wishing something would happen. Sitting up on the grease rack wasn't as much fun as he had thought it would be.

While Henry was wishing something would happen, a police car stopped in front of the Supermarket next door to the service station. The officer got out and hurried into the market.

Boy, oh, boy, thought Henry. Now something is happening. Maybe somebody's holding up the Supermarket. If he comes out shooting, I better duck.

"Three M eighty-five, stand by," blared the radio in the police car.

Jeepers, thought Henry, I bet that means headquarters is going to send help. If the burglars get out and try to escape, I'm in a good place to watch where they go. I'll be a lookout

and keep my eagle eye on the door just in case any suspicious-looking people come out.

Henry slid down in the seat and peered over the edge of the car door with his eagle eye. He saw a lady with a baby in a Taylor-tot come out of the Supermarket. She was followed by a man on crutches. They didn't look the least bit suspicious. Wait a minute, thought Henry. That man is on crutches. Maybe the crutches are a disguise. Maybe when he gets around the corner he'll throw them away and begin to run. I better watch him.

Pish-tush went the grease gun.

"Thirteen L ten meet thirteen A nine," blared the radio in the police car. Here comes help, thought Henry.

Just at that moment Ribsy pointed his nose into the air and sniffed. Then he trotted purposefully toward the police car. Now what's Ribsy up to, wondered Henry, forgetting to keep his eagle eye on the man on crutches. The officer had not slammed the door of the police car shut when he got out. Henry was horrified to see Ribsy push it wider open with his nose and jump into the front seat.

"Here, Ribsy," Henry called "You get of of there!"

Ribsy jumped out of the police car. In his mouth was a brown paper bag.

Henry groaned. A dog that robs police cars! Now he really was in trouble. "Ribsy, you drop that!" he ordered.

Obediently Ribsy dropped the bag. He looked at Henry, wagged his tail, and tore open the bag with his paws and teeth.

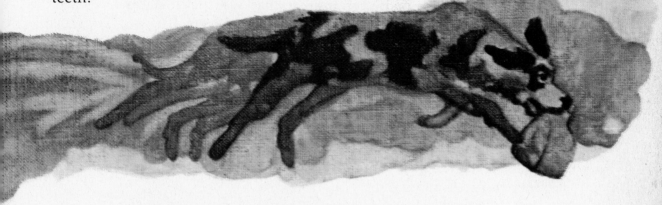

Henry looked down at the pavement. It was too far to jump. Anyway, he had promised his father he wouldn't open the car door. There must be some way he could attract attention. "Say, mister," he called to Al, who was working under the car.

Pish-tush went the grease gun. *Pish-tush, pish-tush.*

"Ribsy!" yelled Henry. The dog looked up and wagged his tail. He had a sandwich in his mouth.

"Drop that!" ordered Henry. Ribsy swallowed the sandwich in two gulps and poked his nose into the paper bag again.

Henry hoped the policeman would stay in the Supermarket a long time. He didn't want him to see the thief who had stolen his lunch. Henry wondered what happened to dogs that stole lunches, especially policemen's lunches.

At that moment the policeman came out of the Supermarket with a bag in his hand. He looked at the open door of his car. Then he saw Ribsy. "Here, you!" he shouted.

Looking guilty, Ribsy picked up the paper bag and ran between the gasoline pumps. The policeman ran after him. "Come back here," he yelled, and tripped on the hose from the pump. Ribsy ran under the car that was getting gas. "Come out from under there," ordered the policeman.

Al hung the hose on the pump, and the driver of the car started the motor. The sound frightened Ribsy into running out.

Ribsy, followed by Al and the policeman, ran around behind the station, where Henry could not see him. He listened to two pairs of feet running back and forth on the cement. Then Ribsy appeared from behind the station and ran under the grease rack.

When the policeman appeared, Henry was horrified to see him put his hand on the gun on his hip.

"Don't shoot," begged Henry. "Please don't shoot my dog. I know he shouldn't have stolen your lunch, but please don't shoot him."

The policeman looked startled to see Henry peering out of the car above his head. "I'm not going to shoot your dog," he said kindly. I'm just trying to get my lunch back if there's anything left of it."

"I saw you put your hand on your gun and I thought . . ." Henry began.

"I was just trying to keep it from flopping against me when I ran," explained the officer.

Just the same, Henry could not help feeling Ribsy had had a narrow escape. "I'm afraid there isn't much left of your lunch, sir," said Henry politely.

Then, to Henry's relief, Mr. Huggins returned. "What's the trouble?" he wanted to know, when he saw the policeman talking to Henry.

"I just stepped into the market to buy a pint of milk to drink with my lunch," began the officer, and went on to explain what had happened.

Mr. Huggins snapped his fingers at Ribsy, who came out from under the grease rack. Looking guilty, he dropped the tattered bag at Mr. Huggins' feet. Part of a cupcake rolled out onto the cement.

"Not much left, is there?" said Mr. Huggins. Then he looked at Ribsy. "Aren't you ashamed of yourself?"

Ribsy's tail and ears drooped. Henry could see his dog really was ashamed. He hoped the policeman noticed how sorry he looked. "What happens to dogs that rob police cars?" Henry asked. "Do they get arrested or get a ticket or something?"

The policeman laughed. "No, nothing like that. But he'll probably get a stomach-ache from eating too much."

After Mr. Huggins had insisted on paying for the lunch, the officer drove away and Al lowered the car. "You old dog," said Henry crossly.

Beverly Cleary

Activities

1. The story of Henry and Ribsy had a beginning, a middle, and an ending. In the beginning you met the main characters. In the middle Ribsy gets into trouble. In the ending the officer lets Ribsy go. Now try to think of another ending for the story. Write five or six more sentences that tell what finally happened to Henry and Ribsy in your new ending.

2. Henry kept hearing the sound of the grease gun go *pish-tush*. There are many sounds that we hear each day. For example, windshield wipers might make a *squish-squash* sound. Make up funny words to describe the sounds for three different things. Say them to the class and let them guess what you are imitating.

Looking Back

Some of the groups of words below are sentences. Other groups are not. Write **sentence** if the group of words is a sentence. If a group of words is not a sentence, write **not a sentence.** *pages 2–3*

1. A bus.
2. The driver honks his horn.
3. Fell all night.
4. Rain washes the bus.

Write each of the following sentences. Begin each sentence with a capital letter. End each sentence with the correct punctuation mark. Decide whether each sentence is **declarative,** a **question,** a **command,** or an **exclamation.** *pages 4–7*

5. what a storm that was
6. did you see the tree fall
7. look out the window
8. the tree has fallen across the road

Write each sentence below. Draw a line between the subject part and the predicate part. Draw one line under the subject part. Draw two lines under the predicate part. *pages 10–11*

9. Four yellow hens ran off the farm.
10. A farmer chased the hens.
11. The animals headed for town.

Write each noun in each sentence. After each noun, write whether it names a **person, place, thing,** or **idea.** Write whether it is **common** or **proper.** *pages 38–39, 48–49*

12. Laurie saw a footprint on the ground.
13. A friend followed the girl to a cave.
14. Bill admired the beauty of Overlook Mountain.

Write the plural form of each noun. *pages 40–43*

15. beach   17. child   19. fly
16. fox   18. man

Change the word at the end of the sentence to make a possessive noun. Write the possessive noun. *pages 52–53*

20. Irene saw the ___ car.   (teacher)
21. The ___ faces showed smiles.   (children)
22. The ___ drivers waved.   (cars)

Write the action verb. Then write the object of the verb. *pages 72–75*

23. Ronnie saw a cat.   25. Ronnie brought a bowl.
24. The cat licked its paw.   26. The cat drank milk.

Write each sentence. Use the correct form of the verb in the present tense. *pages 76–77*

27. Tony ___ his lunch.   (eat)
28. The children ___ in the park.   (run)
29. Pete ___ to the field.   (hurry)

Read each sentence. Then write the verb in the past tense. *pages 78–79, 86–87*

30. Roy asks for a flower.
31. A flower grows here.
32. I give it to a friend.
33. My friend plants a seed.

Read each sentence. Write the correct form of the verb *have*. *pages 82–83*

34. We ___ a serious problem.   (present)
35. Sue ___ colds.   (past)
36. She ___ a sore throat.   (present)

Looking Back

Write the correct past tense form of each verb in parentheses.
pages 84–86

37. Peter has ___ Sue often.   (phone)
38. They have ___ for hours.   (talk)
39. Sue has ___ her book report.   (begin)
40. Peter has ___ his math.   (do)

Read each pair of sentences. In the second sentence replace the underlined words with pronouns. Write whether each pronoun is a **subject** or an **object** pronoun.   *pages 112–119*

41. Cheryl met friends at the station.
<u>Cheryl</u> recognized <u>the friends</u> quickly.
42. Bob wore a new jacket.
<u>The jacket</u> fits <u>Bob</u> perfectly.
43. Greg carried the bags.
<u>Greg</u> took <u>the bags</u> to the bus.

Write the correct possessive pronoun for each blank.   *pages 122–123*

44. Cindy bought new shoes.
The red ones are ___ .   (her, hers)
45. Alison has blue shoes.
___ shoes are shiny.   (Her, Hers)

Draw a line between the subject part and predicate part in each of the following sentences. Draw one line under the simple subject. Draw two lines under the simple predicate.   *pages 152–157*

46. A group of children invented a new game.
47. The new game has a secret name.
48. Three children in the class wrote a story about the game.

Write each sentence. Write whether the sentence has a compound subject or a compound predicate. *pages 162–165*

49. Polly and Tim had a party.
50. Roy came to the party and played the piano.
51. Jan and her brothers played a magic trick.
52. The children played games and sang songs.

Write each adjective in these sentences. After each adjective, write the noun it describes. *pages 192–193*

53. A young musician plays a shiny flute in the bright sun.
54. A brown dog with sad eyes listens carefully.
55. A large crowd of happy people gathers around.

Write the correct form of the adjective. Remember some adjectives use **more** or **most**. *pages 194–195, 200–201*

56. Norman has a ___ voice than Dick.   (soft)
57. Lily sang the ___ note of all.   (high)
58. The trumpet made a ___ sound than the flute.   (loud)
59. The oboe makes the ___ sound of all.   (more beautiful, most beautiful)
60. Jim is a ___ player than Bob.   (more careful, most careful)
61. His fingers have the ___ touch of all.   (more delicate, most delicate)

Write each of these adjectives with an **er** ending. *pages 194–197*

62. noisy   **64.** flat   **66.** sad   **68.** hot
63. fast   **65.** dim   **67.** happy   **69.** roomy

Write each of these adjectives with an **est** ending. *pages 194–197*

70. slim   **71.** warm   **72.** juicy   **73.** small

Looking Back

Write each verb. Write whether the verb is an **action verb** or a **linking verb.** *pages 226–227*

74. Nadia is a dancer.
75. She dances on her toes.
76. She practices daily.

77. Antonio was an acrobat.
78. He hung from his toes.
79. I am near him.

Write the word that follows the linking verb. (Do not count words such as *a* or *an*). Write whether the word is a **noun** or an **adjective.** Then write the word to which the noun or adjective is linked. *pages 228–229*

80. Ruth is a doctor.
81. She is happy.
82. Some patients are children.

83. Ruth is alert.
84. Her patients are grateful.
85. She is careful.

Write each sentence using the correct form of the verb. *pages 230–231*

86. Luis ___ baking bread yesterday. (was, were)
87. The children ___ helping him last week. (was, were)
88. He ___ baking cakes now. (am, is, are)

Decide if each verb should be in the present or past tense. *pages 230–231*

89. Tom ___ winning now. (is, was)
90. I ___ winning last week. (am, was)
91. The twins ___ losing two weeks ago. (are, were)
92. They ___ losing today. (are, were)

Write the noun in each sentence that shows possession. Write whether it is **singular** or **plural.** *pages 238–239*

93. The parents watched the students' game.
94. One student's catch saved the day.

Write each adverb. Then write the word it describes. *pages 260–261*

95. The creature grinned strangely.
96. It jumped wildly.
97. We stared around.

Use the correct form of the adverb in parentheses. *pages 262–263*

98. Jerry ran ___ than Earl did. (long)
99. Claire ran the ___ of all. (long)
100. She came ___ to breaking the record. (close)
101. Jerry came ___ to the record than Earl. (near)

Use **more** or **most** to complete each sentence correctly. *pages 262–263*

102. Jerry practiced ___ frequently than Earl. (more, most)
103. Claire practiced ___ happily of all. (more, most)

Change each adjective to an adverb. Write the adverb. *pages 262–265*

104. swift   **106.** crazy   **108.** complete
105. odd   **107.** dainty   **109.** soft

Write each sentence. Use capital letters where necessary. *pages 266–267*

110. dr. boulez opened the boulez laboratory in july.
111. ms. smith and mr. j. r. fox arrived from england on monday.

If a sentence has a compound subject, write **compound subject.** If a sentence has a compound predicate, write **compound predicate.** If the sentence is a compound sentence, write **compound sentence.** *pages 290–293*

112. Harry and Ann went to the aquarium.
113. The dolphins entertain, and their trainer rewards them.
114. They jump and catch fish high in the air.

Write each underlined word. Then write whether the word is a **noun, pronoun, adjective, verb,** or **adverb.** *pages 296–297*

115. <u>Harry</u> and Ann <u>feed</u> their <u>dog</u> <u>daily</u>.
116. <u>They</u> play with <u>him</u> and take him for <u>long</u> <u>walks</u>.
117. They <u>brush</u> his <u>soft</u> fur <u>frequently</u>.
118. His <u>fur</u> is <u>wet</u> from the <u>rain</u>.

I. Grammar

SENTENCES

Definition

A **sentence** is a group of words that states a complete idea. page 2 MORE PRACTICE, page 348

Virginia painted a lovely picture.

James lost his shoes.

Parts of Sentences

The **subject part** of a sentence names whom or what the sentence is about. The subject part may have one word or more than one word. page 10 MORE PRACTICE, pages 349, 356

A large circus arrives in town every spring.

The tall girl on the high wire performs many tricks.

The **simple subject** of a sentence is the main word in the subject part. page 154 MORE PRACTICE, page 356

The little girl played outside.

The boy with the crutches liked school.

A **compound subject** has two or more simple subjects that have the same predicate. The subjects are joined by and. page 162 MORE PRACTICE, pages 357, 364

Mary and her friends skated on the pond.

Snow and sleet fell during the night.

The **predicate part** of a sentence tells what action the subject part does. The predicate part may have one word or more than one word. page 10 MORE PRACTICE, pages 349, 356

The Parker family planted a garden.

Many flowers bloomed beside the fence.

The **simple predicate** is the main word or group of words in the predicate part. page 156 MORE PRACTICE, page 356

The horse jumped over the bush.

The parents clapped at the end of the speech.

A **compound predicate** is a predicate that has two or more verbs that have the same subject. The verbs are joined by <u>and</u>. page 162
MORE PRACTICE, page 357, 364

Betty <u>fed</u> the pig and <u>hugged</u> it.

The pig <u>squealed</u> and <u>squirmed</u> in Betty's arms.

The **object of a verb** receives the action of the verb. It answers the question <u>whom?</u> or <u>what?</u> after an action verb. page 74 MORE PRACTICE, page 352

Anthony broke his <u>glasses</u>.

The visitor opened the <u>door</u>.

Kinds of Sentences

A **declarative sentence** is a sentence that makes a statement or tells something. page 4 MORE PRACTICE, pages 348, 365

The teacher read a story to the class.

The children looked at the beautiful pictures.

A **question sentence** is a sentence that asks something. page 4 MORE PRACTICE, pages 348, 365

What did you do in school today?

Do you know which country grows the most rice?

A **command sentence** is a sentence that tells or asks someone to do something. page 4 MORE PRACTICE, pages 348, 365

Honk your bicycle horn.

Wait for me at the center desk.

An **exclamation sentence** is a sentence that shows excitement or strong feeling. page 5 MORE PRACTICE, pages 348, 365

How the trees bend in the wind!

What an awful sound the wind makes!

A **simple sentence** is a sentence that has one subject part and one predicate part. page 292 MORE PRACTICE, page 364

The children played games.

Miranda watched the game from behind a tree.

A **compound sentence** is a sentence that contains two simple sentences joined by <u>and</u>. page 292 MORE PRACTICE, page 364

Paul read a book, <u>and</u> Joan watched TV.

Mr. Frantz cleaned the garage, <u>and</u> Natalie mowed the lawn.

PARTS OF SPEECH

Noun

A **noun** is a word that names a person, place, thing, or idea. page 39 MORE PRACTICE, pages 350, 365

The <u>ships</u> sailed from the <u>harbor</u>.

<u>William</u> tripped over a <u>rope</u>.

The <u>friendship</u> of the <u>children</u> delighted the <u>teacher</u>.

A **singular noun** is a noun that names one person, place, thing, or idea. page 40 MORE PRACTICE, page 350

The <u>horse</u> raced around the <u>field</u>.

A <u>turtle</u> lives in our <u>pond</u>.

A **plural noun** is a noun that names more than one person. place, thing or idea. page 40 MORE PRACTICE, page 350

The <u>children</u> have two <u>dogs</u>.

The <u>dogs</u> live in small <u>houses</u>.

A **common noun** is a noun that names any person, place, thing, or idea. page 48 MORE PRACTICE, page 351

A little <u>shepherd</u> cried for the lost <u>sheep</u>.

The <u>dog</u> followed the <u>canary</u>.

A **proper noun** is a noun that names a special person, place, thing, or idea. A proper noun can be one word or more than one word. page 48 MORE PRACTICE, page 351

<u>John Campos</u> lives on <u>Green Street</u>.

<u>Claudia</u> attends the <u>Lincoln Middle School</u>.

A **possessive noun** is a noun that names who or what has something. page 52 MORE PRACTICE, page 351

The <u>woman's</u> hand touched my cheek.

Who hid <u>Andre's</u> hat?

Verb

An **action verb** is a word that names an action. It may contain more than one word. page 72 MORE PRACTICE, pages 352, 365

The boy <u>hides</u> behind the chair.

The girl <u>finds</u> the boy.

The **present tense** of a verb names an action that happens now. page 76 MORE PRACTICE, page 352

The plant <u>needs</u> water and plant food.

Chickens <u>eat</u> corn and grains.

The **past tense** of a verb names an action that already happened. page 78 MORE PRACTICE, page 352

The Pilgrims <u>celebrated</u> the first Thanksgiving.

The team <u>played</u> well yesterday.

A **helping verb** helps the main verb to name an action or make a statement. pages 84-87 MORE PRACTICE, page 352, 353

Astronauts <u>have</u> landed on the moon.

Marsha <u>has</u> picked the beans.

The **past tense** of a verb with **have** names an action that began in the past and is still going on. The **past tense with have** uses the helping verb **have** or **has** and the main verb in the past tense. page 84 MORE PRACTICE, page 353

The children <u>have dug</u> a hole.

The pony <u>has jumped</u> over the wall.

The **present tense** of the helping verb **be** (**am, is, are**) and a main verb ending with **ing** name an action that continues in the present. page 236 MORE PRACTICE, page 361

I <u>am selling</u> buckets of fish.

You <u>are helping</u> the salesperson.

The cat <u>is eating</u> the fish.

The **past tense** of the helping verb **be** (**was, were**) and a main verb ending with **ing** name an action that began in the past and continued for a time. page 236 MORE PRACTICE, page 361

The sun <u>was shining</u> this morning.

Many people <u>were playing</u> outdoors in the sun.

A **linking verb** is a verb that connects the subject part with a noun or adjective in the predicate part. It tells what the subject is or is like. page 226 MORE PRACTICE, page 360

Today <u>is</u> Halloween.

Our costumes <u>are</u> scary.

Pronoun

A **pronoun** is a word that takes the place of one or more nouns. page 112 MORE PRACTICE, page 354, 365

Denise played on the sidewalk.

She fell and scratched her hand.

Two strangers spoke to Frank.

They asked him for the time.

Adjective

An **adjective** is a word that describes a noun or pronoun. page 192 MORE PRACTICE, page 358, 365

Little Adam tipped his red hat.

The silly clown jumped over a tiny stick.

Adverb

An **adverb** is a word that describes an action. page 260 MORE PRACTICE, pages 362, 365

The monkeys chattered noisily.

The elephant walked slowly.

II. Usage

USING VERBS

When the subject is a singular noun or it, he, or she, an **s** is added to form the present tense verb. page 77 MORE PRACTICE, pages 352, 355

The cat races around the room.

It leaps onto the sofa.

When the subject is a plural noun or I, you, we, or they, the verb doesn't change in the present tense. page 77 MORE PRACTICE, pages 352, 355

The rabbits eat lettuce in our garden.

They hop away.

When a subject is a singular noun and the predicate is compound, add an **s** to the main verb in the predicate to form the present tense. page 166 MORE PRACTICE, page 357

Amy <u>buys</u> and <u>sells</u> antiques.
Mabel also <u>repairs</u> and <u>paints</u> furniture.

When a compound subject is joined by <u>and</u>, the verb does
not change in the present tense. page 166 MORE PRACTICE, page 357
The <u>ducks</u> and <u>geese</u> <u>swim</u> in the pond.
<u>Ruth</u> and <u>Dorothy</u> <u>watch</u> from the bank.

When the subject is a singular noun or it, he, or she, the
present tense of have is **has**. page 82 MORE PRACTICE, page 352
The <u>dog has</u> a bone.
He <u>has</u> a ball.
She <u>has</u> a truck.
It <u>has</u> a worm.

When the subject is a plural noun or I, you, we, or they, the
present tense of have is **have**. page 82 MORE PRACTICE, page 352
The children <u>have</u> toys.
I <u>have</u> a cold.
You <u>have</u> the flu.
We <u>have</u> fun.
They <u>have</u> a horse.

Use special forms of the **past** tense for these verbs. page 86 MORE
PRACTICE, page 353

Present	Past	Past with Helping Verb		
begin	began	(has)	(have)	begun
break	broke	(has)	(have)	broken
do	did	(has)	(have)	done
drink	drank	(has)	(have)	drunk
fly	flew	(has)	(have)	flown
give	gave	(has)	(have)	given
grow	grew	(has)	(have)	grown
lose	lost	(has)	(have)	lost
run	ran	(has)	(have)	run
sit	sat	(has)	(have)	sat

Handbook

Plants <u>grow</u> best in sunlight.

The violets <u>grew</u> new blooms last week.

The ivy <u>has grown</u> very fast.

Use the forms of **be** in the present and past tense as shown
in this chart.   page 226   MORE PRACTICE, page 360

Present		Past	
I	**am**	I	
She		She	
He	**is**	He	**was**
It		It	
You		You	
We	**are**	We	**were**
They		They	

USING PRONOUNS

A **subject pronoun** is a pronoun that is used as the subject
of a sentence.   page 114   MORE PRACTICE, page 354

Elsie and Helen went to the library.

<u>They</u> borrowed two books.

The canary lived in a golden cage.

<u>It</u> sang all day long.

An **object pronoun** is a pronoun that is used as the object of
a verb.   page 116   MORE PRACTICE, page 354

The boy kicked the ball across the yard.

Sonya kicked <u>it</u> almost to the street.

Jason delivered the newspapers.

The dealer stacked <u>them</u> on his bicycle.

This chart shows the use of subject pronouns and object pronouns. page 118 MORE PRACTICE, page 355

Subject Pronouns		Object Pronouns	
I	we	me	us
you		you	
she, he, it	they	her, him, it	they

A **possessive pronoun** is a pronoun that names who or what has something. page 122 MORE PRACTICE, page 355
Mary washed <u>her</u> new bicycle.
The children found <u>their</u> baseball.

USING ADJECTIVES

An adjective ending in **er** compares two nouns. An adjective ending in **est** compares more than two nouns. page 194 MORE PRACTICE, page 358
The flute makes a <u>softer</u> sound than the trombone.
The drums play the <u>loudest</u> music in the band.

Use **more** before some adjectives when comparing two nouns. page 200 MORE PRACTICE, page 359
Swimming was <u>more fun</u> at camp than canoeing.
Sailing was <u>more difficult</u> than canoeing.

Use **most** before some adjectives when comparing more than two nouns. page 200 MORE PRACTICE, page 359
The President has the <u>most difficult</u> job of all the jobs in the country.
The President lives in the <u>most beautiful</u> home in America.

USING ADVERBS

Add **er** to some adverbs when comparing two actions. Add **est** to some adverbs when comparing more than two actions. page 262 MORE PRACTICE, page 362
Laurel can swim <u>faster</u> than her pet dog.
Audry tried <u>hardest</u> of all the children.

Use **more** before some adverbs when comparing two actions. Use **most** before some adverbs when comparing more than two actions.   page 262   MORE PRACTICE, **page 362**

The sun shines <u>more brightly</u> today than yesterday.

It shone <u>most brightly</u> of all on Tuesday.

III. Mechanics

CAPITALIZATION

Use a **capital letter** to begin the first word of every sentence.   page 6   MORE PRACTICE, **pages 348, 363**

<u>T</u>he rocketship prepared for landing.

<u>W</u>hat leaped from the rocketship?

Use a **capital letter** to begin each important word of a proper noun. A proper noun is a noun that names a special person, place, or thing.   page 266   MORE PRACTICE, **page 363**

<u>M</u>atthew <u>H</u>enson explored the <u>A</u>rctic.

The explorers traveled on a ship called the <u>G</u>reenland.

Use a **capital letter** to begin each important word in the title of a book. Always begin the first word of a title with a capital letter.   page 266   MORE PRACTICE, **page 363**

Have you read *<u>T</u>he <u>P</u>rince and the <u>P</u>auper?*

<u>T</u>he <u>S</u>ecret of the <u>H</u>idden <u>S</u>taircase is my favorite book.

Use a **capital letter** for each initial in a person's name. Use a period after the initial.   page 266   MORE PRACTICE, **page 363**

James <u>E</u>. Carter was elected President.

<u>T</u>. <u>A</u>. Edison invented the electric light bulb.

Use a **capital letter** to begin the names of the months and days of the week.   page 266   MORE PRACTICE, **page 363**

We will begin our vacation on <u>M</u>onday, June 26.

Our class play will be on the last <u>F</u>riday in <u>M</u>ay.

Handbook

PUNCTUATION

Use a **period** (.) at the end of a declarative or a command sentence. page 6 MORE PRACTICE, pages 348, 365

The king of the beasts shook his mane.

Run away if you ever meet a lion.

Use a **question mark** (?) at the end of a question sentence. page 6 MORE PRACTICE, pages 348, 365

Where is the library?

Do you have a book for your report?

Use an **exclamation mark** (!) at the end of an exclamation sentence. page 6 MORE PRACTICE, page 348, 365

What a silly costume you have!

How scary her mask is!

Use a **comma** (,) to separate each noun in a series of three or more nouns. page 168 MORE PRACTICE, pages 359, 365

Tom, Carol, and Sherry played in a band.

Theodore played piano, violin, and drums.

Use a **comma** to separate each verb in a series of three or more verbs. page 168 MORE PRACTICE, pages 359, 365

The children hopped, skipped, and jumped on the sidewalk.

Mother cut, sewed, and fitted Jane's new outfit.

Use a **comma** in a compound sentence to separate the two simple sentences. The comma is placed before <u>and</u>. page 292 MORE PRACTICE, page 364

The camel looked at the tourists, and the people stepped back.

The elephant stretched its trunk, and the children gave it peanuts.

Add an **apostrophe** and **s** ('s) to form the possessive of most singular nouns. page 52 MORE PRACTICE, page 361

The bird's nest was full of eggs.

The neighbor's dog chased the hat.

Add an **apostrophe** (') to form the possessive of plural nouns that end with **s**. page 52 MORE PRACTICE, page 361

Some animals wandered through the scouts' camp.

The cowboys' horses grazed by the river.

Handbook

Add an **apostrophe** and **s** ('s) to form the possessive of plural nouns that do not end with **s**. page 53 **MORE PRACTICE**, page 361

This store sells women's clothes on the third floor.

The shop displays children's clothing in the window.

Use an **apostrophe** (') to join two words together to make one word called a **contraction**. page 240 **MORE PRACTICE**, page 361

He's excited about the holiday.

Jane doesn't like the beach.

CAPITALIZATION AND PUNCTUATION IN CONVERSATIONS

Use punctuation marks named **quotation marks** to show the exact words that a person speaks. Use them to show where the conversation starts and where it stops. page 176

"This machine is going to talk," Mr. Edison said.

Tell who is speaking by giving the name or title of the person before or after the spoken words. Use conversation words such as asked, shouted, and cried to show how the person is speaking. Whenever a conversation begins with a new speaker, indent the first word. page 176

"This machine is going to talk," **Mr. Edison said.**

Use a comma to divide the spoken words from the person who is saying them. Always use it before the quotation marks. page 177

"This machine is going to talk**,**" Mr. Edison said.

Use a question mark before the quotation mark if the speaker asks a question. page 177

The worker asked, "Mr. Edison, what is this thing**?**"

Use a capital letter to begin the first word of the quotation. page 177

"**M**ary had a little lamb," he shouted.

If the conversation words and the speaker's name follow the quotation, do not capitalize the first word after the quotation. Always capitalize proper nouns. page 177

"Mary had a little lamb," **he** shouted.

Place a period at the end of the complete quotation.

"Mary had a little lamb," he shouted. page 177

IV. Spelling

SPELLING NOUNS

To make most singular nouns plural, add **s**. page 40   MORE PRACTICE, page 350

cow	horse	bed
cows	horses	beds

If a singular noun ends with **s**, **ss**, **x**, **ch**, **sh**, or **z**, add **es** to form the plural. page 40   MORE PRACTICE, page 350

box	bus	bench	dish
boxes	buses	benches	dishes

Many singular nouns ending in **f** or **fe** add **s** to form the plural in the usual way. page 43   MORE PRACTICE, page 350

roof	safe	cliff
roofs	safes	cliffs

For some singular nouns ending in **f** or **fe**, change the **f** to **v** and add **s** or **es** to form the plural. page 43   MORE PRACTICE, page 350

life	shelf	loaf	wife
lives	shelves	loaves	wives

If a singular noun ends with a consonant and **y**, change the **y** to **i** and add **es** to form the plural. page 42   MORE PRACTICE, page 350

butterfly	country	sky
butterflies	countries	skies

If a singular noun ends with a vowel and **y**, add **s** to form the plural. page 42   MORE PRACTICE, page 350

key	boy	day
keys	boys	days

SPELLING VERBS

If a verb ends in a consonant and **y**, change the **y** to **i** and add **es** to make the correct form of the present tense. page 88 MORE PRACTICE, page 353

try	worry	study
tries	worries	studies

If a verb ends in a consonant and **y**, change the **y** to **i** and add **ed** to form the past tense. page 89 MORE PRACTICE, page 353

study	hurry	try
studied	hurried	tried

If a verb ends in a vowel and **y**, add **s** to make the correct form of the present tense. page 88 MORE PRACTICE, page 353

play	say	obey
plays	says	obeys

If a verb ends in a vowel and **y**, add **ed** to form the past tense. page 89 MORE PRACTICE, page 353

play	obey	stay
played	obeyed	stayed

If a one-syllable verb ends with a consonant, vowel, consonant, double the last consonant and add **ed** to form the past tense. Verbs that end in **w**, **x**, or **y** are exceptions to this rule. page 89 MORE PRACTICE, page 353

shop	beg	knit
shopped	begged	knitted

SPELLING ADJECTIVES

If an adjective ends with a consonant and **y**, change the **y** to **i** and add **er** or **est** to make the correct form of the adjective. page 196 MORE PRACTICE, page 358

happy	funny	pretty
happier	funnier	prettier
happiest	funniest	prettiest

If a one-syllable adjective ends with consonant, vowel, consonant, double the last consonant and add **er** or **est** to make the correct form of the adjective. Adjectives that end in **w, x,** or **y** are exceptions to this rule.   page 197   MORE PRACTICE, page 358

dim	hot	big
dimmer	hotter	bigger
dimmest	hottest	biggest

SPELLING ADVERBS

Add **ly** to some adjectives to form an adverb.   page 264   MORE PRACTICE page 363

quiet	sudden	final
quietly	suddenly	finally

Change **y** to **i** and add **ly** to form an adverb from an adjective that ends in **y**.   page 264   MORE PRACTICE, page 363

happy	busy	easy
happily	busily	easily

V. Vocabulary

A **compound noun** is a noun made up of two or more other words.   page 44   MORE PRACTICE, page 350

The campers went on a <u>hayride</u>.
Peter explored the <u>lakeside</u>.

An **abbreviation** is the short form of a word.   page 50   MORE PRACTICE, page 351

Abbreviations Used in Writing	Title Stands for	Abbreviations Used in Addresses, Lists	Stands for
Mr.	a man	Ave.	Avenue
Dr.	Doctor	Blvd.	Boulevard
Rev.	Reverend	Dr.	Drive
Sr.	Senior	Rd.	Road
Jr.	Junior	Rte.	Route
Ms.	a woman	St.	Street
Mrs.	a married woman	Co.	Company
		Inc.	Incorporated

A **prefix** is a letter or group of letters added to the beginning of a word. page 90, 202 MORE PRACTICE, pages 353, 359

Prefix	Meaning	Example
mis	badly, in the wrong way	Did you know you misspelled my name?
re	again	Please rewrite my name.
un	opposite of	Jack untied his shoelaces.

A **suffix** is one or more letters added to the end of a word. pages 54, 202 MORE PRACTICE, pages 351, 359

Suffix	Meaning	Example
er	one who	printer (one who prints)
or	one who	sailor (one who sails)
ness	the state of being	happiness (state of being happy)
less	without	senseless (without sense)
y	having	thirsty (having thirst)
ful	full of	careful (full of care)
less	without	harmless (without harm)

A **synonym** is a word that has nearly the same meaning as another word. page 92 MORE PRACTICE, pages 353, 359

The large hall filled with people.

The big hall filled with people.

The silent audience broke into applause.

The quiet audience broke into applause.

An **antonym** is a word that means the opposite of another word. page 232 MORE PRACTICE, pages 360–361

Susan began reading the book on Monday.

She finished reading it on Friday.

The train arrives in the station at ten.

The train leaves at eleven.

Homonyms are words that sound alike but have different spellings and different meanings. page 126 MORE PRACTICE, page 355

They're playing with their gifts.

The two waiters wanted to go home, too.

A **homograph** is a word that is spelled the same way as another word but has a different meaning. page 158 MORE PRACTICE, page 356

Lena lowered her head in the wind.

Be sure to wind your watch.

Helen left her umbrella behind.

Make a left turn at the crossroads.

A **contraction** is a word made up of two words. The words are joined together to make one word. page 240 MORE PRACTICE, page 361

This chart shows contractions of pronouns with the present tense of **be,** pronouns with **have** and **has,** and pronouns with **had.**

Contraction	Short For	Contraction	Short For
I'm	I am	I've	I have
you're	you are	you've	you have
he's	he is	he's	he has
she's	she is	she's	she has
it's	it is	it's	it has
we're	we are	we've	we have
they're	they are	they've	they have

Contraction	Short For
I'd	I had
you'd	you had
he'd	he had
she'd	she had
it'd	it had
we'd	we had
they'd	they had

Handbook

VI. Special Forms

FRIENDLY LETTER

Use this form to write a friendly letter. page 62

Heading ⟶
> 63 Barrow Street
> Boston, Massachusetts 68102
> January 14, 1978

Greeting ⟶ Dear Kenny,

Body ⟶
We had a lot of fun in the snow last week. A howling blizzard swept through our town on Monday. Jo Ann, Tommy, Amy, and I built a huge snow fort with a wall that was five feet high. It had a long, dark tunnel, too. Mom gave us delicious sandwiches and a thermos of hot, creamy chocolate for a picnic. Later we had an exciting snowball fight, but the dog kept catching the snowballs! I wish you could have been with us.

Closing ⟶ Your friend,

Signature ⟶ Charles

Use this form to address an envelope.

Return Address ⟶
Charles Kinnly
63 Barrow Street
Boston, Massachusetts 68102

Address ⟶
Kenny Brody
8657 Gulf Road
El Paso, Texas 68705

BUSINESS LETTER

Use this form to write a business letter. page 100

Heading→

                                                130 Hugh Street

                                                Omaha, Nebraska 58412

                                                May 17, 19___

Inside→ Brown's Sporting Goods

Address 473 Ocean Avenue

Johnson, New York 11005

Greeting→ Dear Brown's Sporting Goods:

    I want to order a warm-up suit. I read your ad about the sale in this morning's newspaper. I want a suit that is red with blue stripes. My size is small. I am sending a check for the sale price of $20.00.

                                      Yours truly,

Closing→

Signature→   *Jan L. Hanson*

                                      Jan L. Hanson

BOOK REPORT

Follow these steps to write a book report. A book report tells about a story in two or three summary paragraphs. page 312

1. Write the title and author of the book.
2. In the first summary paragraph, describe the main character and tell the setting where the character lives.
3. In the second summary paragraph, tell one or two important events that happened in the story.

**Stuart Little
by E.B. White**

Stuart Little is the second son in the Little family. Just over two inches tall, he looks like a mouse. He lives in New York City with his father and mother, his brother George, and Snowball the cat. Stuart dresses very well and often carries a cane. He even has little ice skates made from paper clips.

Stuart has many adventures. Once he was rolled up in a window shade. Another time he was almost dumped into the ocean with a load of garbage. His greatest adventure happens when he decides to go out into the world to search for his friend Margalo. Margalo had run away because of a mysterious note.

OUTLINES

Use this form to arrange ideas into an outline. page 272

Fur Traders in the West

I. Fur traders in the West
   A. Found new lands
   B. Found new routes for pioneers
II. Fur traders in the mountains
   A. Called mountaineers
   B. Learned many Indian skills

Use these steps to write the outline.

1. Show the main idea in the title.
2. Identify the main headings of an outline by using Roman numerals. Develop these main headings into the topic sentences for your paragraph.

   Fur traders were the first explorers in the American West.

3. Put a period after the Roman numeral for each main heading.
4. Identify the subheadings of an outline by using capital letters. Develop these subheadings into the detail sentences for the paragraphs in your report.

    They found many new lands as they traveled west.

5. Put a period after the capital letter for each subheading of an outline.
6. Use the same structure throughout the outline. Main headings and subheadings may be written in phrases or sentences.

Handbook

More Practice

Learning About Sentences, pages 2–3

Some of the groups of words below are sentences. Other groups are not. Write **sentence** if the group of words is a sentence. If a group of words is not a sentence, write **not a sentence.**

1. The Mendez family drives away.
2. The dog runs away.
3. The police.
4. José Mendez looks around.
5. Nilda Mendez writes a sign.
6. Hangs the sign in town.
7. Knocks on doors.
8. The sad family.

Four Kinds of Sentences, pages 4–5

Read each sentence. Decide what kind it is. Write whether each sentence is **declarative,** a **question,** a **command,** or an **exclamation.**

1. Will the family find the dog?
2. How unhappy they are!
3. They hear a noise.
4. What is that sound?
5. Open the door.
6. The dog is at the door.
7. How did it get home?
8. Give the dog some food.

Sentence Signals, pages 6–7

Write each of the following sentences. Begin each sentence with a capital letter. End each sentence with the correct punctuation mark.

1. a new boy joins our class
2. his name is Kevin
3. where did he come from
4. he came from another city
5. make him feel welcome
6. how unfriendly he is
7. come back
8. why does he walk away
9. the boy solves the mystery
10. the real Kevin appears

Subject Parts and Predicate Parts, pages 10–11

Write the subject part of each sentence.

1. Mrs. Kornfeld loses her ring.
2. The detective finds a feather.
3. A friend sees a tree.
4. Mr. Kornfeld sees a nest in the tree.
5. The detective smiles.

Write the predicate part of each sentence.

6. Birds sit on eggs in the nest.
7. One bird brings food.
8. The detective puts a shiny penny near a window.
9. Another bird takes the penny.
10. The detective finds the ring in the nest.

Understanding New Words in Sentences, pages 12–13

Read each sentence. Write the underlined word in each sentence. Then write what you think each underlined word means.

1. Kiko was sick yesterday. Her underline{absence} from school was noted by her teacher.
2. Joel Jackson is an underline{apprentice} to a printer. He is learning the printing business. He will be able to get a job as a printer.
3. Sandford is very underline{timid}. He is even too shy to ask people the time.
4. The boat was underline{submerged} in the lake. It went under the water. It took twelve workers to get it out.
5. This tea was voted underline{superior}. The quality of the tea was better than all the others. Five out of six judges liked it best.

Nouns, pages 38–39

Write each noun. After each, write **person, place, thing,** or **idea.** Then write **singular** if the noun is singular and **plural** if it is plural.

1. The children visited the museum.
2. Maria looked at the Egyptian mummies.
3. Judy admired the precious stones.
4. The museum gave pleasure to the children.

Forming Plural Nouns, pages 40–43

Write the plural form of each noun.

1. zoo	4. ray	7. box	10. life
2. roof	5. child	8. crate	11. leaf
3. lunch	6. fig	9. woman	12. family

Compound Nouns, pages 44–45

Write each compound noun. Draw a line between the two words. Then write what each compound noun means.

1. A heavy rainstorm hit the area.
2. The downpour caused a lot of damage.
3. Many backyards filled with water.
4. People drove on the sidewalk.

Write a compound noun to replace the underlined words.

5. The tourists boarded a boat that sails.
6. The light of the moon gave a soft glow.
7. At the time of night the group could see the city's lights.

Common and Proper Nouns, pages 48–49

Write each noun. Write whether it is **common** or **proper**.

1. The ship traveled into the port.
2. The tourists saw the Panama Canal.
3. Mrs. Potts pointed to the Andes Mountains.
4. The Hawaiian Islands appeared on the horizon.

Abbreviations, pages 50–51

Change each underlined word to an abbreviation. Write the new phrase.

1. The Good Idea <u>Company</u>
2. 3:00 <u>post meridiem</u>
3. <u>Friday, February</u> 2
4. 8:36 <u>ante meridiem</u>
5. <u>Mister</u> Adam Jones
6. Mill <u>Road</u>

Possessive Nouns, pages 52–53

Change the word at the end of the sentence to make a possessive noun. Write the possessive noun.

1. The passengers board Captain ___ airplane.   (River)
2. The ___ baggage arrived.   (attendants)
3. The ___ dinners were prepared.   (travelers)
4. The ___ engine started.   (plane)

Suffixes, pages 54–55

In each sentence find each word that has the suffix **er, or, ness,** or **less.** Write each word and then write what it means.

1. The concert began with a banjo player.
2. A singer sang a folk song.
3. One song told of a friendless child.
4. The performers spread gladness.

Action Verbs, pages 72–73

Read each sentence. Write the action verb.

1. The air hummed with excitement.
2. Runners raced around the track.
3. Our team broke the old record.
4. Jenny set a new record.

Objects of Verbs, pages 74–75

Read each sentence. Write the verb and the object of the verb.

1. The coach blows her whistle.
2. The runners take their places.
3. The starter raises the gun.
4. The starter pulls the trigger.
5. The runners start the race.
6. The winner crosses the line.

Present Tense, pages 76–77

Write the correct form of the verb in the present tense.

1. The fan ___ to the game. (run)
2. Sandy ___ for the basket. (shoot)
3. He ___ two points. (score)
4. Amanda ___ in the air. (leap)
5. She ___ the ball. (catch)
6. The fans ___ . (clap)

Past Tense, pages 78–79

Read each sentence. Write the verb in the past tense.

1. Ralph chases the ball.
2. It lands in his glove.
3. The rain pours all day.
4. The players work hard.

Present and Past of *Have*, pages 82–83

Read each sentence. Write the correct form of the verb *have*.

1. Wendy ___ good cards. (present)
2. The girls ___ the aces. (past)
3. Dyani ___ two kings. (past)
4. Marcia ___ bad cards. (past)
5. You ___ a good hand. (present)
6. Hamid ___ a queen. (present)

The Past Tense with _Have_, pages 84–85

Write the correct past tense form of each verb in parentheses.

1. Tom has ___ the house this summer.   (paint)
2. His sisters have ___ him.   (help)
3. They have ___ the old paint.   (scrape)

More About the Past Tense, pages 86–87

Write the correct past tense form of each verb in parentheses.

1. The players have ___ badly.   (do)
2. Perry has ___ the water.   (drink)
3. One skater ___ her stick.   (break)
4. Maya ___ well tonight.   (do)
5. The coach ___ angry.   (grow)
6. The team has ___ the game.   (lose)

Forms of Verbs: Present, page 88

Write the correct form of the verb in the present tense.

1. The coach ___ to the ball field.   (hurry)
2. The coach ___ the weather carefully.   (study)
3. The captain ___ about rain.   (worry)

Forms of Verbs: Past, page 89

Write each of these verbs in the past tense.

1. obey   2. study   3. drag   4. share

Prefixes, pages 90–91

Change the underlined words to one word that has a prefix.

1. Leona <u>placed in the wrong way</u> her keys.
2. Her daughter <u>did the opposite of lock</u> the door for her.

Synonyms, pages 92–93

Write the verb in parentheses that closely names the action.

1. The fans ___ with excitement.   (scream, speak)
2. Many eager fans ___ onto the field.   (walk, race)

Pronouns, pages 112–113

Read each pair of sentences. The second sentence in each pair has one or more pronouns. Write each pronoun. Then write the noun or nouns each pronoun replaces.

1. Nancy wrote a report about ants.
   She wrote it in the library.
2. Nancy studied articles about ants.
   She found them in several different books.
3. Joe White helped Nancy with the report.
   He told her lots about ant life.

Pronouns as Subjects, pages 114–115

Read each pair of sentences. In the second sentence some words are underlined. Write the subject pronoun that can be used in place of the underlined words.

1. Jason drives a truck. The truck has a CB radio.
2. Jason drives across the country. Jason drives long distances.
3. Other drivers call Jason. The drivers ask about the weather.

Pronouns as Objects, pages 116–117

Read each pair of sentences. In the second sentence some words are underlined. Write the object pronoun that can be used in place of the underlined words.

1. One driver called Jason on the CB radio.
   The driver asked Jason for help.
2. Jason answered the driver's call.
   Jason answered the call in less than a minute.
3. The driver told Jason about two flat tires.
   Glass on the road caused the tires to go flat.

Using Subject and Object Pronouns, pages 118–119

Read each sentence. Write the correct pronoun.

1. Sue said to Mr. Ray, " ___ need help."   (I, me)
2. "Tell ___ about the problems," answered Mr. Ray.   (I, me)
3. Sue told ___ about the worst problems.   (he, him)
4. Mr. Ray helped ___ quickly.   (she, her)

Possessive Pronouns, pages 122–123

Read each sentence. Write the correct possessive pronoun.

1. The students read ___ reports.   (their, theirs)
2. Carl read ___ first.   (his, theirs)
3. Then Andrea read ___ .   (her, hers)
4. It told about ___ trip to Mexico.   (her, hers)

Using Pronouns, pages 124–125

Write the correct form of the present tense of the verb.

1. Nancy enjoys television.
   She ___ television every evening.   (watch)
2. Nancy looks for programs about nature. ·
   They ___ Nancy many new facts.   (teach)
3. Nancy tells the club members about the nature programs.
   They ___ very carefully.   (listen)

Spelling Sound-Alikes, pages 126–127

Read each sentence. Write the correct word for each blank space.

1. "Do ___ friends visit you often?"   (you're, your)
2. "Yes, ___ good to see them."   (its, it's)
3. They bring ___ books.   (their, there, they're)
4. ___ fun to read.   (Their, There, They're)

Reviewing Sentences, pages 152–153

Write the subject part of each of the following sentences.

1. Many people invent new things.
2. These inventions help us.
3. Some discoveries keep us warm.
4. Other inventions keep us cool.

Write the predicate part of each of the following sentences.

5. The Chinese invented many things.
6. A Greek man made a press for fruit.
7. Johannes Gutenberg worked on a printing press.

Simple Subjects, pages 154–155

Write the subject part. Draw one line under the simple subject.

1. A Scottish inventor made a steam engine.
2. Many people used the engine for many things.
3. Trains ran on steam by 1804.

Simple Predicates, pages 156–157

Write the predicate part. Draw one line under the simple predicate.

1. Alice read about some inventors.
2. She told the class about Michael Faraday.
3. Kim studied the life of Samuel Morse.

Words That Look Alike, pages 158–159

Two sentences with underlined words are followed by two meanings. Write the letter of the correct meaning next to each number.

1. Who invented the bat and ball?
   (a) baseball stick
2. Do you mean a bat that flies?
   (b) animal

Compound Subjects, pages 162–163

Write the subject part of each sentence. If the subject is compound, write **compound.**

1. Alexander Graham Bell and Thomas Edison worked hard.
2. The telephone first rang in 1876.
3. Homes and offices needed telephones.

Compound Predicates, pages 164–165

Write the predicate part of each sentence. If the predicate is compound, write **compound.**

1. People called and talked on the telephone.
2. They made meals and cleaned rooms by the electric lights.
3. People looked at telephones.
4. They read books and played games by the lights.

Agreement of Compound Subjects and Predicates, pages 166–167

Write the correct form of each verb in the present tense.

1. Lucy ___ and ___ a list of inventions.   (find) (read)
2. Lucy and her parents ___ the museum.   (visit)
3. The guard ___ and ___ them many things.   (stop) (show)

Using Commas in Writing, pages 168–169

Write each sentence. Add commas where they are needed.

1. Alexander Graham Bell worked as a scientist teacher and inventor. He also liked music and flying.
2. Bell lived in Canada England and America.
3. He studied invented and helped others during his life.

More Practice

Adjectives, pages 192–193

Write each adjective that appears in each sentence. After each adjective, write the noun it describes.

1. The new group performs during assembly.
2. The talented students practice after school.
3. The teacher is a famous singer.
4. The group sings favorite songs.
5. Four girls sing in a quartet.
6. The boys practice pretty songs.
7. The music echoes in the huge auditorium.
8. The teacher looks out at the empty seats.
9. The teacher pulls the heavy curtain.
10. A curious visitor stops and listens.

Adjectives That Compare, pages 194–195

Write each sentence with the correct form of the adjective.

1. The visitor listened for a ___ time than I did.   (long)
2. The songs were the ___ songs on the radio.   (late)
3. The group seemed ___ than the other singing group.   (loud)
4. This was a much ___ group than the other.   (large)
5. The group sang the ___ song of all.   (short)

Adjectives That End in y, page 196

Write each of these adjectives with an **er** and then with an **est** ending.

1. happy
2. mushy
3. noisy
4. lazy
5. heavy
6. juicy
7. roomy
8. busy
9. sunny

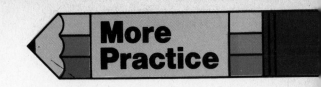

Using More and Most to Compare, pages 200–201

Write the correct form of the adjective that goes in each sentence.

1. Eva has the ___ voice in the whole group.   (more pleasing, most pleasing)
2. The tenors sound ___ than the baritones.   (more joyous, most joyous)
3. The soprano singer has the ___ voice of all.   (more delicate, most delicate)
4. Dan has a ___ voice than the other bass singer.   (more pleasant, most pleasant)

Prefixes and Suffixes, pages 202–203

Write each underlined word. Then write the meaning of the word.

1. Chip doesn't have a <u>squeaky</u> voice.
2. The audience listened to the <u>delightful</u> song.
3. They were <u>unaware</u> of his nervousness.
4. He was not <u>careless</u> with the notes.

Adjectives That Mean the Same Thing, pages 204–205

Read the words after each sentence. Write the word that is the synonym for the underlined word.

1. The group gave a <u>brilliant</u> performance.   (splendid, dull, boring)
2. The boys and girls applauded in the <u>crowded</u> auditorium. (empty, full, small)
3. The <u>happy</u> faces pleaded for another song.   (hopeless, unhappy, joyful)
4. A <u>slender</u> girl in the front row jumped up and down. (thin, wealthy, tired)

Linking Verbs, pages 226–227

Write the verb in each sentence. If the verb names an action, write **action verb** after the verb. If the verb is a linking verb, write **linking verb** after the verb.

1. Jan works very hard.
2. She is a musician.
3. She plays the violin.
4. Jan practices every day.
5. Her days are pleasant.
6. She practiced last week.

Nouns and Adjectives After Linking Verbs, pages 228–229

Write the word that follows the linking verb. (Do not count words such as *a, an, the*). If the word is a noun, write **noun.** If the word is an adjective, write **adjective.** Then write the word to which the noun or adjective is linked.

1. George is a racer.
2. Sometimes the job is dangerous.
3. George is fearless.
4. His parents were spectators.
5. His mother was quiet.
6. George was calm.

Using Linking Verbs in the Past and Present Tenses, pages 230–231

Write each sentence. Use the correct form of the linking verb.

1. Tina and Chuck ___ comedians.   (is, are)
2. Tina ___ funnier than Chuck.   (is, are)
3. I ___ a fan of theirs.   (is, am)
4. Tina and Chuck ___ good last night.   (was, were)
5. Chuck ___ funnier than Tina this time.   (was, were)

Antonyms, pages 232–233

Write the word that is an antonym for the underlined word.

1. Jon <u>finished</u> college this year.   (started, quit, completed)

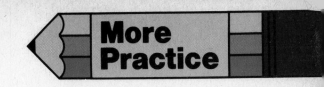
2. His parents <u>arrived at</u> his graduation. (watched, left, awaited)
3. They smiled at their son. (grinned, laughed, frowned)

Verbs Ending in *ing*, pages 236–237

Decide if each verb should be in the present or past tense. Write the form of the verb **be** that belongs in each blank.

1. My job ___ starting today. (is, are)
2. I ___ working now for a florist. (am, was)
3. Now he ___ teaching me a lot. (is, was)
4. Today these flowers ___ beautiful. (are, were)
5. I ___ watering a plant last night. (am, was)
6. Yesterday it ___ dying. (was, were)
7. Now we ___ watching it carefully. (are, were)

Using Apostrophes in Possessives, pages 238–239

Write the noun in each sentence that shows possession. If the noun is singular, write **singular.** If the noun is plural, write **plural.**

1. Katie works as a printer's helper.
2. She helps her father's friend.
3. The workers' jobs are difficult.

Using Apostrophes in Contractions, pages 240–241

Read each sentence. Write each underlined word as a contraction.

1. <u>We have</u> seen the trapeze artist.
2. <u>It is</u> interesting to watch the performers.
3. <u>They are</u> very good at their work.
4. <u>I am</u> a keen observer.

Adverbs, pages 260–261

Write the adverb in each sentence and the word it describes.

1. I visited once.
2. Mr. Atkins greeted me eagerly.
3. He laughed sometimes.
4. He talked often.
5. His dog barked wildly.
6. He ran everywhere.
7. Mr. Atkins spoke angrily.
8. The dog cried softly.
9. Mr. Atkins patted him gently.
10. The dog's tail wagged happily.

11. He ate then.
12. He chewed noisily.
13. He finished later.
14. His eyes closed slowly.
15. He slept deeply.
16. Mr. Atkins laughed again.
17. I looked around.
18. I jumped suddenly.
19. I laughed loudly.
20. A thing moved quickly.

Using Adverbs to Compare, pages 262–263

Read each sentence. Use **er** or **est** to make the correct form of the adverb.

1. Mr. Atkins ran ___ than a flash.   (quick)
2. He raced ___ than his son.   (fast)
3. He ran the ___ in the family.   (fast)
4. Mrs. Atkins tried the ___ .   (hard)
5. She practiced ___ than Mr. Atkins.   (hard)

Read each sentence. Use *more* or *most* to make the correct form of the adverb.

6. Mrs. Atkins improved the ___ rapidly in the family.
7. Soon she ran ___ rapidly than her daughter.
8. She ran ___ carefully than her son.
9. Mr. Atkins ran the ___ smoothly of all.
10. He bought new sneakers ___ recently of all.

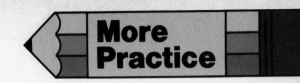

Forming Adverbs from Adjectives, pages 264–265

Change each adjective to an adverb. Write the adverb.

1. A doll swung ___ . (merry)
2. Its eyes shone ___ . (bright)
3. I walked to it ___ . (slow)
4. I touched it ___ . (curious)
5. It moved ___ . (light)
6. Mr. Atkins worked ___ . (busy)
7. He painted ___ . (swift)
8. He sewed ___ . (careful)
9. We talked ___ . (eager)
10. I heard ___ . (clear)
11. The toys sat ___ . (silently)
12. The dog watched ___ . (sleepy)
13. Mr. Atkins whistled ___ . (soft)
14. He hammered ___ . (quick)
15. The dog barked ___ . (sudden)
16. Mr. Atkins spoke ___ . (cross)
17. I patted the dog ___ . (quiet)
18. I enjoyed my visit ___ . (great)

Reviewing Capital Letters, pages 266–267

Write each word in each sentence that should begin with a capital letter.

1. mr. edwin t. atkins has an interesting job.
2. my visit to his shop was quite an adventure.
3. he has three toy houses called oak manor, hillside manor, and the house of flowers.
4. they are all in dameron, maryland.
5. mr. e. atkins makes things for television and movies.
6. my friend, j. d. copeland, read about this work.
7. it was in a book called *monster makers*.
8. j.d. and I are going to write a book called *giggly ghost*.
9. we will take it to mr. atkins.
10. maybe we will surprise mr. ed and his make-believe things.

More Practice

Reviewing Compound Subjects and Predicates, pages 290–291

Read each sentence. If the subject is compound, write **compound subject.** If the predicate is compound, write **compound predicate.**

1. Cindy and Karen stayed home with their mother.
2. Mr. Schultz and Otto went fishing on a big boat.
3. Otto fished and drank water all day.
4. The sky and the water were very blue.

Compound Sentences, pages 292–293

Read each sentence. If a sentence is not compound, write **not compound.**

1. The girls got up early, and their father loaded the car.
2. The girls made a nice lunch.
3. Kay caught the first fish, and the captain held it up.

Read each pair of simple sentences. Make them into one compound sentence. Write the compound sentence.

4. Bees buzzed among the flowers. Black wasps covered the grapes on the terrace.
5. Edda stretched out upon a lounge chair. Her cat curled up at her feet.
6. A wasp landed on the arm of Edda's chair. Edda shooed it away with her book.
7. Later, the wasp landed near the cat. The cat swatted it with her paw.
8. The wasp buzzed angrily. Edda abandoned her place on the terrace.
9. Edda put her chair in the yard near the flowers. This time the bees bothered her.

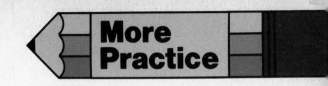
Parts of Speech in Sentences, pages 296–297

Write each underlined word. Write whether the word is a
noun, pronoun, verb, adjective, or **adverb.**

1. The <u>MacLeans</u> <u>owned</u> some rich farm land.
2. <u>They</u> raised <u>cows</u>, <u>horses</u>, and some <u>noisy</u> ducks.
3. <u>Sometimes</u> the <u>ducks</u> got loose and <u>quacked</u> <u>wildly</u>.

Reviewing Punctuation for Sentences, pages 298–299

Write each sentence with the proper end punctuation. Then
write whether the sentence is **declarative,** a **question,** a
command, or an **exclamation.**

1. What is your cat's name
2. His name is Whiskers
3. Look at his face
4. What a funny face it is

Write each sentence. Add the commas where they are needed.

5. Lana the Chimp learned to read write and use a machine.
6. She pushes a key and a word comes on a screen.
7. Lana asked the machine for food candy and water.

Words with Several Meanings, pages 300–301

Read each sentence. Study the meanings. Write the letter of
the correct meaning next to each number on your paper.

1. An <u>iron</u> lock was on the cage.
2. Will you <u>iron</u> this dress?
   (a) kind of metal   (b) press out wrinkles
3. Spot hurt his <u>eye</u>.
4. Put the thread through the <u>eye</u>.
   (a) hole in a needle   (b) organ for seeing
5. The <u>felt</u> kitten is cute.
6. Joe <u>felt</u> the material.
   (a) kind of cloth   (b) touched

INDEX

104, 125, 128, 141, 148, 171, 183, 323, 326, 332, 354

of *have*, 82, 104, 148, 323, 333, 354

linking verbs in, 230, 362

Pronouns, 112–119, 120, 121, 122, 124, 126, 128, 129, 140, 141, 148, 149, 240, 296, 297, 324, 332, 334–335, 356–357

    contractions of, with forms of *be* and *have*, 240, 243, 363

    defined, 112

    list of, 112

    object, 116, 118, 121, 141, 148, 324, 356, 357

    possessive, 122, 126, 128, 129, 140, 149, 324, 357

    subject, 114–115, 118, 120, 124, 140, 148, 324, 356, 357

Pronunciation, 172

    pronunciation key, 172

Proper nouns, 48, 56, 66, 266, 271, 281, 327, 330, 353, 365

    capitalization of beginning of each important word, 266, 271, 281, 327, 365

    defined, 48

Proverb, defined, 30

Punctuation

    apostrophe, 52, 238–241, 337–338, 363

    colon, 101

    comma, 51, 63, 101, 168, 171, 177, 183, 292, 299, 302, 337, 338, 359, 367

    exclamation mark, 6, 9, 146, 298, 302, 322, 337, 350, 367

    period, 6, 9, 50, 146, 177, 266, 298, 302, 322, 337, 350, 367

    question mark, 6, 9, 146, 177, 298, 302, 322, 337, 338, 350, 367

    quotation marks, 176, 183, 338

Question mark, 6, 9, 146, 177, 298, 302, 322, 337, 338, 350, 367

Question sentence, 4, 8–9, 28, 146, 298, 302, 315, 329, 350, 367

    defined, 4

Quotations, 176–177, 183

    punctuation with, 176–177, 183, 338

    See also Conversation

Quotation marks, 176, 183

Reasons, statement of, in paragraph, 134, 135, 141, 217

Reference works, 58–59, 96, 98, 172–173, 208, 244, 248, 274, 308

    almanac, 96, 98, 208

    atlas, 208

    dictionary, 58–59, 172–173

    encyclopedia, 96, 98, 208

    note-taking from, 244, 248, 274, 276, 304

    periodicals, 208

    records, films, and filmstrips, 248

    for two-page report, 248

    See also Library

Report, two-paragraph, 246–251, 253, 272–279, 281

    gathering information for, 248

irregular past tense, 86

linking, 226–231, 234–235, 242, 252, 326, 331, 362

object of, 74–75, 80, 104, 148, 323, 329, 354

past tense, 78, 81, 82, 86, 104, 128, 148, 231, 323, 324, 326, 331, 340, 354, 355

past tense of *be*, 37, 331, 363

past tense with *have*, 84, 86, 87, 333

present perfect tense, 86, 87

present progressive and past progressive tenses, 236–237

present tense, 76–77, 80, 82, 88, 104, 125, 141, 148, 171, 183, 230, 323, 326, 331, 332, 340, 354, 355

synonyms of, 92

tense of, 76

See also Predicate

Vocabulary

antonyms, 232, 235, 252, 363

homographs, 158, 161, 182, 300, 358, 367

homonyms, 126, 129, 357

prefixes, 90–91, 95, 105, 202, 355, 361

suffixes, 54–55, 57, 67, 147, 202, 353, 361

synonyms, 92, 204, 207, 217, 361

understanding new words, 12, 351

words with multiple meanings, 158, 161, 182, 300, 358, 367

Words

with multiple meanings, 158, 161, 182, 300, 358, 367

understanding new words, 12, 351

meanings of, 59

99004-300 3-82 30M